EXPERIMENTAL STUDIES ON THE NATURE OF SPECIES

V. BIOSYSTEMATICS, GENETICS, AND PHYSIOLOGICAL ECOLOGY OF THE ERYTHRANTHE SECTION OF MIMULUS

WILLIAM M. HIESEY
MALCOLM A. NOBS
OLLE BJÖRKMAN

CARNEGIE INSTITUTION OF WASHINGTON PUBLICATION 628
WASHINGTON, D. C.
1971

© Carnegie Institution of Washington 1971

Standard Book Number 0-87279-639-6

Library of Congress Catalog Card Number 40-14859

PORT CITY PRESS, BALTIMORE, MARYLAND

PREFACE

Earlier volumes of this series have reported investigations aimed at clarifying relationships between and within species of higher plants with special reference to their evolution and fitness to natural habitats. The present work is an extension of previous studies with major emphasis on the study of mechanisms underlying natural selection. In addition to field, transplant, and cytogenetic methods previously employed, quantitative physiological and biochemical measurements are included, as well as a beginning in the culture of excised tissues. The combined use of these methods brings to light relationships between biosystematics, morphology, physiology, and biochemistry that suggest new areas for investigation.

The choice of *Mimulus* as a vehicle for the present investigations was made with special consideration of the exacting requirements that need to be met in carrying on such an integrated, multiple-point program of experimental investigations as is reported in this volume. The ideal organism for any kind of biological inquiry is seldom found, but the *Erythranthe* section of *Mimulus* has proved to be a close approach to the ideal for the kinds of investigations described.

The major parts of this volume include (1) a biosystematic review of the *Erythranthe* section of *Mimulus*; (2) a genetic analysis of selected key forms of several species, including a study of the inheritance of growth responses of contrasting ecological races when transplanted to different altitudes; and (3) comparative physiological and biochemical studies on forms originating from contrasting environments, with particular emphasis on the study of photosynthetic characteristics. A review of studies with excised tissues is presented in Chapter IV. The concluding Chapter V reviews the present status of experimental studies aimed at furthering our understanding of plant evolution, with emphasis on physiological and biochemical approaches.

Acknowledgments

It is a pleasure to record the help of a number of people in executing the experiments described in this volume, in the analysis of data, and in the preparation of this publication.

The late Dr. Jens Clausen was active in early discussions leading to the selection of *Mimulus* as an experimental subject. Dr. Robert K. Vickery, while a graduate student at Stanford, made early key hybridizations in *Mimulus* during 1951–1955 which helped to pave the way for the present study. The late Harold W. Milner devoted much time and effort in the early development of apparatus for making measurements on photosynthesis. Dr. Ruth E. Elliott, now at Auckland, New Zealand, helped in the initiation of experiments on excised tissues which were effectively continued by Mrs. Warren Standeven (Kathy Picken).

Mr. Frank Nicholson, in addition to working on this and other laboratory projects, did much of the work of propagation and maintenance of greenhouse and garden cultures of experimental plants at Stanford.

Besides contributing greatly through his technical skill in the building of equipment and apparatus, Mr. Richard W. Hart prepared most of the diagrams and graphs used in this book. The drawings of species used in Chapter I were prepared by Mrs. Pamela Radford, who also assisted in the laboratory. Mrs. Marylee H. Eldredge did much work in processing data and in typing early drafts of this manuscript. Mrs. Karen Roberts typed the final manuscript. During the last two years Mr. Mark Lawrence designed and constructed precision electronic equipment used in physiological measurements.

At the transplant stations over various years we are indebted to Dr. Thomas Pray, Mr. Steven N. Gilborn, Mr. Andrew M. Lenz, Mr. Oakley Shields, Miss Jane Reese, Mr. Joseph S. Chang, and Mr. Steven Wood for their help during summer growing seasons. We are also grateful for the help of Mrs. Arline K. Kapphahn of the User Service Group of the Stanford Computation Center in programming genetic data, and to the Center for use of IBM computer facilities. To our colleagues named in later pages who have provided us with valuable original collections of plant materials we wish to express our sincere thanks.

DEPARTMENT OF PLANT BIOLOGY
CARNEGIE INSTITUTION OF WASHINGTON
    STANFORD, CALIFORNIA
        December 15, 1969

CONTENTS

CHAPTER   PAGE

I. BIOSYSTEMATIC RELATIONSHIPS WITHIN THE ERYTHRANTHE SECTION OF MIMULUS 1

The genus *Mimulus* and the place of the *Erythranthe* section, 1. Key to species of the section *Erythranthe*, 4. Cytogenetic relationships between and within species, 12. The *M. cardinalis–lewisii* complex, 12. Partial genetic barriers within *M. lewisii*, 12. Partial genetic barriers within *M. cardinalis*, 14. Flower structure in relation to differential pollination in *M. cardinalis* and *M. lewisii*, 15. The *M. verbenaceus–eastwoodiae–nelsonii* complex, 23. An amphiploid between *M. nelsonii* and *M. lewisii*, 23. Attempted crosses with species outside the section *Erythranthe*, 24. Conclusions concerning the biosystematic relationships within the *Erythranthe* section, 24.

II. GENETIC AND TRANSPLANT STUDIES 26

METHODS 26

Transplant experiments, 26. Crossing experiments, 26. Recording and processing of data, 30. Index values, 30.

CLASSES OF HERITABLE CHARACTERS THAT DISTINGUISH SPECIES AND ECOLOGICAL RACES 30

Morphological characters, 31. Physiological characters, 31.

INTERSPECIFIC COMBINATIONS 31

Essentially nonmodifiable morphological characters that distinguish entities of the *Erythranthe* section, 32. 1. Petal reflexing, 32. 2. Petal width, 39. 3. Corolla aperture, 41. 4. Pistil length, 43. 5. Number of dentations on leaves, 45. 6. Leaf ratio, 48. Flower color characters, 48. 7. Yellow upper epidermis in petal lobes, 50. Shifts in F_2 segregation ratios of "yellow upper" in populations established at Stanford and Timberline, 52. 8. Yellow lower epidermis in petal lobes, 54. 9. Rose, 54. 10. Light areas, 56. 11. Star, 58. Modifiable characters as expressed in different environments, 58. Intraspecific combinations, 60.

RESPONSES OF PARENTAL AND HYBRID COMBINATIONS AT THE TRANSPLANT STATIONS 63

Growth and survival of species and races and F_1 hybrids at Stanford, Mather, and Timberline, 63. Vigor of intraspecific F_1 hybrids as expressed at Stanford, Mather, and Timberline, 67. Vigor of interspecific hybrids at the transplant stations, 70. Expression of phenological characteristics at Stanford, Mather, and Timberline, 71. Winter activity at Stanford, 76. Frost susceptibility at Timberline, 76. Modifiable characters, 78. Genetic coherence, 78. Coherence as expressed in F_3 progenies, 84. Responses of cloned F_3 progenies at Stanford, Mather, and Timberline, 86. Genetic composition of transplant garden "weedlings," 86. Summary of the genetic structure of the *Erythranthe* section, 89.

CHAPTER	PAGE
III. COMPARATIVE PHYSIOLOGICAL STUDIES ON ECOLOGICAL RACES AND SPECIES	91

Unscrambling the variables, 91. Measurements of physical parameters in natural environments, 93. Transpiration measurements in controlled cabinets, 96. Use of controlled growth facilities, 100. Photosynthetic performance as a means of comparing ecologic races and species, 102. Methods for measuring photosynthetic properties of leaves, 105.

EFFECTS OF LIGHT INTENSITY............ 106

Effect of light intensity during growth on subsequent photosynthetic efficiency as measured under low light intensities, 107. Effect of light intensity during growth on subsequent photosynthetic efficiency as measured under high light intensities, 112. Comparisons between clones of *M. cardinalis* and *M. lewisii* grown under different light intensities, 115. Effect of light intensity on the production of dry matter, 121.

EFFECTS OF O_2 AND CO_2 CONCENTRATION ON PHOTOSYNTHESIS AND GROWTH   124

Method of gas control in growth cabinets, 131. Growth responses of *Mimulus* under different O_2 and CO_2 concentrations, 132. Modifications induced on *Mimulus* by varying O_2 concentration, 137. Growth experiments with varied CO_2 concentrations, 138.

EFFECTS OF TEMPERATURE............ 148

Effects of temperature on growth, 148. Effect of temperature on photosynthetic and biochemical characteristics, 157.

PHOTOSYNTHETIC PERFORMANCE OF PARENTAL AND HYBRID COMBINATIONS   163

Hybrids between *M. lewisii* and *M. cardinalis*, 163. Amphiploid between *M. nelsonii* and *M. lewisii*, 170.

PHOTOSYNTHETIC PERFORMANCE OF ECOLOGICAL RACES OF MIMULUS COMPARED WITH OTHER SPECIES............ 175

Ecotypic differentiation in the *Solidago virgaurea* complex, 175. Photosynthetic differentiation in *Solanum*, 177. Differences in pathways of photosynthetic CO_2 fixation in *Atriplex*, 178.

Photosynthetic differentiation in algae, 179. General conclusions, 182.

IV. GROWTH OF EXCISED TISSUES OF MIMULUS UNDER ASEPTIC CONDITIONS	184

Media employed, 184. Plant materials and establishment of cultures, 184. Examples of experiments, 187.

V. DEVELOPMENT OF APPROACHES IN EXPERIMENTAL STUDIES ON THE NATURE OF SPECIES	194

Levels of experimental approach, 194. The present status of physiological and biochemical inquiries, 196. Future investigations, 197.

LITERATURE CITED	198
INDEX	205

I
BIOSYSTEMATIC RELATIONSHIPS WITHIN THE ERYTHRANTHE SECTION OF MIMULUS

A prerequisite for experimental studies on mechanisms underlying natural selection and evolution in higher plants is an understanding of the biosystematic relationships of the materials under study. Of special importance is the choice of plant materials that must meet many requirements in order to be successfully used in the diverse experiments that need to be made. The chief requirements are:

1. The plant group should include distinct entities that clearly merit recognition as separate species.

2. At least some of the species should be widely distributed in diverse habitats and consist of recognizable ecological races.

3. The members should preferably all be diploid with the same chromosome number and be capable of gene interchange to different degrees, depending on their genetic affinities.

4. The members should have flowers that can be easily manipulated in controlled crossing experiments, and be capable of yielding a large number of offspring from a single pollination.

5. The life cycle from seed germination to flowering should be short enough to facilitate genetic experiments extending through several generations within a reasonable period of time.

6. The members should be fast-growing perennials that can be easily propagated vegetatively into clones having identical genotypes for use in transplant, controlled environment, and physiological experiments.

7. The size and structure of leaves and stems of all members should be suitable for quantitative physiological measurements on intact living plants under precisely controlled conditions.

With requirements such as these in mind, early surveys (cf. Clausen, Keck, and Hiesey, 1947) led to search among species of several genera. Starting with some of the early exploratory collections, Dr. Robert K. Vickery, Jr., began as a graduate student to explore broad cytogenetic relationships within the genus *Mimulus* (Vickery, 1951). Among many crossing experiments, the production of vigorous, fertile, F_1 and F_2 hybrid progeny between a wild form of *Mimulus cardinalis* from near the seacoast of central California and a form of *M. lewisii* from the high Sierras pointed to the likelihood that members of the *Erythranthe* section would be suitable for such experimental studies. Subsequent years of study have confirmed this conclusion.

THE GENUS MIMULUS AND THE PLACE OF THE ERYTHRANTHE SECTION. The genus *Mimulus* of the Scrophulariaceae, or Figwort family, consists of approximately 140 species, most of wihch are herbaceous annual and perennial plants of moist or wet habitats, although some (sections *Diplacus* and *Tropanthus*) are semishrubs that grow in relatively arid situations. Most of the species of *Mimulus* occur in North and South America with some representatives in Australia, New Zealand, Asia, South Africa and Madagascar. The concentration of species is greatest in California.

The history of the taxonomy of *Mimulus* has been reviewed by Adele Grant (1924) and Vickery (1952) and will be only outlined here with special reference to the section *Erythranthe*. The genus was first described by Linnaeus in *Acta Upsaliensis* in 1741, and in 1753 he described *M. ringens* L., which occurs in the eastern half of the United States. Additional species were described later by Linnaeus (1763) and Willdenow (1800). The first species that is included in the group now recognized as the *Erythranthe* section was *M. lewisii*. It was collected by Meriwether Lewis on the Lewis and Clark Expedition near the Continental Divide in southeastern Idaho, probably in the vicinity of Lemhi Pass, and was described by Pursh (1814).

Nearly a century after Linnaeus' first publication, Bentham (1835) recognized 25 species, 10 of which were new, including *M. cardinalis* Dougl. ex Benth., the second member to be described in our study group. Later treatments added new species and elevated some of those previously described to the status of separate genera. Nuttall (1838), for example, segregated the semishrubby group *Diplacus,* and Spach (1840) transferred *M. cardinalis* to the genus *Erythranthe*; Bentham (1846) reinstated *M. cardinalis* in *Mimulus,* but separated another group of three species under the genus *Eunamus.* Gray (1886) placed both *Diplacus* and *Eunamus* back in *Mimulus* with the rank of sections, and grouped the remainder of the species under two other sections, *Eumimulus* and *Mimuloides.* Later in the same year he established the section *Oenoe*.

The section *Erythranthe* was established in 1885 by E. L. Greene and included both *M. cardinalis* and *M. lewisii,* the only two members of the section (as it is now accepted) which were known at that time. Greene also included *M. parishii,* a new annual desert species, which he said could almost as well be included in his next new section, *Simiolus*.

The third species of the *Erythranthe* section was first collected in 1895 by Alice Eastwood near Bluff City along the San Juan River in southern Utah. Although she referred this collection to *M. cardinalis,* she noted that the plants were smaller and had more dentate and more villous leaves than California representatives of this species. This collection was apparently destroyed in the San Francisco earthquake in 1906. In 1913 P. A. Rydberg visited the same locality and recognized that Miss Eastwood had collected a new species, *M. eastwoodiae,* which he named in her honor. In 1909 E. L. Greene had described *M. verbenaceus* from Arizona and *M. rupestris* from Mexico, both of which we now recognize as members of the section.

Subsequently, some taxonomists raised some of the sections of *Mimulus* back to the status of genera, while others reduced them again to sections within the genus. In the most extensive taxonomic treatment made on the genus, Adele Grant (1924) recognized a total of 114 species grouped under 10 sections. She considered the section *Erythranthe* to consist of four species, *M. cardinalis* Dougl., *M. rupestris* Greene, *M. verbenaceus* Greene, and *M. nelsonii* Grant, the last of which she described as new. She placed *Mimulus lewisii* and *M. eastwoodiae* together with a number of other species in a new section *Paradanthus* on the basis of corolla morphology.

The first genetic information on *Mimulus* was reported by Brožek (1926) who studied the inheritance of flower spotting and other characters on horticultural forms referred to by the names *M. tigrinis*, *M. triginoides* and *M. quinqueovulaneus* of the section *Simiolus*. Earlier plant hybridizers included crossings between *M. cardinalis* and *M. lewisii* for horticultural purposes (Focke, 1881). Brožek (1929, 1930, 1931, 1932) later worked extensively on a Mendelian analysis of flower color inheritance in a horticultural form identified as *M. cardinalis* Dougl. These studies will be referred to again in the next chapter.

Since 1950 extensive cytogenetic studies have been made in *Mimulus* by Dr. Vickery and his students at the University of Utah. These have resulted in great clarification of the general biosystematic relationships within the entire genus, although chief emphasis has been placed on questions relating to speciation and evolution within the *Mimulus guttatus–glabratus* complex of the section *Simiolus*.

From their cytogenetic investigations Vickery and his associates have arrived at a clear picture of the genetic distinctness of most of the taxonomic sections of the genus that were recognized by Grant (Vickery, 1966). A notable exception is that Grant, on the basis of morphological characters, placed *M. lewisii* and *M. eastwoodiae* in a new section, *Paradanthus*, composed of a varied assortment of species, rather than in the *Erythranthe*. Subsequent cytogenetic evidence (Vickery, Mukherjee, and Wiens, 1958; 1963) clearly establishes the placement of both *M. lewisii* and *M. eastwoodiae* in the *Erythranthe* section.

SPECIES OF THE ERYTHRANTHE SECTION. Although the species of the *Erythranthe* section have previously been described, concepts regarding the relationships between this and other sections, and between the components of the section, have been modified considerably as evidence from biosystematic studies has accumulated. It is therefore helpful to review the taxonomy of the group in the light of the currently available information in order to establish a basis for the discussion and integration of the transplant, genetic, and physiological data presented in subsequent chapters.

The members of the *Erythranthe* section are all herbaceous perennials that have rootstocks or creeping stolons, conspicuous flowers with red, orange, pink, lavender or purple corollas, and stems with opposite leaves that differ widely in shape and size among the species. All the members of the section grow in moist habitats, either along stream banks or near springs or seeps in mountainous areas. As a group, the *Erythranthe* are readily distinguishable from other sections of the genus.

As presently understood, the section consists of the following *Mimulus* species: *M. cardinalis* Dougl., *M. lewisii* Pursh., *M. verbenaceus* Greene, *M. nelsonii* Grant, *M. eastwoodiae* Rydg., and *M. rupestris* Greene.

Typical forms of all of the above species except *M. rupestris* are illustrated in figures 2 to 6. As is evident from these drawings, each of the species is of distinct appearance. They can easily be distinguished from one another by means of the simple key that follows.

KEY TO SPECIES OF THE SECTION ERYTHRANTHE.
A. Anthers not reflexed, loculi in the same axis as the filaments or slightly crescent shaped
   a. Style and stamens strongly exerted, petals reflexed, color of corollas vermilion to intensely orange-red .... 1. *M. cardinalis*
   aa. Style and stamens included, petals spreading but never reflexed, color of corollas pale pink to deep rose-magenta .... 2. *M. lewisii*
AA. Anther lobes reflexed, horseshoe-shaped at the tips of the filaments
   a. Stems stout, spreading by coraloid rhizomes
     b. Stems erect, leaves elliptic, mostly erect or spreading .... 3. *M. verbenaceus*
     bb. Stems arching, leaves lanceolate to oblanceolate, recurved and arching ...... 4. *M. nelsonii*
   aa. Stems delicate, mostly prostrate, mainly spreading by stolons
     b. Leaves ovate to cuneate, coarsely and irregularly toothed all along the margins ....
                                                                                      5. *M. eastwoodiae*
     bb. Leaves elliptical to oblanceolate, saliently and regularly toothed only along the upper half..
                                                                                          6. *M. rupestris*

The distribution of the species shown in figure 1 is based on a study of herbarium collections at the University of California at Berkeley; the California Academy of Sciences, San Francisco; the Dudley Herbarium, Stanford; the Rancho Santa Ana Botanic Garden, Claremont; the herbarium of the University of Washington, Seattle; and the Washington State University Herbarium at Pullman. Grant (1924) included an extensive citation of herbarium collections and references to specific localities, so we will limit our discussion primarily to experimental materials used in our studies, which are listed in table 2.

It is evident from figure 1 that *M. cardinalis* and *M. lewisii* have the most widespread geographical distribution, and that *M. verbenaceus* has a more limited range. The remaining three species, *M. eastwoodiae, M. nelsonii,* and *M. rupestris,* are restricted endemics.

The numerous characters that distinguish the species of the *Erythranthe* section are to a degree linked genetically with physiological qualities that determine their capacity to survive in contrasting environments, as described in Chapters II and III. Brief general descriptions of each of the six species follow.

1. *Mimulus cardinalis* Dougl. in Benth. Scroph. Ind. 28, 1835.

M. cardinalis occurs along the Pacific Coast from lower California to Oregon, and inland to Arizona and Nevada. It grows at altitudes ranging from near sea level to 2,500 m. *M. cardinalis* consists of a large number of ecological races

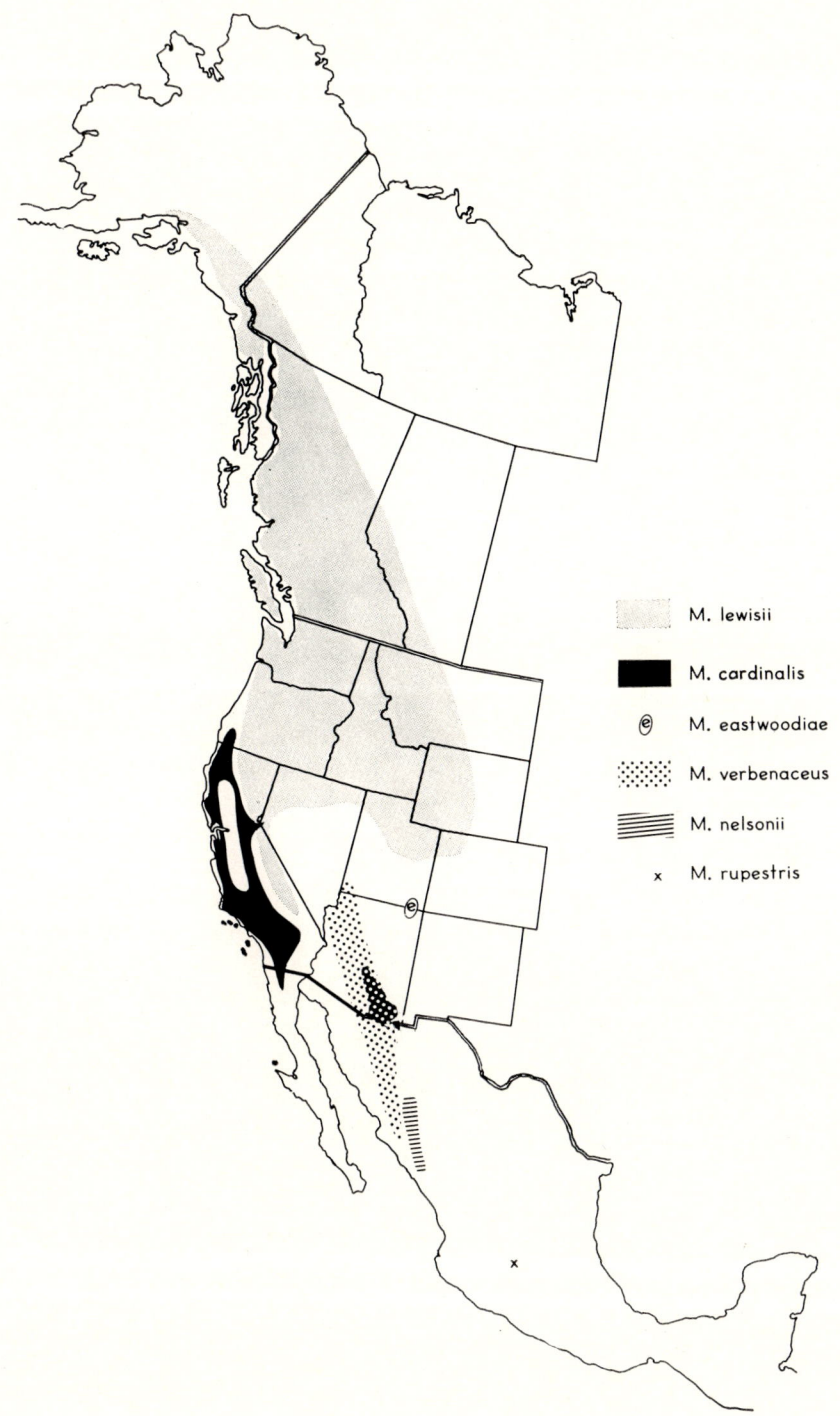

Figure 1. Geographical distribution of species of the *Erythranthe* section of *Mimulus*.

Figure 2. *Mimulus cardinalis* Dougl. drawn from clone 6546-5, originally from Los Trancos Creek, coastal central California. Stem approximately half natural size; anther, × 25; seed, × 50.

that may differ in minor morphological characters such as pubescence and thickness of leaves, anthocyanin markings on leaves, shading of flower color, habit of growth, and width of leaves. Individuals within given local populations also vary among themselves, but to a lesser degree.

A form occurring at high altitudes in Arizona has narrower leaves than other races, and is genetically differentiated by a mild sterility barrier that appears to be the result of a reciprocal translocation between two pairs of chromosomes (figure 9, lower right).

The flowers of *Mimulus cardinalis* are typically scarlet, but vary from pale reddish-yellow to yellow. Yellow-flowered forms have been reported by Grant (1924, p. 142) but have not been included in the present study.

2. *Mimulus lewisii* Pursh., Fl. Am. Sept. 2:427, pl 20, 1814.

The distribution of *M. lewisii* tends to complement that of *M. cardinalis*, *M. lewisii* being widespread at higher elevations and latitudes and extending to climates with more severe winters (figure 1). The southern limit is the Kings Canyon region in the southern Sierra Nevada of California. From there it extends northward through the Sierra Nevada and Cascade Ranges to southern coastal Alaska and eastward to Alberta, Idaho, Montana, Wyoming, Utah, and Colorado. Like *M. cardinalis*, *M. lewisii* is composed of ecological races that differ in color of corollas, in size, shape of leaves, and in stem and branching characteristics.

Forms from the Sierra Nevada of California are readily distinguishable from those further to the north and east in having narrower and less dentate leaves and pale pink flowers in contrast with the deep purple-flowered forms of the north and east. A partial genetic barrier exists between the Sierran and the northern forms, and is the result of two pairs of reciprocal translocations, as explained in more detail on page 12. Conceivably, the Sierran plants could merit taxonomic recognition as a subspecies, but in the present report we prefer to regard them as two regionally and cytologically differentiated races.

3. *Mimulus verbenaceus* Greene Leaflets Bot. Obs. & Crit. 2:2, 1909.

M. verbenaceus is less widely distributed than either *M. cardinalis* or *M. lewisii*, and occurs in interior regions from southern Utah to Arizona, and south to Mexico. It is found in open moist places along streams and seeps. There is considerable diversity in form among various races that occur at altitudes ranging from 600 m to around 2,250 m. The species overlaps in distribution with *M. cardinalis* in Arizona (cf. figure 1). Genetically, however, *M. verbenaceus* is more closely related to *M. eastwoodiae* and *M. nelsonii* than to *M. cardinalis*. It differs from *M. eastwoodiae* and *M. nelsonii* in leaf and flower characters, as shown in figures 4, 5, and 6.

Figure 3. *Mimulus lewisii* Pursh drawn from clone 7405-4, originally from the Harvey Monroe Hall Natural Area in the central crest of the Sierra Nevada of California. Stem approximately half natural size; anther, × 20; seed, × 60.

Figure 4. *Mimulus verbenaceus* Greene drawn from clone 7143-1, originally from the Bright Angel Trail, Grand Canyon, Arizona. Stem approximately two-thirds natural size; anther, × 20; seed, × 80.

4. *Mimulus nelsonii* Grant Ann. Mo. Bot. Gard. Vol. 11. 1924.

M. nelsonii has distinctive characters in having narrowly lanceolate, dark green leaves generally with anthocyanous cross bands in varying patterns and

Figure 5. *Mimulus eastwoodiae* Rydberg drawn from clone 7144-1, originally from Arches National Monument, Utah. Stem approximately natural size; anther, × 25; seed, × 85.

long, crimson corollas. It is distributed at higher altitudes in the central highlands of Mexico (figure 1) and as presently known occurs only over a limited geographical range. It appears to intergrade with *M. verbenaceus* in Mexico.

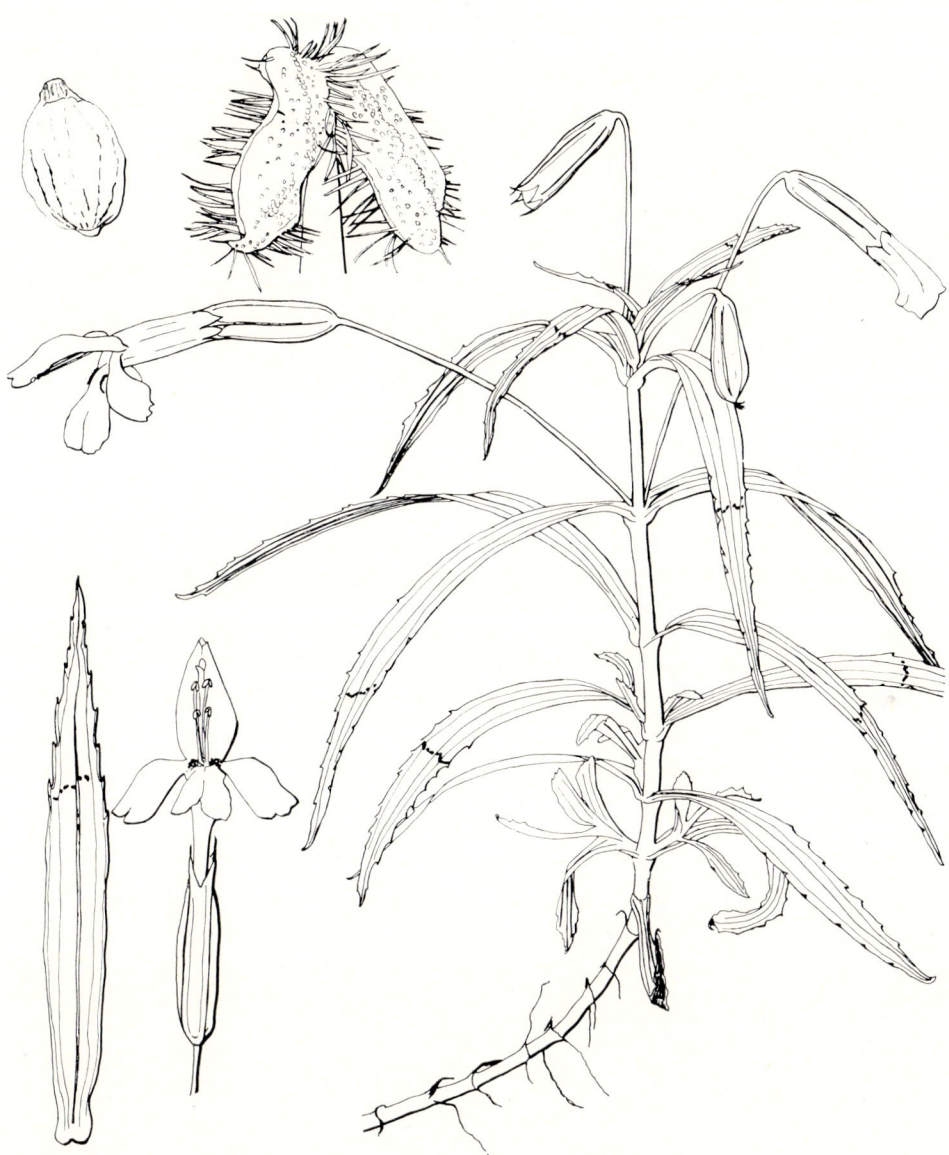

Figure 6. *Mimulus nelsonii* Grant drawn from clone 7422-13, originally from near El Salto, in the highlands of Mexico. Stem approximately two-thirds natural size; anther, × 25; seed, × 40.

5. *Mimulus eastwoodiae* Rydb. in Bull. Torr. Bot. Club 40:483, 1913.

Mimulus eastwoodiae is of very restricted distribution in southeastern Utah and northeastern Arizona, as indicated in figure 1. It occurs in special kinds of habitats in moist, shaded places, often in wet caves or under overhanging rocks in cliffy places in an otherwise arid climate. Its stoloniferous habit, as contrasted to the rhizomes characteristic of other species of the *Erythranthe* section, and its relatively small, highly dentate leaves and small flowers readily distinguish it from other species of the *Erythranthe* (figure 5).

6. *Mimulus rupestris* Greene, Leaflets Bot. Obs. & Crit. 2:3, 1909.

This species is thus far known to occur only on the site of Pringle's original collection in 1900, at about 2200 m elevation on wet cliffs at the Sierra de Tepoxtlan. It appears to be closely related to *M. verbenaceus, M. nelsonii* and *M. eastwoodiae.* No living material of *M. rupestris* has been available for the present investigations.

CYTOGENETIC RELATIONSHIPS BETWEEN AND WITHIN SPECIES. All of the species of the *Erythranthe* section as described above are diploid with $n=8$ chromosomes (figure 8). Extensive crossing experiments (table 1) within and between these species bring to light the existence of two genetically distinct components, as indicated in the diagram in figure 7. One consists of what may be regarded as the *Mimulus cardinalis–lewisii* complex, the other as the *M. verbenaceus–eastwoodiae–nelsonii* complex. First-generation hybrids within either group are fertile, in contrast with hybrids between the two groups, which are essentially sterile. There are differences in degree of fertility among hybrids within each of these two major groups, depending upon the particular combinations that are crossed, as shown in table 1. Some of these differences appear to be of significance in indicating biosystematic and evolutionary relationships and will be discussed later.

THE M. CARDINALIS–LEWISII COMPLEX. The very close genetic relationship between *M. cardinalis* and *M. lewisii* makes possible extensive cytogenetic and transplant studies with members of this group and combinations of hybrids between them. Chapter II is largely devoted to such studies, with special emphasis on the inheritance of characters of importance for survival in different kinds of environments. It seems significant that what appears to be parallel genetic barriers have evolved both within *Mimulus cardinalis* and within *M. lewisii,* as described below.

PARTIAL GENETIC BARRIERS WITHIN M. LEWISII. As indicated in figure 7, *M. lewisii* may be considered to be composed of two morphologically and geographically distinct forms. One group occurs northward from the Warner Mountains in California through British Columbia to Alaska and eastward to the Rocky Mountains. The other is native to the Sierra Nevada of California. When any of the former group are crossed among themselves in any combination, all the F_1 hybrids show regular pairing and high pollen fertility (table 1). The same is true when any of the races of *M. lewisii* from the Sierra Nevada

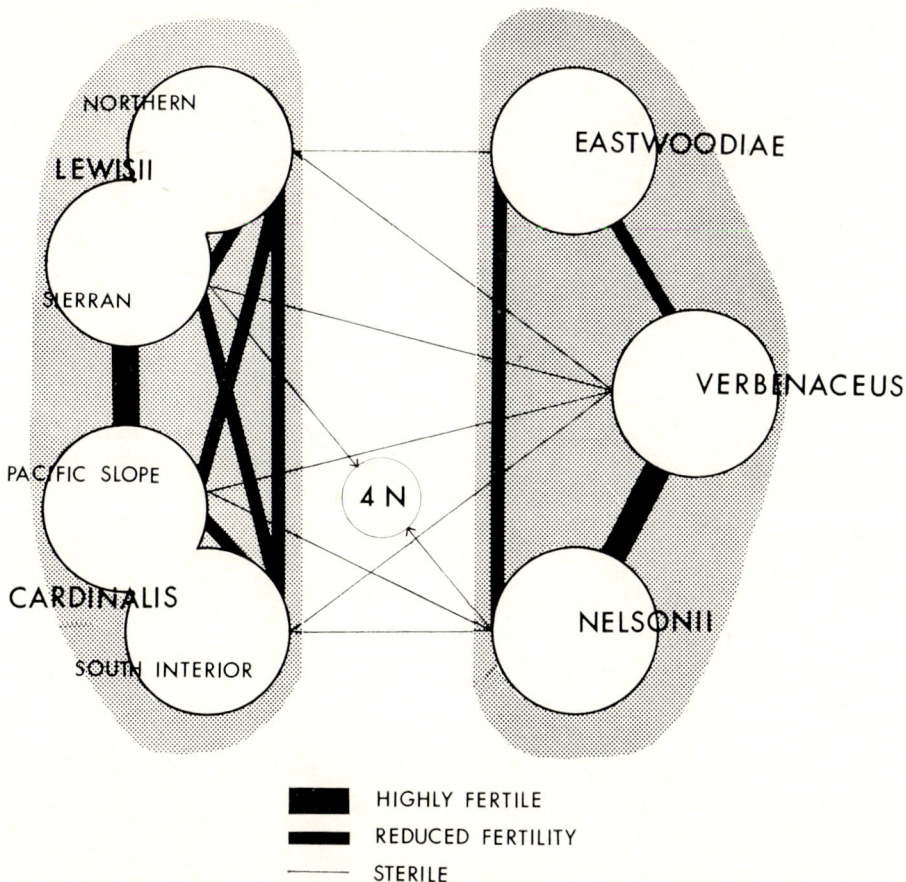

Figure 7. Degrees of interfertility between the major entities within the *Erythranthe* section of *Mimulus*. The shaded areas indicate taxa included within the two species-complexes. The tetraploid ($4n$) refers to the amphiploid between *M. nelsonii* and *M. lewisii*. See also figures 9, 11, and 12.

are intercrossed. Pollen fertilities in both instances range from 82 to 94 per cent. In F_1 hybrids between any of the members of the northern and of the Sierran group, however, there are consistent irregularities in chromosome pairing. Two sets of quadrivalents, either in rings or chains during first metaphase of meiosis (cf. figure 9, upper right) are characteristic, and pollen fertilities range from 33 to 56 per cent (table 1).

These cytogenetic differences are accompanied by combinations of morphological characters that make the two forms readily distinguishable. The most obvious difference is flower color. The corollas of the Sierran forms are mostly pale pink in contrast with the purplish to rose-magenta flowers of the northern race. The leaves are narrower and more lanceolate in the Sierran forms as contrasted with the northern races which are usually more ovate, shorter, and have longer-stalked glandular trichomes.

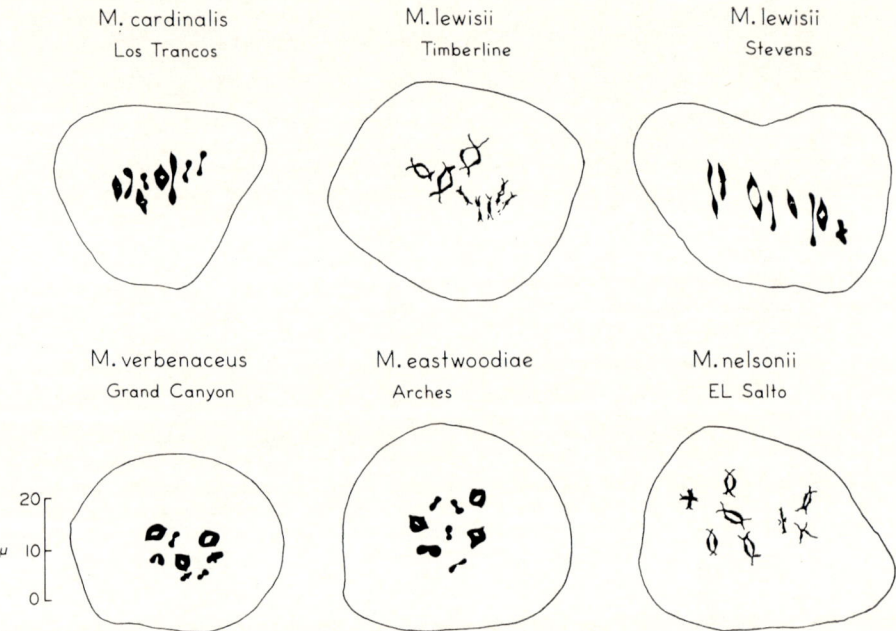

Figure 8. Smear preparations of pollen mother cells of species of the *Erythranthe* section of *Mimulus*, all having $n=8$ chromosomes with regular meiosis.

The northern forms of *M. lewisii* also differ physiologically from the Sierran forms as evidenced by their responses to transplanting at the Stanford, Mather, and Timberline field stations.

PARTIAL GENETIC BARRIERS WITHIN M. CARDINALIS. Within *M. cardinalis* there are likewise two groups that have evolved minor genetic incompatibilities between them. A race of *M. cardinalis* from the Santa Catalina Mountains of Arizona when crossed with races from the Pacific coast or from the central Sierra Nevada yields F_1 hybrids that show reduced pollen fertility of 60 to 80 per cent as compared with 90 to 95 per cent in crosses between different forms from California (table 1). This partial sterility also is accompanied by some meiotic irregularity in approximately 50 per cent of the pollen mother cells.

FLOWER STRUCTURE IN RELATION TO DIFFERENTIAL POLLINATION IN MIMULUS CARDINALIS AND M. LEWISII. In view of the high degree of interfertility between *M. cardinalis* and *M. lewisii*, the differences between these species in corolla-tube shape and in relative positions of anthers and pistils that favor different pollinating agents are of biosystematic importance.

The red-orange flowers of *M. cardinalis* have reflexed corolla lobes, and the

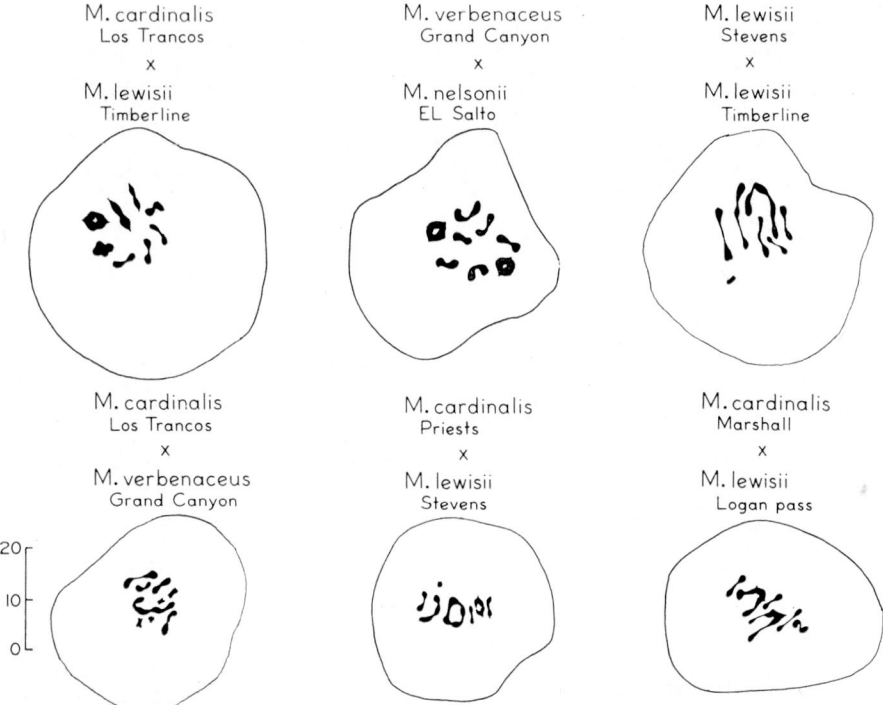

Figure 9. Examples of meiotic chromosomal pairing in F_1 hybrids between members of the *Erythranthe* section of *Mimulus*. Smear preparations of pollen mother cells.
Top row: left and center, regular pairing; right, irregular pairing between northern and southern races of *M. lewisii*.
Bottom row: other combinations with irregular pairing.

thick-walled corolla tube is strongly compressed laterally so that the width of its aperture rarely exceeds 4 mm. From this slot-like opening the long style and stamen filaments are exerted to a distance of about 16 mm above the corolla aperture, the stigma exceeding the anthers by about 4 mm (cf. plate I, also the floral diagram in figure 13). The bright color of the flowers attracts hummingbirds whose long beaks fit naturally into the narrow corolla tubes while gathering the nectar secreted at the base. During this process pollen from the exerted anthers is dusted freely on the foreheads of the hummingbirds

TABLE 1

Pollen Fertility, Seed Set, and Meiotic Behavior in Species, Intraspecific, and Interspecific Hybrids of the *Erythranthe* Section of *Mimulus*

Species and Races	Percent Normal Pollen	Percent Normal Seed Set	Meiotic Behavior
Mimulus cardinalis			
Races:			
Los Trancos	94	86	8 II, regular
Priests Grade	96	89	8 II, regular
Yosemite	96	84	8 II, regular
San Antonio Peak	95	81	8 II, regular
Baja California	95	86	8 II, regular
Marshall Gulch	92	72	8 II, regular
F_1 Hybrids			
Los Trancos × Priests Grade	94	87	8 II, regular
Los Trancos × Yosemite	94	88	8 II, regular
Los Trancos × San Antonio Pk.	92	91	8 II, regular
Los Trancos × Baja California	95	84	8 II, regular
Priests Grade × Yosemite	94	86	8 II, regular
Priests Grade × Baja California	95	86	8 II, regular
Yosemite × San Antonio	93	81	8 II, regular
Yosemite × Baja California	93	83	8 II, regular
Marshall Gulch × Los Trancos	82	42	6 II, 1 IV
Marshall Gulch × Priests Grade	76	61	6 II, 1 IV
Marshall Gulch × Yosemite	63	50	6 II, 1 IV
Marshall Gulch × Baja California	74	38	6 II, 1 IV
Mimulus lewisii			
Races:			
Yosemite	90	91	8 II, regular
Tamarack	91	88	8 II, regular
Porcupine	(male sterile)	...	...
Timberline	89	89	8 II, regular
Warner Mountains	95	86	8 II, regular
Mt. Rainier	94	88	8 II, regular
Stevens Pass	86	84	8 II, regular
Logan Pass	96	82	8 II, regular
F_1 Hybrids			
Yosemite × Tamarack	92	86	8 II, regular
Porcupine × Yosemite	89	92	8 II, regular
Yosemite × Timberline	92	88	8 II, regular
Timberline × Tamarack	93	84	8 II, regular
Tamarack × Timberline	92	83	8 II, regular
Porcupine × Timberline	91	86	8 II, regular
Warner Mts. × Stevens Pass	87	82	8 II, regular
Warner Mts. × Stevens Pass	94	86	8 II, regular
Warner Mts. × Logan Pass	95	84	8 II, regular
Mt. Rainier × Stevens Pass	94	88	8 II, regular
Mt. Rainier × Logan Pass	94	85	8 II, regular
Stevens Pass × Logan Pass	93	79	8 II, regular
Timberline × Warner Mts.	33	40	4 II, 2 IV
Timberline × Mt. Rainier	62	55	4 II, 2 IV

(*Continued on following page*)

TABLE 1—*Continued*

Species and Races	Percent Normal Pollen	Percent Normal Seed Set	Meiotic Behavior
Timberline × Stevens Pass	58	43	4 II, 2 IV
Timberline × Logan Pass	46	52	4 II, 2 IV
Mimulus cardinalis–lewisii combinations			
F₁ Hybrids			
Los Trancos × Yosemite	78	78	8 II, regular
Los Trancos × Tamarack	76	80	...
Los Trancos × Porcupine	73	86	8 II, regular
Los Trancos × Timberline	76	89	8 II, regular
Priests Grade × Timberline	68	81	...
Yosemite × Yosemite	80	71	8 II, regular
Yosemite × Tamarack	81	77	...
Yosemite × Porcupine	83	82	...
Yosemite × Timberline	77	92	8 II, regular
San Antonio Pk. × Yosemite	78	89	8 II, regular
San Antonio Pk. × Tamarack	83	86	...
San Antonio Pk. × Timberline	76	88	...
Baja California × Yosemite	74	87	...
Baja California × Tamarack	84	88	...
Baja California × Porcupine	82	87	...
Baja California × Timberline	82	89	8 II, regular
Marshall Gulch × Timberline	48	54	6 II, 1 IV
Los Trancos × Warner Mts.	40	50	4 II, 2 IV
Los Trancos × Mt. Rainier	37	36	...
Los Trancos × Stevens Pass	42	48	4 II, 2 IV
Los Trancos × Logan Pass	34	30	...
Priests Grade × Warner Mts.	22	28	...
Priests Grade × Mt. Rainier	28	26	4 II, 2 IV
Priests Grade × Stevens Pass	26	23	4 II, 2 IV
Priests Grade × Logan Pass	24	26	...
Yosemite × Mt. Rainier	33	46	...
Yosemite × Stevens Pass	34	30	...
San Antonio Pk. × Logan Pass	30	27	4 II, 2 IV
Baja California × Warner Mts.	30	8	4 II, 2 IV
Baja California × Mt. Rainier	34	13	4 II, 2 IV
Baja California × Stevens Pass	28	19	...
Baja California × Logan Pass	29	16	4 II, 2 IV
Marshall Gulch × Warner Mts.	31	4	...
Marshall Gulch × Mt. Rainier	(sublethal)		
Marshall Gulch × Stevens Pass	(sublethal)		
Marshall Gulch × Logan Pass	23	12	4 II, 2 IV
Mimulus cardinalis–verbenaceus combinations			
F₁ Hybrids			
Los Trancos × Grand Canyon	21	12	4 II, 1 IV, 4 I
Priests Grade × Grand Canyon	14	12	5 II, 1 IV, 2 I
Yosemite × Grand Canyon	21	14	4 II, IV, 4 I
San Antonio Pk. × Grand Canyon	14	...	...
Baja California × Grand Canyon	12	11	6 II, 1 IV
Marshall Gulch × Grand Canyon	...	...	...

(*Continued on following page*)

TABLE 1—*Continued*

Species and Races	Percent Normal Pollen	Percent Normal Seed Set	Meiotic Behavior
Mimulus lewisii–verbenaceus combinations			
F₁ Hybrids			
Timberline × Grand Canyon	20	1	6 II, 1 IV
Mt. Rainier × Grand Canyon	14	0	6 II, 1 IV
Logan Pass × Grand Canyon	14	11	6 II, 1 IV
Mimulus cardinalis–eastwoodiae combinations			
F₁ Hybrids			
Los Trancos × Arches	(unsuccessful)	...	...
Yosemite × Arches	10	1	4 II, 1 IV, 4 I
San Antonio Pk. × Arches	5	4	4 II, 1 IV, 4 I
Baja California × Arches	6	3	...
Mimulus lewisii–eastwoodiae combinations			
F₁ Hybrids			
Yosemite × Arches	9	1	4 II, 1 IV, 4 I
Tamarack × Arches	8	3	...
Timberline × Arches	8	6	4 II, 1 IV, 4 I
Mimulus cardinalis–nelsonii combinations			
F₁ Hybrids			
Los Trancos × El Salto	15	...	5 II, 1 IV, 2 I
Priests Grade × El Salto	11	6	...
Yosemite × El Salto	12	8	...
San Antonio Pk. × El Salto	12	10	...
Baja California × El Salto	10	17	5 II, 1 IV, 2 I
Marshall Gulch × El Salto	12	...	...
Mimulus lewisii–nelsonii combinations			
F₁ Hybrids			
Timberline × El Salto	22	5	3 II, 2 IV, 2 I
Mt. Rainier × El Salto	12	2	4 II, 1 IV, 4 I
Logan Pass × El Salto	13	3	3 II, 2 IV, 2 I
Mimulus verbenaceus			
Race:			
Grand Canyon	90	88	8 II, regular
F₁ Hybrid			
verbenaceus Grand Canyon × *eastwoodiae* Arches	84	81	8 II, regular
Mimulus eastwoodiae			
Race:			
Arches	76	67	8 II, regular
F₁ Hybrid			
eastwoodiae Arches × *nelsonii* El Salto	80	82	8 II, regular
Mimulus nelsonii			
Race:			
El Salto	...	73	8 II, regular
F₁ Hybrid			
verbenaceus Grand Canyon × *nelsonii* El Salto	93	83	8 II, regular

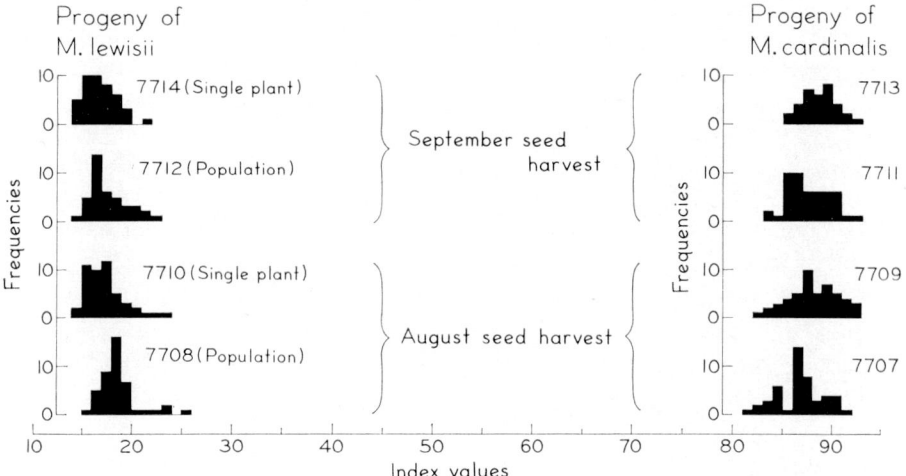

Figure 10. Constancy of progenies grown at Stanford derived from seed harvested on plants of *Mimulus lewisii* and *M. cardinalis* growing intermixed and flowering simultaneously in a natural habitat in the central Sierra Nevada. See text, and figure 28.

so that they become effective pollinating agents as they visit different flowers. Both in the experimental gardens and in natural populations two hummingbird species, *Calypte anna* T. L. (Anna) and *Selasphorus rufus* T. L. (Rufus) were observed to be habitual visitors of *M. cardinalis* throughout the flowering season and appear to be the most common pollinators of this species.

In contrast with *M. cardinalis*, *M. lewisii* has pale pink to deep rose flowers that have erect or spreading corolla lobes. The walls of the corolla tubes are thin, membranaceous and flexible, and the corolla tubes are 10 to 13 mm across. The style and anther filaments are much shorter than in *M. cardinalis* and are

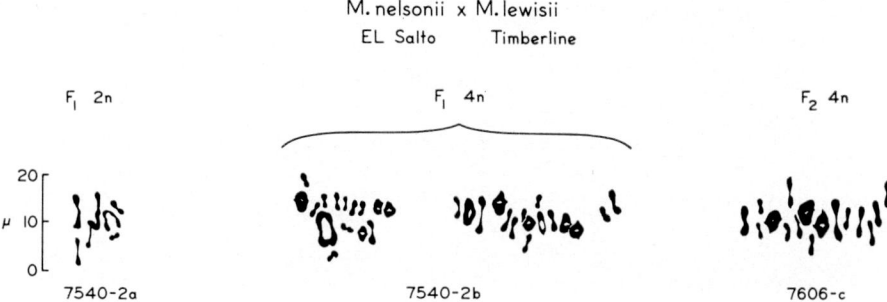

Figure 11. Chromosomal pairing during first metaphase of hybrid derivatives of *Mimulus nelsonii* × *M. lewisii*. *Left*, irregular pairing in the diploid sector ($n=8$) of an F_1 hybrid; *center*, partially irregular and regular pairing in the tetraploid sector ($n=16$) of the same F_1 individual; *right*, regular pairing in the self-perpetuating amphiploid of the tetraploid F_1.

included well within the corolla tube about 4 mm below the corolla tube opening (cf. figure 13). The flowers of *M. lewisii* are ideally suited for pollination by bees. These insects are able to crawl down the wide corolla tubes when gathering nectar at the base. In this operation pollen is released on their bodies and is carried from flower to flower. Both honeybees and wild bumblebees have been observed to act as pollinators, the latter especially at high altitudes in natural habitats of *M. lewisii*. In the Timberline population three species, *Bombus centralis* Cresson, *B. balteatus* Dahlbom, and *B. flavifrons* Cresson have been taken from corollas of *M. lewisii*.

Although *M. lewisii* is frequently visited by hummingbirds, and *M. cardinalis* by bees, and both species, in turn, by other insects including carpenter bees, butterflies, sphinx moths, ants, and beetles, cross-pollination between the two species has been found to be extremely rare both in the experimental gardens and in natural populations.

Mimulus cardinalis and *M. lewisii* seldom occur together under natural conditions because of their different habitat requirements. Consequently, they are essentially nonoverlapping in distribution (cf. figure 1). At mid-elevations on the western slope of the Sierra Nevada, however, seeds of *M. lewisii* from high elevations are occasionally carried by streams to lower sites occupied by *M. cardinalis* and establish ephemeral populations. Progeny tests have been made from two such sites located about 30 miles apart in Yosemite National Park. One was on the floor of Yosemite Valley along the banks of the Merced River at approximately 1300 m elevation. At this site a small but essentially constant population of about 22 individuals of *M. cardinalis* was studied from 1956 through 1960. During the summer of 1957 three individuals of *M. lewisii* became established in this colony, and again in 1959 five individuals of this species were observed. In both years the plants of *M. cardinalis* and *M. lewisii* flowered simultaneously at this site. Progeny tests consisting of 200 seedling plants harvested from each species on both years failed to yield any F_1 hybrids,

Plate I. Floral characters in *Mimulus lewisii* and *M. cardinalis* and their inheritance in the first- and second-generation hybrids.

Upper row: left, *M. lewisii* originally from the Harvey Monroe Hall Natural Area at 3200 m elevation; *right*, *M. cardinalis* from near sea-level in central California; *center*, their F_1 hybrid.

Lower rows: Sample of second-generation plants showing various recombinations of pigmentation in the petals and floral structure: 7135-35, a *cardinalis*-like derivative having yellow carotenoid pigments in all petal tissues, and vegetatively also like *M. cardinalis* (parent of the F_3 population 7428, Plate II, *bottom*); 7111-17, an intermediate derivative lacking carotenoid pigments in the petal lobes and vegetatively like the F_1; 7111-16, a recombination essentially like *M. lewisii* in pigmentation, floral, and vegetative characteristics (parent of the F_3 population 7541, Plate II, *top*); 7135-60, a recombination like the F_1, but with yellow carotenoid pigments in the mesophyll of the petal-lobe tissues; 6700-246, a recombination having carotenoid pigments in the lower epidermis and in the mesophyll but not in upper epidermis, and unusual in that the stamens exceed the styles; 6699-303, a *M. cardinalis*-like recombination in flower structure, but lacking carotenoid pigments in the upper epidermis.

Plate II. Examples of patterns of variation in floral characteristics in three F_3 populations of *M. lewisii* × *M. cardinalis*.

  Top: Array of progeny from 7111-16, a *lewisii*-like F_2 individual (see Plate I).
  Center: Array from 7135-34, an F_1-like F_2 derivative.
  Bottom: Array from 7135-35, a *cardinalis*-like F_2 plant (see Plate I).
Note the genetic coherence expressed in the linkage between floral pigments and floral structure, especially in the degree of exertion of the anthers and pistils.

Figure 12. Flowers of *Mimulus nelsonii*, clone 7422-12 (*upper left*), *M. lewisii*, clone 7405-4 (*upper right*), and their F_1 hybrid (*upper center*).
Below: Flowers from the diploid sector of the F_1 hybrid 7540-2 (*left*) and the tetraploid sector of the same plant (*right*).

nor were any hybrids found in the area of the original site during subsequent years.

A second locality studied in 1968 and 1969 was on a small island and gravel bar along the South Fork of the Tuolumne River at about 1400 m elevation. Here nearly equal numbers of both species were present with 53 plants of *M. cardinalis* and 44 of *M. lewisii*. As in the previous locality, flowering of the

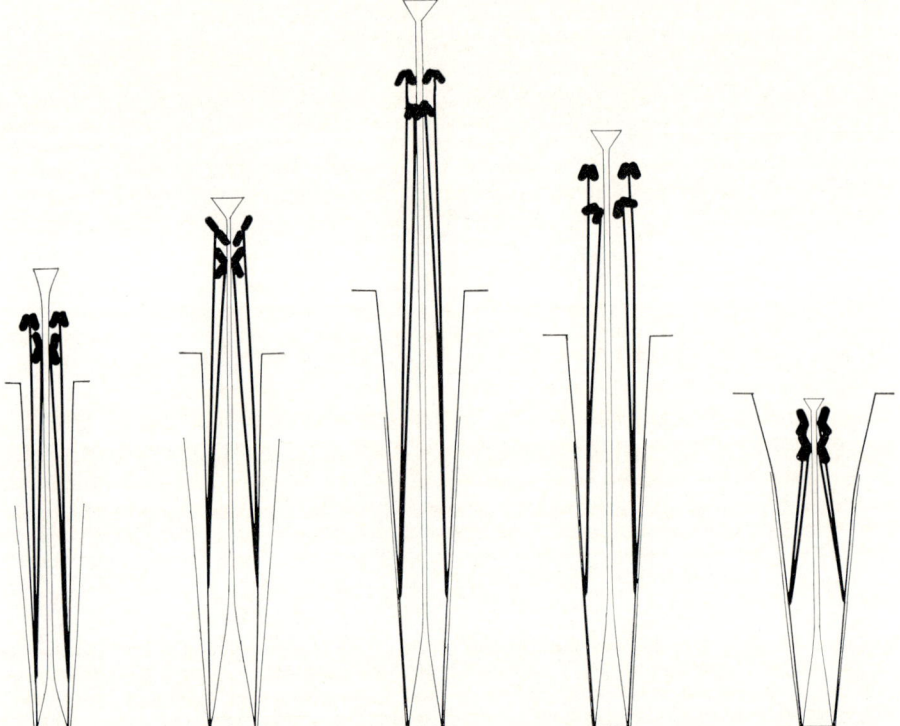

Figure 13. Diagrams of longitudinal sections of flowers of different species of the *Erythranthe* section of *Mimulus* showing differences in the exertion of anthers and stigmas in relation to corolla tubes.
Left to right: *Mimulus eastwoodiae, M. cardinalis, M. nelsonii, M. verbenaceus,* and *M. lewisii*.

two species was simultaneous, starting in mid-June and continuing through September. Seed set on all plants of both species was excellent, with from 80 to 90 per cent of the flowers having full seed capsules. Seed samples for progeny tests were collected on both species twice during the season. The first collection was made during the early part of August when the seeds of most of the earlier flowers were ripe; the second was made in September when most of the plants were past flowering and in ripe fruit. From each species at each date two kinds of samples were taken. One consisted of all the ripe capsules from a single plant of each species that grew within 30 cm of each other. The second consisted of a single ripe capsule from each of the remaining plants in the entire population of the two species.

The seeds thus collected were germinated and grown at Stanford, the seedlings being space-planted in rows in a garden. When the resulting populations were in full flower, individual seedlings were scored on the basis of their morphology on an index scale, as explained on page 30, low values falling within the range of *M. lewisii,* and high values within the range of *M. cardinalis.* The frequency histograms shown in figure 10 summarize the results of this study. As is evident from the figure, not a single hybrid between *M. lewisii* and *M. cardinalis* was found. Moreover, thorough search at the site of their origin in 1969 failed to reveal the presence of any hybrids. The population of *M. cardinalis* remained essentially stable with 56 plants present, but the frequency of *M. lewisii* dropped from 44 individuals in 1968 to only 13 in 1969.

From these tests it is evident that the combined effect of ecological isolation and differential pollinating agents serves as an extremely effective barrier to natural intercrossing between these morphologically very distinct but genetically highly interfertile species.

THE M. VERBENACEUS–EASTWOODIAE–NELSONII COMPLEX. Crosses between any of these morphologically distinct species, in any combination, yield vigorous F_1 hybrids that in some instances show slightly reduced fertility over crosses made within either of the three species (cf. table 1). Conspicuous morphological differences between *Mimulus verbenaceus* and *M. nelsonii* are found, for example, to segregate widely in the F_2 generation, and show many kinds of recombinations, as described in Chapter II.

AN AMPHIPLOID BETWEEN M. NELSONII AND M. LEWISII. The relative genetic distinctness between the *M. cardinalis–lewisii* complex, on one hand, and the *M. eastwoodiae–verbenaceus–nelsonii* complex, on the other, is further demonstrated by the formation of a stable new tetraploid amphiploid derivative between *M. nelsonii* and *M. lewisii*. The amphiploid was derived by pollinating a clone of *M. nelsonii* (7422-12, El Salto) with *M. lewisii* (clone 7405-4, Timberline). Among a population of 92 vigorous F_1 plants, one was a sectorial chimera that spontaneously produced a segment of tetraploid tissue in addition to normal diploid tissue. Flowers produced on the diploid sector were sterile, whereas those on the tetraploid sector yielded a high percentage of viable seeds. These gave rise to a stable, non-segregating F_2 population of amphiploid progeny. Figure 11 shows drawings of irregular meiotic pairing between the parental chromosomes in pollen mother cells of the diploid sector of the F_1 hybrid, examples of both irregular and regular pairing in the tetraploid sector of the F_1, and regular normal pairing in the tetraploid amphiploid F_2 derivative. Figure 12 illustrates flowers of the parents and sterile F_1 hybrid (above) and diploid and tetraploid flowers of the sectorial chimera from which the amphiploid originated.

The amphiploid derivatives, unlike the *M. lewisii* parent, grow vigorously in the Stanford garden and appear as a uniform, constant-breeding population. So far as we are aware this is the only known instance of polyploidy within the *Erythranthe* section. In other sections of the genus, as for example section *Simiolus,* studied extensively by Vickery and his associates, polyploidy is a prominent feature of speciation. Mukherjee and Vickery (1962) reported in this section an example of what may have been amphiploidy in an interspecific cross between inter-sterile *M. tilingii* and *M. guttatus,* but the genetic reproducibility of this combination was not tested.

ATTEMPTED CROSSES WITH SPECIES OUTSIDE THE SECTION ERYTHRANTHE. In his extensive crossing experiments Vickery (1966) attempted a number of hybridizations between *M. cardinalis* and various forms of *M. guttatus, M. ringens, M. luteus,* and *M. primuloides,* and also between *M. lewisii* and the same group of species. In none of these instances were viable F_1 hybrids produced. The present authors have confirmed this negative evidence from numerous attempts to obtain progeny in combinations between *M. cardinalis* and *M. primuloides, M. guttatus, M. moschatus, M. dentatus,* and other species outside the *Erythranthe* section.

CONCLUSIONS CONCERNING THE BIOSYSTEMATIC RELATIONSHIPS WITHIN THE ERYTHRANTHE SECTION. The biosystematic evidence indicates that the *Erythranthe* section has evolved as an evolutionary assemblage separate from other species of *Mimulus* over long periods of geological time. The separation between the *M. cardinalis–lewisii* complex and the *M. verbenaceus–eastwoodiae–nelsonii* complex, although occurring considerably later in the evolutionary time scale, is undoubtedly also of ancient origin although the genomes of the two complexes still function harmoniously when combined in an amphiploid.

The question as to how the *Erythranthe* should be dealt with taxonomically suggests two possible choices. One is to recognize the entities named above as valid species, including perhaps the sixth as yet little known *M. rupestris* collected by Pringle. Another alternative is to consider the *M. cardinalis–lewisii* complex to be a single biological species, and the *M. verbenaceus–eastwoodiae–nelsonii* complex to be a second species.

Most taxonomists undoubtedly prefer to follow the classical approach and to attach specific names to such recognizably distinct entities as *M. lewisii* and *M. cardinalis,* and to *M. verbenaceus, M. eastwoodiae* and *M. nelsonii.* In the absence of cytogenetic evidence, Kearney and Peebles (1942) regarded *M. verbenaceus* as a variety of *M. cardinalis* on the basis of morphological similarity.

From a biosystematic point of view we are inclined to regard the *Erythranthe* section as being composed of only two biologically distinct species, as reflected in the diagram, figure 7. Support for this view can be most clearly seen from the genetic evidence presented in table 1. Whether or not the nomenclature should be altered to reflect this concept is an open question. We have chosen to follow the classical classification for the purpose of emphasizing the morphological and ecological contrasts between *M. cardinalis* and *M. lewisii* in our presentation of the available experimental evidence relating to the genetic structure and composition of these and other members of the section.

II
GENETIC AND TRANSPLANT STUDIES

This chapter summarizes data obtained from transplant experiments at the Stanford, Mather, and Timberline sites combined with inter- and intra-specific crossings between entities of various ranks within the *Erythranthe* section of *Mimulus,* as outlined in Chapter I. These results were accumulated through the years from 1952 through 1969 from cultures involving many thousands of plants. To attempt a detailed account of all the experiments and recorded observations would lengthen this report unduly. We will therefore endeavor to portray the most salient features that have emerged and to interpret their significance as they relate to mechanisms of natural selection and evolution in higher plants.

METHODS

SOURCES OF EXPERIMENTAL MATERIALS. Many of the *Mimulus* plants were either obtained as transplants dug from their natural habitats, as described in earlier studies of this series (cf. Clausen, Keck, and Hiesey, 1948; Clausen and Hiesey, 1958) or were grown from seed collected from plants in their natural habitats. Seeds collected from distant areas were kindly furnished to us by other botanists, including Dr. R. K. Vickery, Jr., Dr. Kenton Chambers, Dr. Richie Bell, Dr. Dennis Breedlove, and Miss Jane Reese (cf. table 2), to whom the authors are most grateful. Table 2 lists the principal collections of *Mimulus* used in the present studies.

TRANSPLANT EXPERIMENTS. The time-honored method of establishing vegetatively propagated clones of individual plants, which are subsequently grown in gardens at the altitudinal stations at Stanford (elevation 30 m), Mather (1400 m), and Timberline (3050 m) for the purpose of determining expression of growth, survival, and response patterns in contrasting climates, has supplied a substantial part of the data in these investigations. For details describing the transplant stations and methods of transplanting, the reader is referred to the earlier publications of this series, especially Clausen, Keck, and Hiesey (1940, 1948) and Clausen and Hiesey (1958). In *Mimulus* the transplant experiments proved to be especially useful for comparing the survival and overall growth performance of species and races originally from contrasting climates, and of first-, second-, and third-generation progeny derived from crosses between them.

CROSSING EXPERIMENTS. Controlled pollinations between the various members of the *Erythranthe* section are easily made. The single stigma and the well-separated and easily removed anthers that are attached to the corolla tubes are readily emasculated with simple tools. A single seed capsule may, in fertile combinations, yield up to 600 or more offspring. Mature seeds germinate readily when grown in soil in seed-pans in a greenhouse. After germination, the

TABLE 2

Cultures of *Mimulus* Used in Crossing and Transplant Experiments

Culture Number	Origin	Reference Code	Elevation, meters	Latitude, degrees N.	Longitude, degrees W.
Mimulus cardinalis Dougl.					
6542	Los Trancos Creek, San Mateo County, California	Trancos	30	37° 19'	122°23'
6578	Canyon del Diablo, San Pedro Martir, Baja California. K. Chambers 531	Baja	600	31° 7'	115° 21'
6694	Yosemite Valley, Mariposa County, California	Yosemite	1200	37° 43'	119° 40'
6998	Woodfords, Alpine County, California. F. J. Fisher	Woodfords	2000	38° 45'	119° 50'
7114	Little Wolf Creek, Grass Valley, Nevada County, California	Grass Valley	800	39° 12'	121° 3'
7116	North Crane Creek, Yosemite National Park, Tuolumne County, California	Crane	1400	37° 47'	119° 50'
7117	Middle Fork of Tuolumne River, Yosemite National Park, Tuolumne County, California	Middle Fork	2100	37° 49'	119° 45'
7120	San Antonio Peak, San Gabriel Mts., Los Angeles County, California. Verne Grant 9760	San Antonio	2200	34° 16'	117° 38'
7142	Beaver Creek, Siskiyou County, California	Siskiyou	700	42° 56'	122° 49'
7210	Priests Grade, Tuolumne County, California	Priests	400	37° 48'	120° 17'
7211	Jacksonville, Tuolumne County, California	Jacksonville	240	37° 51'	120° 22'
7245	Marshall Gulch, Santa Catalina Mountains, Pima County, Arizona. J. Reese	Marshall Gulch	2440	32° 26'	110° 46'
7246	Bear Wallow, Santa Catalina Mountains, Pima County, Arizona. J. Reese	Bear Wallow	2280	32° 25'	110° 43'

(*Continued on following page*)

TABLE 2—*Continued*

Culture Number	Origin	Reference Code	Elevation, meters	Latitude, degrees N.	Longitude, degrees W.
Mimulus lewisii Pursh					
6632	East of Stevens Pass, Chelan County, Washington	Stevens	760	47° 40'	120° 25'
6541	Harvey Monroe Hall Natural Area, Mono County, California	Timberline	3200	37° 59'	119° 19'
6686	Merced River, Yosemite National Park, Mariposa County, California	Yosemite	1200	37° 43'	119° 40'
7122	Tamarack Flat, Yosemite National Park, Mariposa County, California	Tamarack	1900	37° 31'	119° 43'
7123	Smoky Jack, Yosemite National Park, Mariposa County, California	Smoky Jack	2300	37° 50'	119° 41'
7124	Porcupine Flat, Yosemite National Park, Mariposa County, California	Porcupine	2400	37° 48'	119° 34'
7125	Murphy Creek, Yosemite National Park, Mariposa County, California	Tenaya	2500	37° 50'	119° 27'
7127	Warren Creek, Mono County, California	Warren	2800	37° 57'	119° 13'
7128	East side of Ebbetts Pass, Alpine County, California. F. J. Fisher	Ebbetts	2100	38° 35'	119° 47'
7129	East side of Donner Pass, Nevada County, California. F. J. Fisher	Donner	2000	39° 19'	120° 13'
7145	Big Cottonwood Canyon, Wasatch Mts., near Alta, Salt Lake City, Utah. R. K. Vickery	Alta	2650	40° 35'	*ca.* 111° 37'
7146	Mt. Rainier, Mt. Rainier National Park, Pierce County, Washington. N. K. Potts	Rainier	1200–1500	46° 47'	121° 45'
7212	East side of Logan Pass, Glacier National Park, Glacier County, Montana. R. Johnson	Logan	2000	48° 45'	113° 20'
7256	Warner Mts. near Lily Lake, Modoc County, California. Haller 1462	Warner	2000	41° 58'	120° 14'

(*Continued on following page*)

TABLE 2—*Continued*

Culture Number	Origin	Reference Code	Elevation, meters	Latitude, degrees N.	Longitude, degrees W.
7643	Jarbidge Mts., Elko County, Nevada. O. Shields	Jarbidge	2400	45° 45'	115° 28'
7644	Wheeler Peak, White Pine County, Nevada. O. Shields	Wheeler	3200	39° 3'	114° 19'
Mimulus verbenaceus Greene					
7143	Bright Angel Trail, Grand Canyon, Coconino County, Arizona. Earl Jackson	Grand Canyon	610	36° 6'	112° 6'
7548	Above Weeping Rock, Zion National Park, Washington County, Utah. J. Reese	Zion	1500	37° 16'	112° 57'
7638	Canyon de Tarahinure, Surotato, Sinaloa, Mexico. D. Breedlove 15600	Sinaloa	1550		
7639	Canyon de Tarahinure, Surotato, Sinaloa, Mexico. D. Breedlove 15616	Surotato	920		
Mimulus eastwoodiae Rydg.					
7144	Arches National Monument, Grand County, Utah. R. K. Vickery 339	Arches	1300	*ca.* 38° 40'	*ca.* 109° 35'
7420	Mystery Canyon, San Juan County, Utah. T. Morley	Mystery	*ca.* 1300	*ca.* 37° 19'	*ca.* 112° 56'
7421	Rainbow Bridge, Bridge Canyon, San Juan County, Utah. T. Morley	Rainbow	*ca.* 1000	*ca.* 37° 4'	*ca.* 110° 57'
Mimulus nelsonii Grant					
7422	Road between Mazatlan and El Salto, Durango, Mexico. C. Richie Bell 17703	El Salto			
7640	Between Mazatlan and Durango, Durango, Mexico. Dennis Breedlove	Mazatlan			
7641	Between Villa Union and Durango, Durango, Mexico, on highway 40. H. G. Baker 7641	Durango	2400		

seedlings may be transplanted to flats in which they may be grown to a size sufficient for transfer either to pots or to field plots. Clones of individual plants can readily be established through vegetative propagation either by dividing root stocks or by making cuttings from growing shoots, and can be used in any number of experiments involving physiological and biochemical studies in controlled environments.

RECORDING AND PROCESSING OF DATA. Records pertaining to each individual and to propagules made from it were kept in notebooks at Stanford and at the altitudinal field stations. Genetic data on as many as 24 specific characters have been recorded over the years. The results at each transplant station, averaged over a period of years, have been coded and transferred to IBM cards for statistical analysis with the help of computers. This is a technique especially useful for studying correlations in inheritance between various combinations of characters in second- and third-generation progenies from intra- and interspecific crosses. The methods used for coding characters in *Mimulus* were essentially the same as those described in an earlier study of *Potentilla* (Clausen and Hiesey, 1958, pp. 110–114).

INDEX VALUES. The use of index values has proved to be helpful for comparing the overall characteristics of an individual plant of hybrid origin in terms of its degree of similarity to or difference from either original parent. These values are obtained by simply adding up the total score for that individual of its rating on a scale of 1 to 9 for each of a number of characters that distinguish the parents. This method was introduced by Anderson (1936) and has been used by many workers.

In the present study most of the discussion relating to the inheritance and segregation of specific characters revolves on first-, second-, and third-generation hybrids between *Mimulus lewisii* and *M. cardinalis*. In assigning values for a given character, the expression of that character in *M. lewisii* is assigned a low value (usually from 1 to 3, depending upon the degree of variability of that character within the parental race) and the expression of that same character in *M. cardinalis* a value of 8 or 9. Individual hybrid derivatives of this parentage are assigned values estimated to be close approximations on the basis of such a scale. The sum of 14 or more such values representing selected characters differentiating the parents is then used as the *index value* of that individual.

The scoring for different characters is described in the following pages under the discussion of the inheritance of each character. Index values are used mainly for comparing the phenotypic composition of progenies of different genetic origin.

CLASSES OF HERITABLE CHARACTERS THAT DISTINGUISH SPECIES AND ECOLOGICAL RACES

One may broadly classify characters that distinguish species and races of the *Erythranthe* section of *Mimulus* into two groups:

Morphological characters. These are of great importance and serve as both taxonomic and genetic markers. They include such characters as size and shape of floral and vegetative parts, color and color-patterns in flowers, and growth habit. Among such markers one may distinguish between characters that are relatively stable in expression in a wide range of environments, as, for example, leaf shape and floral characters, and others that are highly modifiable, such as leaf size and number of flowers per inflorescence. Examples of both essentially nonmodifiable and modifiable characters and their mode of inheritance will be described in later paragraphs.

Physiological characters. Differences in capability for survival and growth in the contrasting environments at the Stanford, Mather, and Timberline transplant stations, and variations in phenological responses, including the timing of developmental stages during the seasons, are characters that are often inherited and can be observed in garden cultures. The study of internal functions, on the other hand, requires quantitative measurements under controlled laboratory conditions.

The expression of inherited differences in nearly all physiological characters is usually highly modified by the environments in which the plants are growing. This is true both in experiments for testing survival and growth performance at the transplant stations and in highly refined laboratory measurements under controlled conditions. The degree of modification under known sets of controlled environments may yield information of importance regarding possible mechanisms of natural selection.

That physiological characteristics are of basic importance for determining the natural distribution of species and races of plants in different environments is axiomatic. From a biosystematic and evolutionary point of view, a study of the inheritance of both morphological and physiological characters is of prime importance in determining to what extent, if any, the two kinds of characters may be genetically linked.

The remainder of this chapter will be devoted to the study of the inheritance of characters of species of the *Erythranthe* section of *Mimulus* in relation to morphological and physiological characteristics that can be observed in greenhouse and garden experiments in both inter- and intraspecific combinations. Data relating to quantitatively measured physiological characters under controlled laboratory conditions will be reserved for Chapter III.

INTERSPECIFIC COMBINATIONS

Most of the emphasis in the current study on *Mimulus* has been concentrated on interspecific combinations of the *Erythranthe* section, especially of combinations between *Mimulus cardinalis* and *M. lewisii* which have especially suitable distinguishing traits that can be followed through various generations. Since characters that distinguish *M. cardinalis* and *M. lewisii* are also common to the other species of the *Erythranthe* section, the discussion in the following paragraphs for individual characters applies in varying degree to all interspecific combinations within the section. The major interspecific cultures that have been included in this study are listed in table 3.

Characters that are essentially unmodified by the external environment provide the most satisfactory markers for genetic studies. These will be discussed first.

ESSENTIALLY NONMODIFIABLE MORPHOLOGICAL CHARACTERS THAT DISTINGUISH ENTITIES OF THE ERYTHRANTHE SECTION. As emphasized in Chapter I, morphological characters that distinguish different species and races of the *Erythranthe* section of *Mimulus* are distinctive and can in general be described with clarity. Close study, nevertheless, reveals complexity in almost every character. Eleven characters that have proven to be essentially nonmodifiable when clones are transplanted to different environments, either at the contrasting altitudinal stations at Stanford, Mather, and Timberline, or in controlled growth cabinets, are reviewed below in some detail.

1. *Petal reflexing*

The character "petal reflexing" is based primarily on the orientation of two lateral petal lobes of the lower corolla lip in relation to the axis of the corolla tube. In *M. cardinalis* these lobes are strongly reflexed, and usually addressed backwards against the corolla tube, forming an angle of 180° with respect to the tube axis. In contrast, the corresponding petal lobes of *M. lewisii* are erect or slightly spreading and form an angle less than 60° with respect to the axis of the corolla tube (cf. figure 14, also figures 2 and 3). In *M. nelsonii* the petal lobes of the upper lip are as in *M. cardinalis,* but the lateral petal lobes of the lower lip are not reflexed. *Mimulus verbenaceus* resembles *M. nelsonii* in the reflexing character (figure 4); *M. eastwoodiae,* on the other hand, approaches *M. lewisii* in the nonreflexed orientation of the petal lobes (figure 5).

The inheritance of petal reflexing can most clearly be studied in crosses between *M. cardinalis* and *M. lewisii.* The F_1 hybrids are intermediate in expression in this character, but with a bias towards *M. lewisii.* Second-generation progenies display a wide range of recombinations that encompasses both parental extremes, with a slightly skewed frequency distribution in the direction of *lewisii*-like types. In F_3 progenies the frequency distribution in different classes of expression of this character depends heavily on the particular genotype of the F_2 progenitor.

The classes of progeny derived from crosses between *M. cardinalis* and *M. lewisii* were scored on a scale of 1 to 9 according to the approximate angle formed by the lateral petal lobes of the lower lip with the main axis of the corolla tube, as listed in table 4.

The observed inheritance of petal reflexing in crosses between *M. cardinalis* and *M. lewisii* in F_1, F_2, and F_3 progeny is summarized in table 5. This table

TABLE 3
Interspecific Hybrids in *Mimulus*

Culture No.	Combination *	Generation
1. Combinations between *Mimulus cardinalis* and *M. lewisii*		
6544	6542-1 card Trancos × 6541-1 lew Timberline	F_1
6545	6542-1 card Trancos × 6541-1 lew Timberline	F_1
6546	6542-2 card Trancos × 6541-3 lew Timberline	F_1
6547	6541-3 lew Timberline × 6542-1 card Trancos	F_1
6548	6542-2 card Trancos × 6541 lew Timberline	F_1
6549	6541-4 lew Timberline × 6542-2 card Trancos	F_1
6635	6546-5 card Trancos × 6546-3, F_1 of 6546	B_1†
6636	6541-3 lew Timberline × 6546-3, F_1 of 6546	B_2‡
6637	6546-3, F_1 of 6546 × self	F_2
6638	6547-1, F_1 of 6547 × self	F_2
6695	6546-5 card Trancos × 6632-1 lew Stevens	F_1
6696	6632-1 lew Stevens × 6546-5 card Trancos	F_1
6697	6543-111 card Trancos × 6632-1 lew Stevens	F_1
6698	6632-1 lew Stevens × 6543-111 card Trancos	F_1
6699	6546-3, F_1 of 6546 × self	F_2
6886	6875-2 card Baja × 6632-1 lew Stevens	F_1
6687	6632-1 lew Stevens × 6875-2 card Baja	F_1
6688	6875-2 card Baja × 6684-2 lew Timberline	F_1
6689	6684-2 lew Timberline × 6875-2 card Baja	F_1
6700	6547-1, F_1 of 6547 × self	F_2
6701	6546-5 card Trancos × 6546-3, F_1 of 6546	B_1
6702	6541-3 lew Timberline × 6546-3, F_1 of 6546	B_2
6978	6699-451, F_2 of card Trancos × lew Timberline × self	F_3
6979	6638-141, F_2 of lew Timberline × card Trancos × self	F_3
6980	6638-208, F_2 of lew Timberline × card Trancos × self	F_3
6981	6638-256, F_2 of lew Timberline × card Trancos × self	F_3
6982	6700-240, F_2 of lew Timberline × card Trancos × self	F_3
6983	6699-303, F_2 of card Trancos × lew Timberline × self	F_3
6984	6699-230, F_2 of card Trancos × lew Timberline × self	F_3
6985	6637-122, F_2 of card Trancos × lew Timberline × self	F_3
6986	6638-222, F_2 of lew Timberline × card Trancos × self	F_3
6987	6699-308, F_2 of card Trancos × lew Timberline × self	F_3
6988	6699-432, F_2 of card Trancos × lew Timberline × self	F_3
6989	6638-207, F_2 of lew Timberline × card Trancos × self	F_3
7109	6546-3, F_1 of 6546 × self	F_2
7110	6547-1, F_1 of 6547 × self	F_2
7111	6546-3, F_1 of 6546 × self	F_2
7112	6546-3, F_1 of 6546 × self	F_2
7131	6546-5 card Trancos × 6541-1 lew Timberline	F_1
7132	6546-5 card Trancos × 7104-1 lew Smoky Jack	F_1
7133	6694-105 card Yosemite × 7104-1 lew Smoky Jack	F_1
7134	6694-105 card Yosemite × 6541-1 lew Timberline	F_1

* Abbreviations used: card = *Mimulus cardinalis*, lew = *lewisii*, verb = *verbenaceus*, east = *eastwoodiae*, nels = *nelsonii*. Origins indicated by localities shown under "reference code" in Table 2. The numbers refer to clones that were crossed.
† Backcross on maternal race.
‡ Backcross on paternal race.

(*Continued on following page*)

TABLE 3—*Continued*

Culture No.	Combination *	Generation
7135	6546-3, F_1 of 6546 × self	F_2
7136	6547-1, F_1 of 6547 × self	F_2
7278	6546-5 card Trancos × 7121-5 lew Yosemite	F_1
7279	7121-5 lew Yosemite × 6546-5 card Trancos	F_1
7280	6546-5 card Trancos × 7122-13 lew Tamarack	F_1
7281	7122-13 lew Tamarack × 6546-5 card Trancos	F_1
7282	7124-18 lew Porcupine × 6546-5 card Trancos	F_1
7283	6546-5 card Trancos × 7208-13 lew Timberline	F_1
7284	7208-13 lew Timberline × 6546-5 card Trancos	F_1
7285	6694-105 card Yosemite × 7121-5 lew Yosemite	F_1
7286	7121-5 lew Yosemite × 6694-105 card Yosemite	F_1
7287	6694-105 card Yosemite × 7122-13 lew Tamarack	F_1
7288	7122-13 lew Tamarack × 6694-105 card Yosemite	F_1
7289	7124-18 lew Porcupine × 6694-105 card Yosemite	F_1
7290	6694-105 card Yosemite × 7208-13 lew Timberline	F_1
7291	7208-13 lew Timberline × 6694-105 card Yosemite	F_1
7292	7119-16 card Baja × 7121-5 lew Yosemite	F_1
7293	7121-5 lew Yosemite × 7119-16 card Baja	F_1
7294	7119-16 card Baja × 7122-13 lew Tamarack	F_1
7295	7122-13 lew Tamarack × 7119-16 card Baja	F_1
7296	7124-18 lew Porcupine × 7119-16 card Baja	F_1
7297	7119-16 card Baja × 7208-13 lew Timberline	F_1
7298	7208-13 lew Timberline × 7119-16 card Baja	F_1
7299	7120-15 card San Antonio × 7121-5 lew Yosemite	F_1
7300	7121-5 lew Yosemite × 7120-15 card San Antonio	F_1
7301	7120-15 card San Antonio × 7122-13 lew Tamarack	F_1
7302	7122-13 lew Tamarack × 7120-15 card San Antonio	F_1
7303	7120-15 card San Antonio × 7208-13 lew Timberline	F_1
7304	7208-13 lew Timberline × 7120-15 card San Antonio	F_1
7305	7120-15 card San Antonio × 7212-7 lew Logan	F_1
7306	7212-7 lew Logan × 7120-5 card San Antonio	F_1
7426	7135-30, F_2 of card Trancos × lew Timberline × self	F_3
7427	7135-34, F_2 of card Trancos × lew Timberline × self	F_3
7428	7135-35, F_2 of card Trancos × lew Timberline × self	F_3
7429	7135-39, F_2 of card Trancos × lew Timberline × self	F_3
7430	7135-60, F_2 of card Trancos × lew Timberline × self	F_3
7463	6546-5 card Trancos × 7410-2 lew Warner	F_1
7464	7410-2 lew Warner × 6546-5 card Trancos	F_1
7465	6546-5 card Trancos × 7413-1 lew Rainier	F_1
7466	7413-1 lew Rainier × 6546-5 card Trancos	F_1
7467	7415-1 lew Logan × 6546-5 card Trancos	F_1
7468	6694-105 card Yosemite × 7410-2 lew Warner	F_1
7469	7410-2 lew Warner × 6694-105 Yosemite	F_1
7470	7411-2 lew Stevens × 6694-105 card Yosemite	F_1
7471	7413-1 lew Rainier × 6694-105 card Yosemite	F_1
7472	7119-16 card Baja × 7410-2 lew Warner	F_1

* Abbreviations used: card = *Mimulus cardinalis*, lew = *lewisii*, verb = *verbenaceus*, east = *eastwoodiae*, nels = *nelsonii*. Origins indicated by localities shown under "reference code" in Table 2. The numbers refer to clones that were crossed.
† Backcross on maternal race.
‡ Backcross on paternal race.

(*Continued on following page*)

TABLE 3—Continued

Culture No.	Combination *	Generation
7473	7410-2 lew Warner × 7119-16 card Baja	F₁
7474	7119-16 card Baja × 7411-2 lew Stevens	F₁
7475	7411-2 lew Stevens × 7119-16 card Baja	F₁
7476	7119-16 card Baja × 7413-1 lew Rainier	F₁
7477	7119-16 card Baja × 7415-1 lew Logan	F₁
7478	7415-1 lew Logan × 7119-16 card Baja	F₁
7479	7210-1 card Priests × 7410-2 lew Logan	F₁
7480	7210-1 card Priests × 7411-3 lew Stevens	F₁
7481	7411-3 lew Stevens × 7210-1 card Priests	F₁
7482	7210-1 card Priests × 7413-1 lew Rainier	F₁
7483	7413-1 lew Rainier × 7210-1 card Priests	F₁
7484	7210-1 card Priests × 7415-1 lew Logan	F₁
7485	7415-1 lew Logan × 7210-1 card Priests	F₁
7486	7210-1 card Priests × 7425-1 lew Timberline	F₁
7487	7425-1 lew Timberline × 7210-1 card Priests	F₁
7488	7244-2 card Marshall × 7410-2 lew Warner	F₁
7489	7244-2 card Marshall × 7411-3 lew Stevens	F₁
7490	7411-3 lew Stevens × 7244-2 card Marshall	F₁
7491	7244-2 card Marshall × 7413-1 lew Rainier	F₁
7492	7413-1 lew Rainier × 7244-2 card Marshall	F₁
7493	7244-2 card Marshall × 7415-1 lew Logan	F₁
7494	7415-1 lew Logan × 7244-2 card Marshall	F₁
7495	7244-2 card Marshall × 7424-1 lew Timberline	F₁
7496	7424-1 lew Timberline × 7244-2 card Marshall	F₁
7541	7111-16, F₂ of card Trancos × lew Timberline × self	F₃
7542	7111-37, F₂ of card Trancos × lew Timberline × self	F₃
7543	7112-55, F₂ of card Trancos × lew Timberline × self	F₃
7544	7112-60, F₂ of card Trancos × lew Timberline × self	F₃
7545	7112-80, F₂ of card Trancos × lew Timberline × self	F₃
7596	7464-8, F₁ of lew Warner × card Trancos × self	F₂
7597	7473-1, F₁ of lew Warner × card Baja × self	F₂
7598	7476-6, F₁ of card Baja × lew Rainier × self	F₂
7645	7635-2, F₁ of lew Logan × card Baja × self	F₂
7646	7635-1, F₁ of lew Logan × card Baja × self	F₂

2. Combinations between *Mimulus cardinalis* and *M. verbenaceus*

7213	7113-5 card Trancos × 7143-7 verb Grand Canyon	F₁
7214	7143-7 verb Grand Canyon × 7113-5 card Trancos	F₁
7215	6649-105 card Yosemite × 7143-5 verb Grand Canyon	F₁
7216	7143-5 verb Grand Canyon × 6649-105 card Yosemite	F₁
7217	7119-7 card Baja × 7143-2 verb Grand Canyon	F₁
7218	7143-3 verb Grand Canyon × 7119-7 card Baja	F₁
7219	7119-16 card Baja × 7143-2 verb Grand Canyon	F₁
7220	7143-2 verb Grand Canyon × 7119-16 card Baja	F₁
7328	7120-15 card San Antonio × 7216-3 verb Grand Canyon	F₁
7329	7216-3 verb Grand Canyon × 7120-15 card San Antonio	F₁

* Abbreviations used: card = *Mimulus cardinalis*, lew = *lewisii*, verb = *verbenaceus*, east = *eastwoodiae*, nels = *nelsonii*. Origins indicated by localities shown under "reference code" in Table 2. The numbers refer to clones that were crossed.
† Backcross on maternal race.
‡ Backcross on paternal race.

(*Continued on following page*)

TABLE 3—*Continued*

Culture No.	Combination *	Generation
7497	6546-5 card Trancos × 7143-3 verb Grand Canyon	F_1
7498	6694-105 card Yosemite × 7143-3 verb Grand Canyon	F_1
7499	7143-3 verb Grand Canyon × 6694-105 card Yosemite	F_1
7500	7119-16 card Baja × 7143-3 verb Grand Canyon	F_1
7501	7143-3 verb Grand Canyon × 7119-16 card Baja	F_1
7502	7210-1 card Priests × 7143-3 verb Grand Canyon	F_1
7503	7143-3 verb Grand Canyon × 7210-1 card Priests	F_1
7504	7244-2 card Marshall × 7143-3 verb Grand Canyon	F_1
7505	7143-3 verb Grand Canyon × 7244-2 card Marshall	F_1
7599	7497-7 card Trancos × verb Grand Canyon × self	F_2
7600	7500-3 card Baja × verb Grand Canyon × self	F_2

3. Combinations between *M. cardinalis* and *M. eastwoodiae*

7307	6546-5 card Trancos × 7144-1 east Arches	F_1
7308	7144-1 east Arches × 6546-5 card Trancos	F_1
7309	6649-105 card Yosemite × 7144-1 east Arches	F_1
7310	7144-1 east Arches × 6649-105 card Yosemite	F_1
7311	7144-2 east Arches × 6649-105 card Yosemite	F_1
7312	7119-16 card Baja × 7144-1 east Arches	F_1
7313	7144-1 east Arches × 7119-16 card Baja	F_1
7314	7144-2 east Arches × 7119-16 card Baja	F_1
7315	7120-15 card San Antonio × 7144-1 east Arches	F_1
7316	7144-1 east Arches × 7120-15 card San Antonio	F_1
7317	7144-1 east Arches × 7120-15 card San Antonio	F_1

4. Combinations between *M. cardinalis* and *M. nelsonii*

7512	7119-16 card Baja × 7422-16 nels El Salto	F_1
7513	7422-16 nels El Salto × 7119-16 card Baja	F_1
7514	7244-2 card Marshall × 7422-16 nels El Salto	F_1
7515	7422-16 nels El Salto × 7244-2 card Marshall	F_1
7531	6694-105 card Yosemite × 7422-12 nels El Salto	F_1
7532	7120-15 card San Antonio × 7422-12 nels El Salto	F_1
7533	7422-12 nels El Salto × 7120-15 card San Antonio	F_1
7534	7210-1 card Priests × 7422-12 nels El Salto	F_1
7535	7422-12 nels El Salto × 7210-1 card Priests	F_1
7546	6546-5 card Trancos × 7422-12 nels El Salto	F_1
7547	7422-12 nels El Salto × 6546-5 card Trancos	F_1
7603	7513-1, F_1 of card Baja × nels El Salto × self	F_2
7604	7532-2, F_1 of card San Antonio × nels El Salto × self	F_2

5. Combinations between *M. lewisii* and *M. verbenaceus*

7221	7149-17 lew Timberline × 7143-3 verb Grand Canyon	F_1
7222	7143-3 verb Grand Canyon × 7149-17 lew Timberline	F_1
7223	7149-16 lew Timberline × 7143-19 verb Grand Canyon	F_1
7224	7108-1 lew Timberline × 7143-5 verb Grand Canyon	F_1
7506	7413-1 lew Rainier × 7143-3 verb Grand Canyon	F_1
7507	7143-3 verb Grand Canyon × 7413-1 lew Timberline	F_1

* Abbreviations used: card = *Mimulus cardinalis*, lew = *lewisii*, verb = *verbenaceus*, east = *eastwoodiae*, nels = *nelsonii*. Origins indicated by localities shown under "reference code" in Table 2. The numbers refer to clones that were crossed.
† Backcross on maternal race.
‡ Backcross on paternal race.

(*Continued on following page*)

TABLE 3—*Continued*

Culture No.	Combination *	Generation
7508	7415-1 lew Logan × 7143-3 verb Grand Canyon	F_1
7509	7143-3 verb Grand Canyon × 7415-1 lew Logan	F_1
7510	7143-3 verb Grand Canyon × 7424-5 lew Timberline	F_1
7511	7424-5 lew Timberline × 7143-3 verb Grand Canyon	F_1
7601	7508-2, F_1 of lew Logan × verb Grand Canyon × self	F_2
7602	7511-8, F_1 of lew TL × verb Grand Canyon × self	F_2

6. Combinations between *M. lewisii* and *M. eastwoodiae*

7318	7121-5 lew Yosemite × 7144-1 east Arches	F_1
7319	7144-1 east Arches × 7121-5 lew Yosemite	F_1
7320	7144-2 east Arches × 7121-5 lew Yosemite	F_1
7321	7122-13 lew Tamarack × 7144-1 east Arches	F_1
7322	7144-1 east Arches × 7122-13 lew Tamarack	F_1
7323	7144-2 east Arches × 7122-13 lew Tamarack	F_1
7324	7208-13 lew Timberline × 7144-1 east Arches	F_1
7325	7144-1 east Arches × 7208-3 lew Timberline	F_1
7326	7208-13 lew Timberline × 7144-2 east Arches	F_1
7327	7144-2 east Arches × 7208-13 lew Timberline	F_1

7. Combinations between *M. lewisii* and *M. nelsonii*

7516	7413-1 lew Rainier × 7422-16 nels El Salto	F_1
7517	7413-2 lew Rainier × 7422-16 nels El Salto	F_1
7518	7415-1 lew Logan × 7422-16 nels El Salto	F_1
7519	7415-2 lew Logan × 7422-16 nels El Salto	F_1
7520	7425-1 lew Timberline × 7422-16 nels El Salto	F_1
7521	7422-16 nels El Salto × 7424-1 lew Timberline	F_1
7522	7424-1 lew Timberline × 7422-16 nels El Salto	F_1
7540	7422-12 nels El Salto × 7405-4 lew Timberline	F_1
7605	7516-1, F_1 of lew Rainier × nels El Salto × self	F_2
7606	7540-2, F_1 of nels El Salto × lew Timberline × self	F_2

8. Combinations between *M. eastwoodiae* and *M. nelsonii*

7536	7422-12 nels El Salto × 7144-1 east Arches	F_1
7537	7144-1 east Arches × 7422-12 nels El Salto	F_1
7538	7422-12 nels El Salto × 7144-5 east Arches	F_1
7539	7144-5 east Arches × 7422-12 nels El Salto	F_1
7608	7536-1, F_1 of nels El Salto × east Arches × self	F_2

9. Combinations between *M. verbenaceus* and *M. nelsonii*

7523	7143-3 verb Grand Canyon × 7422-16 nels El Salto	F_1
7524	7422-16 nels El Salto × 7143-3 verb Grand Canyon	F_1
7607	7523-8, F_1 of verb Grand Canyon × nels El Salto × self	F_2

10. Combinations between *M. verbenaceus* and *M. eastwoodiae*

7330	7216-3 verb Grand Canyon × 7144-1 east Arches	F_1
7331	7144-1 east Arches × 7216-3 verb Grand Canyon	F_1
7332	7144-2 east Arches × 7216-3 verb Grand Canyon	F_1

* Abbreviations used: card = *Mimulus cardinalis*, lew = *lewisii*, verb = *verbenaceus*, east = *eastwoodiae*, nels = *nelsonii*. Origins indicated by localities shown under "reference code" in Table 2. The numbers refer to clones that were crossed.
† Backcross on maternal race.
‡ Backcross on paternal race.

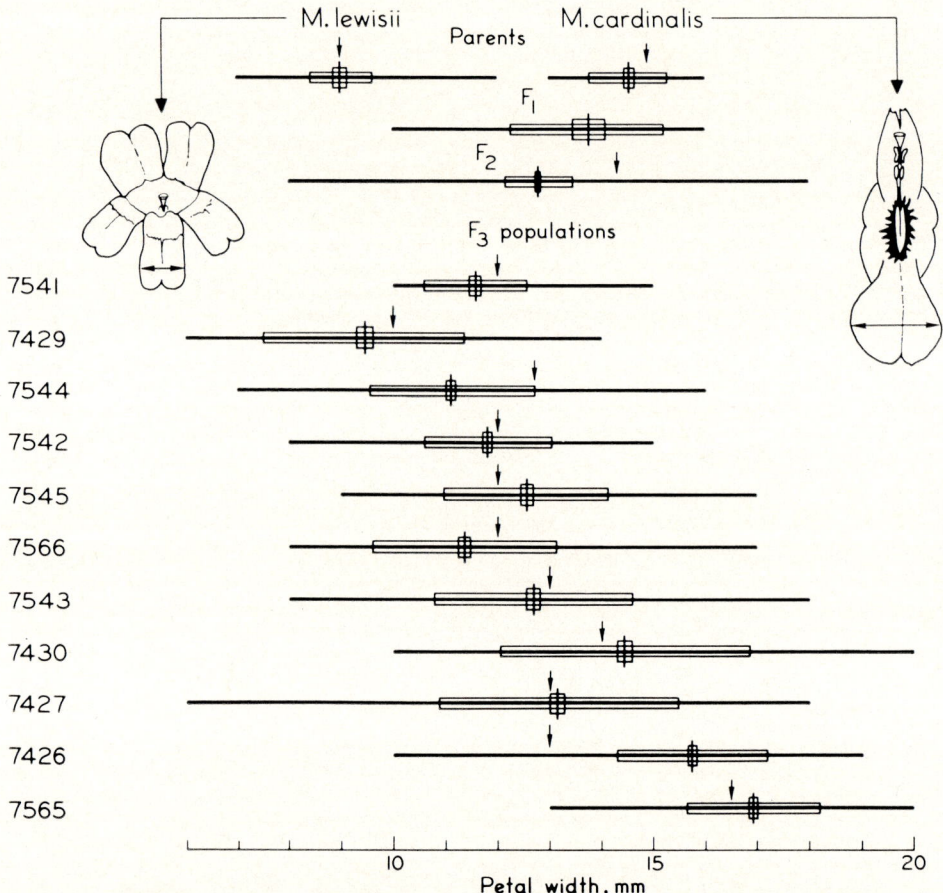

Figure 14. Inheritance of petal width in the cross *M. lewisii* × *M. cardinalis* in F_1, F_2, and F_3 progenies all grown in gardens at Stanford.

The bar diagrams indicate statistical values for populations of each generation, including self-pollinated progeny of the parental individuals. Vertical lines intersecting the horizontal bars represent the means; the thick portions bisected by the means, the standard error; the narrow double line, the standard deviation; and the thin single line, the range of variation within a population. Arrows above each bar diagram indicate the position along the scale of the individual plant giving rise to the progeny through self-pollination.

shows the relative frequencies within the various classes of progeny described above that were derived from the parental, F_1, F_2, and F_3 generations.

From table 5 it is evident that (1) there is variation in the degree of expression of this character in both of the parental species, *M. cardinalis* and *M. lewisii;* (2) the inheritance of petal reflexing is complex, and cannot be referred to simple Mendelian inheritance; and (3) the segregation in F_2 and F_3 progenies is broad and covers the entire range between the parental extremes. In certain F_3 populations, especially in cultures Nos. 7141, 7426, and 7565, there is evidence of restricted segregation, apparently a consequence of genetic coherence, as discussed on pages 78 to 85.

TABLE 4

Scoring of Petal Reflexing into Classes

Class	Angle of Reflexing	Relation to Parents
1	0–20°	lower range of *M. lewisii*
2	21–40°	average range of *M. lewisii*
3	41–60°	upper range of *M. lewisii*
4	61–80°	intermediate between *M. cardinalis* and *M. lewisii*
5	81–100°	intermediate between *M. cardinalis* and *M. lewisii*
6	101–120°	intermediate between *M. cardinalis* and *M. lewisii*
7	121–140°	intermediate between *M. cardinalis* and *M. lewisii*
8	141–160°	lower range of *M. cardinalis*
9	161–180°	typical range of *M. cardinalis*

2. *Petal width*

A measurable character that distinguishes *Mimulus cardinalis* from *M. lewisii* is the width of the central petal lobe of the lower corolla lip (cf. figure 14). Although this character is modifiable to some degree, especially during the latter part of the flowering season, when the flowers tend to become smaller, measurements during comparable stages of flowering are remarkably consistent on plants grown under very different conditions, including measurements made at the altitudinal transplant stations. *Mimulus verbenaceus* and *M. nelsonii* have broad petals and are much like *M. cardinalis*. The petals of *eastwoodiae* are narrow and approach those of *M. lewisii*.

An analysis of the inheritance of petal width in a cross between coastal *M. cardinalis* and subalpine *M. lewisii*, based on average measurements on parental, F_1, F_2, and F_3 populations, is summarized in figure 14. As is evident from the bar graphs, petal width segregates widely in second- and third-generation progeny, and transgresses so heavily in the direction of wide petals as to exceed the range of typical *M. cardinalis*. This is especially evident in the F_3 cultures 7426 and 7565 which have mean values much higher than the mean of the *M. cardinalis* population derived from self-pollination of the *cardinalis* parent used in the original cross.

TABLE 5
Inheritance of Petal Reflexing

Species or Combination	Culture Number	Generation	Number of Plants	Phenotypic Class of Parents	Percentage Frequency of Progeny, by Class *								
					1	2	3	4	5	6	7	8	9
M. cardinalis (selfed)	7113	parent	31	9								19.4	**80.6**
M. lewisii (selfed)	6634	parent	34	2	**50.0**†	47.0	3.0						
M. cardinalis × M. lewisii (and reciprocal)	6546 6547	F_1	17					**64.7**	35.3				
M. cardinalis × M. lewisii	7111 7112	F_2	306	5	0.3	8.8	17.6	35.3	15.7	14.7	4.9	1.6	1.0
(and reciprocal)	7135												
M. cardinalis × M. lewisii	7141	F_3	200	2	12.0	33.5	**51.5**	14.0	1.0				
M. cardinalis × M. lewisii	7429	F_3	291	2	12.0	20.3	19.9	**25.8**	20.3	1.4	0.3		
M. cardinalis × M. lewisii	7544	F_3	241	3	13.7	23.6	24.5	**25.3**	10.0	2.0	0.8		
M. cardinalis × M. lewisii	7542	F_3	330	3	4.2	13.9	22.4	**23.3**	22.1	11.2	1.2	1.5	
M. cardinalis × M. lewisii	7545	F_3	308	4	5.5	10.4	26.0	**31.8**	21.8	3.9	0.6		
M. cardinalis × M. lewisii	7566	F_3	187	3	1.1	9.1	25.6	**43.3**	17.6	3.7	0.5		
M. cardinalis × M. lewisii	7543	F_3	288	5	6.6	6.9	12.5	**18.0**	17.7	11.8	9.4	9.4	7.6
M. cardinalis × M. lewisii	7430	F_3	279	4	1.1	1.4	7.2	14.0	**32.2**	17.9	11.1	7.2	7.9
M. cardinalis × M. lewisii	7427	F_3	281	7		1.1	6.0	13.2	**28.8**	23.1	8.9	8.9	10.0
M. cardinalis × M. lewisii	7426	F_3	299	8				0.3	3.3	31.1	**37.8**	25.8	1.7
M. cardinalis × M. lewisii	7565	F_3	197	7					2.5	29.9	**45.2**	21.8	0.5

* See Table 4 for description of classes.
† Values in boldface type are classes of highest frequency.

The frequency distribution among the various F_3 progenies is related to the genotypic composition of their F_2 parents, as shown by the bar graphs in the lower half of figure 14. Individuals with the widest petal lobes yield progenies that segregate most heavily in this direction, and vice versa. It is also clear from the pattern of the frequency distribution in the F_2 and F_3 progenies that petal width is genetically a complex character that cannot be described in terms of simple Mendelian ratios.

3. *Corolla aperture*

In *Mimulus cardinalis* the corolla tube is compressed laterally, in contrast with *M. lewisii* in which the tube is compressed horizontally (figure 14). This difference can be expressed in terms of a ratio obtained by dividing the vertical length of the aperture in millimeters by the horizontal width. This ratio is a highly constant feature that is not significantly modified either by seasonal ageing in a given environment, or by transplanting to the altitudinal field stations. The species of the *Erythranthe* section that show the greatest contrast in this character are *M. cardinalis*, with a value of 2.2 to 3.0, and *M. lewisii*, with a range between 0.63 and 0.88.

The flowers of *M. verbenaceus* and *M. nelsonii* tend to approach those of *M. cardinalis* in this throat characteristic, whereas those of *M. eastwoodiae* approach *M. lewisii*. An analysis of the inheritance of this character is summarized in table 6. In order to facilitate statistical treatment, the measured values of aperture ratio were converted to a scale of 1 to 9. Plants with values rated at 1 or 2 fall within the range of *M. lewisii*, and those of 8 or 9 within *M. cardinalis*. The intermediate classes were divided into equal increments of expression in determining classes of frequency distribution. This treatment is similar to that used for petal reflexing in table 5.

A marked difference in survival capacity exists between *Mimulus cardinalis* and *M. lewisii* when grown at the altitudinal transplant stations. At the low elevation at Stanford, coastal *M. cardinalis* thrives, in contrast with subalpine *M. lewisii*, which dies. When F_2 seedlings of the hybrid between coastal *cardinalis* and subalpine *lewisii* are germinated and established in the Timberline environment, the plants that survive at the alpine station differ in overall genetic composition from a corresponding sample F_2 population of the same parentage germinated and established at Stanford.

In the character "corolla aperture," for example, there is a shift towards higher frequencies of the wide-throated *lewisii*-like classes among the progeny established at Timberline than among those established at Stanford (cultures 7111, 7112, vs. 7135 in table 6, also table 7). When the class frequencies of all the F_2 plants established at both stations are added together, the group highest in frequency is class 3, a shift from class 4 which was the class of highest frequency among the plants established at Stanford. The frequencies in the adjacent classes of both the Timberline- and Stanford-established populations

TABLE 6
Inheritance of Corolla Aperture

Species or Combination	Culture Number	Generation	Number of Plants	Phenotypic Class of Parents	Percentage Frequency of Progeny, by Class								
					1	2	3	4	5	6	7	8	9
M. cardinalis (selfed)	7113	parent	31	9									100.0
M. lewisii (selfed)	6634	parent	27	2	3.7	96.3							
M. cardinalis × M. lewisii (and reciprocal)	6546 6547	F$_1$	17	...			100.0						
M. cardinalis × M. lewisii	7111* 7112*	F$_2$	150	3	4.0	24.0	**38.0**	19.0	10.0	4.7			
	7135†	F$_2$	153	3	0.7	7.8	25.5	**30.6**	11.8	11.8	6.5	3.3	2.0
	Pooled data		303	3	2.3	15.8	**31.7**	25.1	10.9	8.2	3.3	1.6	1.0
M. cardinalis × M. lewisii	7541	F$_3$	200	1	2.5	**71.0**	24.0	2.0		0.5			
M. cardinalis × M. lewisii	7429	F$_3$	291	2	2.7	21.6	**40.2**	17.5	12.7	4.5	0.7		
M. cardinalis × M. lewisii	7544	F$_3$	237	4	5.1	**44.3**	43.9	4.6	1.3	0.8			
M. cardinalis × M. lewisii	7542	F$_3$	329	2	0.3	7.3	**42.2**	19.2	20.1	9.4	1.5		
M. cardinalis × M. lewisii	7545	F$_3$	295	3	1.7	19.0	**39.3**	25.1	9.2	5.7			
M. cardinalis × M. lewisii	7566	F$_3$	190	2		17.9	**61.0**	20.0	1.1				
M. cardinalis × M. lewisii	7543	F$_3$	288	5	0.7	8.7	**28.1**	14.6	23.6	18.8	2.4	2.4	0.7
M. cardinalis × M. lewisii	7430	F$_3$	277	4	1.8	13.7	**32.8**	17.7	15.2	10.8	6.5	1.1	0.4
M. cardinalis × M. lewisii	7527	F$_3$	281	7		0.4	11.0	20.3	**28.8**	14.6	19.9	3.6	1.4
M. cardinalis × M. lewisii	7426	F$_3$	300	7		0.3	1.0	5.0	37.3	**41.7**	11.3	2.7	0.7
M. cardinalis × M. lewisii	7565	F$_3$	197	8		0.5		3.6	4.6	26.4	**49.7**	13.7	1.5

* Seedlings established at Timberline.
† Seedlings established at Stanford.
‡ Values in boldface type are classes of highest frequency.

likewise reflect the same displacements. The character "corolla aperture" is, therefore, apparently to some degree correlated with the capacity of seedlings to survive in the contrasting climates at Stanford and Timberline during the establishment period.

An outstanding feature in the pattern of inheritance of corolla aperture is the rather strong dominance of the wide-throated characteristic of *M. lewisii* in the F_1, F_2, and most of the F_3 progenies. Second-generation individuals having narrow throats approaching *M. cardinalis* do, however, yield F_3 populations that have high frequencies of narrow-throated classes, as exemplified by cultures Nos. 7527, 7526, and 7565 in table 6. There is no evidence of transgressive segregation in the inheritance of this character.

TABLE 7

Shifts in Class Frequency in the Character "Corolla Aperture" in F_2 Population Samples Established as Seedlings at Stanford and Timberline

Population	Number of Individuals	Classes *								
		1	2	3	4	5	6	7	8	9
Timberline-established (cultures 7111, 7112)	150	6	36	**57** †	29	15	7			
Stanford-established (culture 7135)	153	1	12	39	**47**	18	18	10	5	3

* Classes same as in Table 6. The F_2 seed samples were harvested from the same F_1 individual of the cross *Mimulus cardinalis* Los Trancos × *M. lewisii* Timberline.

† Values in boldface type are classes of highest frequency.

4. *Pistil length*

The length of pistils in various species of the *Erythranthe* section of *Mimulus* differs over a considerable range, *M. lewisii* having the shortest and *M. nelsonii* the longest (see figure 13). This character shows marked stability for a given species at the altitudinal transplant stations, and can be easily measured in nursery and field-grown populations. The inheritance of differences in pistil length between *M. cardinalis* and *M. lewisii* has been studied in detail through the third generation, and the results are summarized in figure 16.

The intermediate expression of this character in F_1 progeny, the wide range of segregation in the F_2, encompassing both parental extremes, and the slightly transgressive segregation in the direction of long pistils found in several of the F_3 progenies reveal the complex nature of this character. The different classes of F_2 phenotypes which gave rise to F_3 progenies reflect marked differences in genotypic composition. This is evident in the trend towards longer pistils in F_3 progenies that have as parents F_2 individuals with successively longer pistils. Pistil length is obviously a character that is genetically complex and

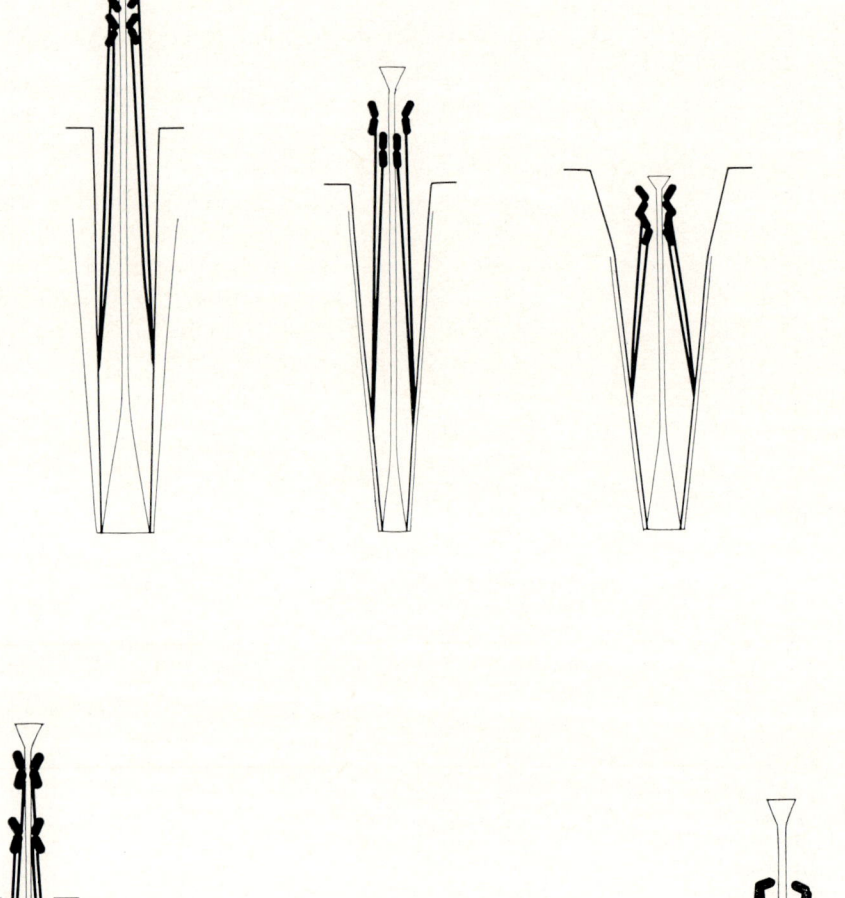

Figure 15. *Above:* Diagrams of longitudinal sections of flowers of parental *Mimulus cardinalis* 6546-5 (*left*), *M. lewisii* 7405-4 (*right*), and their F_1 hybrid 6546-3 (*center*). *Below:* Diagrams of an *M. cardinalis*-like F_2 individual 1135-35 (*left*), an *M. lewisii*-like F_2 derivative 7111-16 (*center*), an an F_1-like F_2 plant 7111-17 (*right*). See Plate II for flowers of F_3 progeny obtained by selfing these F_2's.

governed by multiple genetic factors balanced almost equally between the two parents.

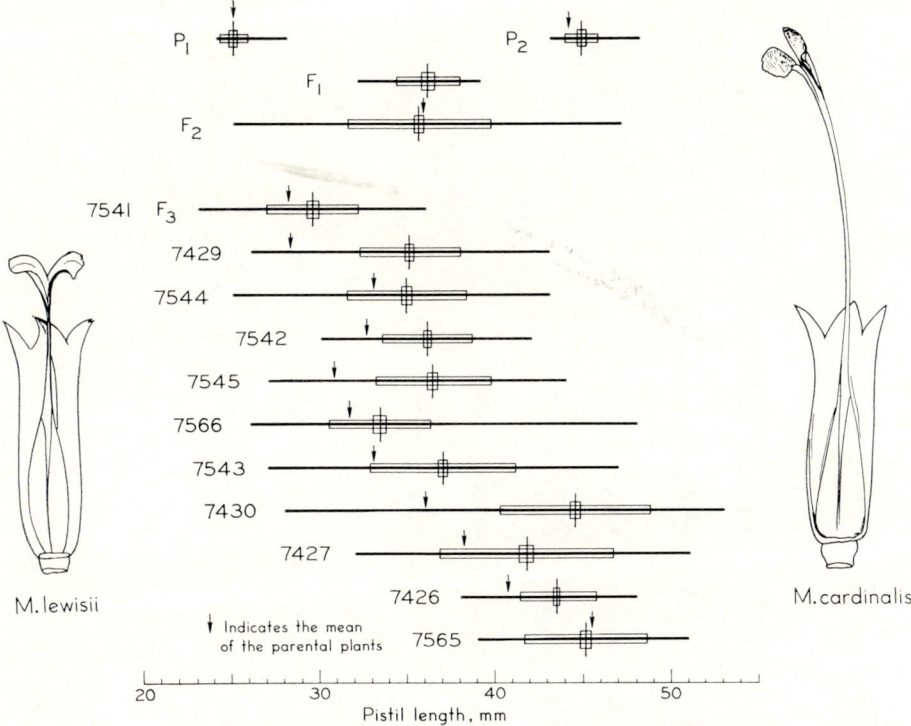

Figure 16. Inheritance of pistil length in hybrid derivatives of *M. lewisii* × *M. cardinalis*. Data from reciprocal crosses were pooled in constructing the bar diagrams. See figure 14 for explanation of the bar diagrams.

5. *Number of dentations on leaves*

Leaves of species of the *Erythranthe* section differ widely in the number of dentations on their margins. There is also often wide variation within species, especially between ecologic races. Forms of *Mimulus lewisii* from the Sierra Nevada of California have 3 to 7 dentations per leaf. Some of the northern forms (Stevens Pass) may have as many as 20 or more, while others may be almost completely entire. *Mimulus verbenaceus* has up to 40 dentations per leaf. For a given clone of a particular race, however, the number of dentations is remarkably constant and is not modified by transplanting to different environments.

Figure 17 shows samples of leaves of *Mimulus cardinalis* Los Trancos, *M. lewisii* Timberline, their F_1 hybrid, and a number of F_3 populations derived from different individuals of the widely segregating F_2 population. The diversity of leaf shapes and of dentation number reflects the complexity of segregation of both characters.

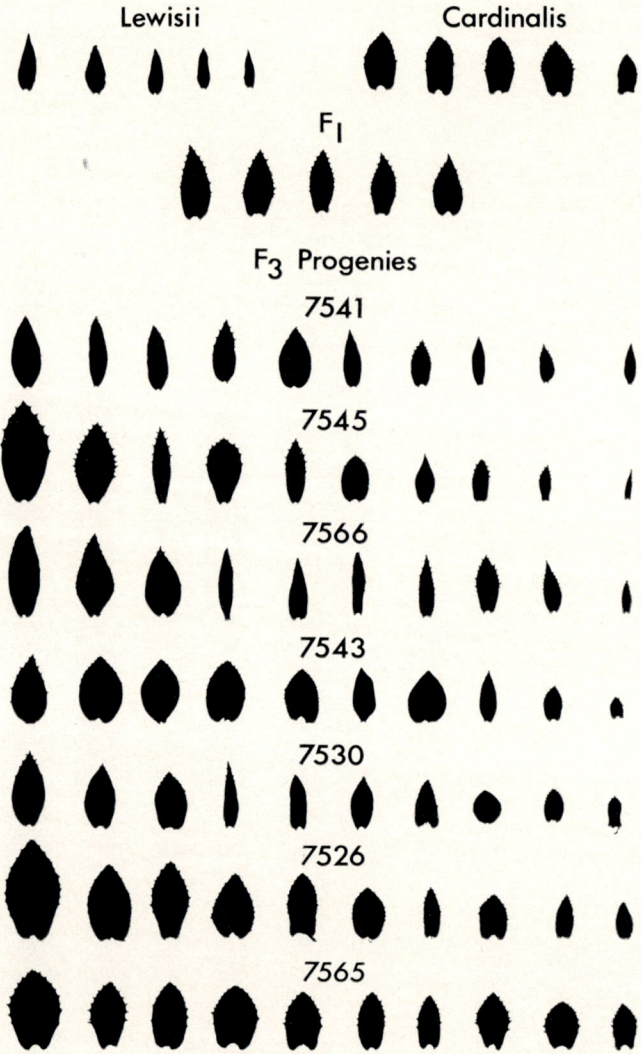

Figure 17. Inheritance of leaf characters in hybrid derivatives of *Mimulus lewisii* and *M. cardinalis*. See also figure 18.

The bar graphs of figure 18 summarize the mode of inheritance of dentation number in the F_1, F_2, and F_3 generations. The F_1 hybrid plants have as many dentations as the *M. cardinalis* parent, reflecting the dominance of many

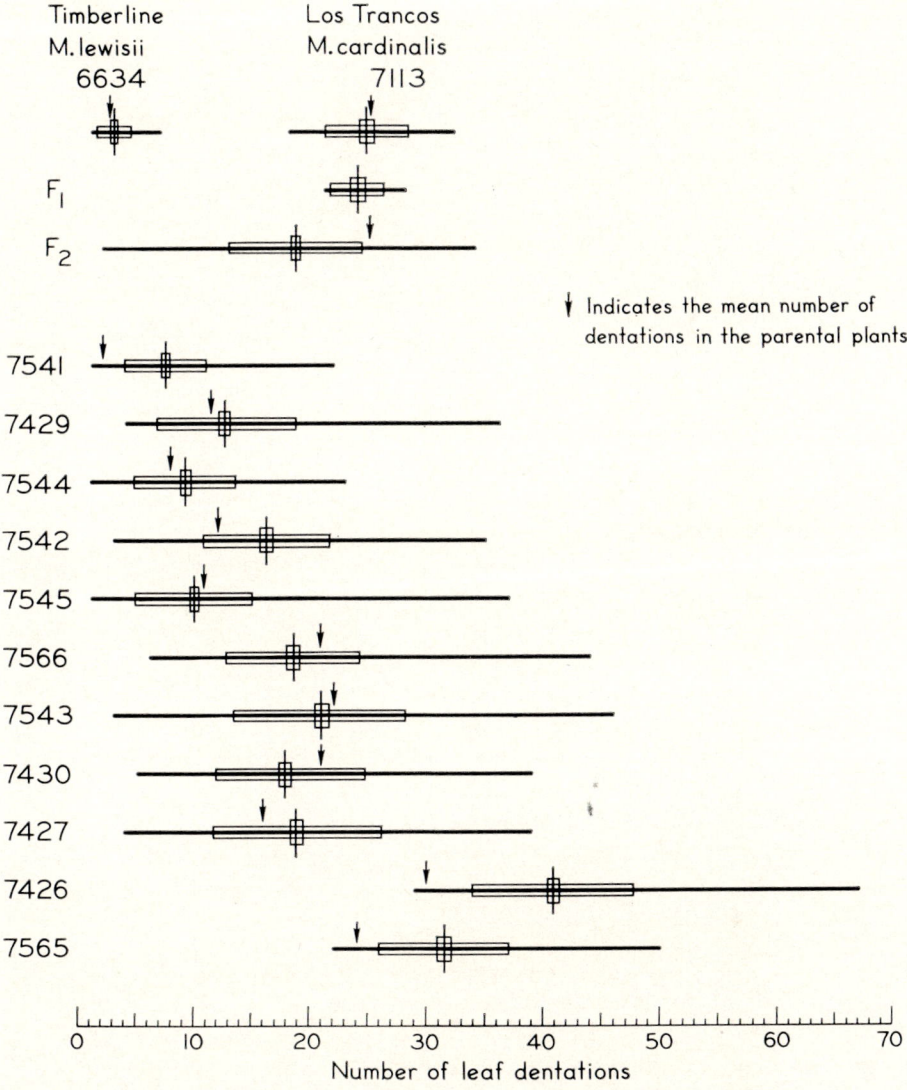

Figure 18. Inheritance of number of dentations on leaf margins in progeny of *Mimulus lewisii* × *M. cardinalis*. Data are pooled from reciprocal crosses. Third-generation progenies are identified by culture numbers at the left.

dentations over few dentations. In the F_2 the frequency distribution is skewed in the direction of high numbers. In the subsequent F_3 progenies derived from a wide spectrum of diverse F_2 phenotypes, the segregations into classes in nearly all populations cover a wide range.

Especially impressive is the extreme degree of transgressive segregation in the direction of high numbers of dentations, shown in figures 17 and 18. In the F_3 culture 7426, for example, the entire population spread falls above the number of leaf dentations found in the original *M. cardinalis* parent. Also evident in figure 17 is the tendency for wider, *M. cardinalis*-like leaves to have a larger number of leaf dentations than narrow-leaved types, although extreme recombinations do occur with fairly high frequency.

6. *Leaf ratio*

Within the section *Erythranthe* the leaves differ widely in size and shape, as shown in Chapter I in figures 2 to 6. In all species, the overall size of leaves is a highly modifiable character, depending upon environmental variables such as light, temperature and moisture. In any particular species or individual, however, leaf shape is remarkably constant and can be expressed as the ratio obtained by dividing the maximum width by the length. Since the leaves of a given individual differ to some extent in their developmental sequence from rosette to inflorescence, the leaf pair subtending the first flower of an inflorescence was selected as a standard for measurement.

The inheritance of leaf shape as expressed by the ratio of width to length has been studied in a number of interspecific crosses, especially in *M. cardinalis* Los Trancos × *M. lewisii* Timberline (table 8). In this combination the leaves of *M. cardinalis* are broadly oval to oblong, the leaf ratio ranging between 0.44 and 0.58. In *M. lewisii* Timberline the leaves are narrower and elliptic lanceolate, with ratios between 0.25 and 0.33. Parental, F_1, F_2, and F_3 populations were scored for this character on an arbitrary scale of 1 to 9, the low values 1 to 4 representing classes with *M. lewisii*, and those 6 to 9, *M. cardinalis*. Table 8 shows the mode of inheritance of this character in F_1, F_2, and F_3 progenies in relation to the parents.

FLOWER COLOR CHARACTERS. Among the more spectacular characters that differentiate some of the species of the *Erythranthe* section are those involving flower color. Studies by Brožek at Prague in Czechoslovakia (1930, 1931, 1932) demonstrated the heritability of differences in flower color in *Mimulus cardinalis* hybrid derivatives grown in Europe as horticultural plants. He also investigated factors contributing to the complexity of expression of flower color in this group of plants. This problem was further pursued by Vickery and Olson (1956) who extracted various pigment components, including carotenoids, xanthophylls, anthocyanins, and anthoxanthins from parental and hybrid populations of *M. cardinalis* and *M. lewisii*. These workers also studied the distribution of some of these pigments in the various floral tissues. More recently

GENETIC AND TRANSPLANT STUDIES

TABLE 8
Inheritance of Leaf Ratio

Species or Combination	Culture Number	Generation	Number of Plants	Phenotypic Class of Parents	Percentage Frequency of Progeny, by Class								
					1	2	3	4	5	6	7	8	9
M. cardinalis	7113	parent	30	7						6.7	10.0	10.0	**73.3**
M. lewisii	6634	parent	27	2	33.3	**40.7***	14.8	11.2					
M. cardinalis × M. lewisii (and reciprocal)	6546 6547	F_1	17	...				5.9	23.5	**35.3**	**35.3**		
M. cardinalis × M. lewisii	7111 7112 7135	F_2	308	4	5.8	6.5	17.5	**20.8**	16.9	11.1	9.7	5.5	6.2
M. cardinalis × M. lewisii	7541	F_3	200	5	2.5	10.5	22.5	**31.5**	19.0	7.5	6.0	0.5	
M. cardinalis × M. lewisii	7429	F_3	292	3	6.8	5.8	11.3	14.8	**19.5**	13.7	8.0	10.1	10.0
M. cardinalis × M. lewisii	7544	F_3	204	1	**19.6**	14.7	12.7	17.2	14.7	11.8	4.4	3.4	1.5
M. cardinalis × M. lewisii	7542	F_3	204	3	2.0	2.9	9.3	10.8	14.7	**17.2**	15.2	11.8	16.1
M. cardinalis × M. lewisii	7545	F_3	227	3	7.5	10.6	11.0	**17.2**	11.0	11.4	11.4	7.1	12.8
M. cardinalis × M. lewisii	7566	F_3	196	4	23.5	**30.6**	20.4	16.8	6.2	1.5	0.5		0.5
M. cardinalis × M. lewisii	7543	F_3	200	6	1.5	2.5	5.0	6.0	6.0	8.5	16.0	12.0	**42.5**
M. cardinalis × M. lewisii	7530	F_3	277	6	2.5	5.0	2.9	9.0	6.8	11.2	11.6	14.2	**36.8**
M. cardinalis × M. lewisii	7427	F_3	278	6				0.7	2.9	6.1	9.7	19.2	**61.5**
M. cardinalis × M. lewisii	7426	F_3	299	6			0.3	1.0	2.0	7.0	14.4	16.4	**58.9**
M. cardinalis × M. lewisii	7565	F_3	200	9					2.0	1.5	14.5	17.0	**65.0**

* Values in boldface type are classes of highest frequency.

Pollock, Vickery, and Wilson (1967) isolated a number of flavonoid components, and characterized the various species of the *Erythranthe* by the presence or absence of different combinations of these components.

The present studies are primarily concerned with the overall inheritance patterns of some of the more clearly definable color differences that serve as markers in differentiating species. By far the most spectacular color differences are found in *M. cardinalis* as compared with *M. lewisii*. Most of the discussion that follows pertains to the differences between these species and hybrid derivatives from them. In this study we have selected five differentiating color characters for study.

In general, second-generation progeny between *M. cardinalis* and *M. lewisii* segregate a spectacular array of derivatives ranging from intense vermilion through shades of orange to yellow, amber and apricot, and include varying shades of clear pink and rose (see Plate I). Standard color charts are inadequate for scoring this range of variation.

Within such an F_2 population, three major categories may be separated by simple observation: (1) vermilion shades of orange to nearly yellow; (2) shades of pink with a distinct amber sheen; and (3) shades of clear pink to brilliant rose without an amber sheen. These three categories have corresponding distinctive histological differences with respect to pigment distribution.

In the first category, yellow chromoplasts occur within the lower two-thirds of the cytoplasm surrounding the vacuole of the cells of the upper epidermis, and rose anthocyanin pigments occur in the vacuoles (see figure 19). The physical mixing of the yellow carotenoids in the plastids and the rose anthocyanin pigments in the vacuoles gives a visual color impression ranging from orange to vermilion.

In plants of the second category, the upper epidermis contains only colorless plastids, but yellow chromoplasts may be present in the mesophyll or in the lower epidermis, or both, in different concentrations. Magenta to pink anthocyanins may be distributed in the vacuoles of the cells of the upper epidermis, the mesophyll, or in any combination of these tissues in varying concentrations and in differing shades of color.

Flowers of plants in the third category contain no yellow carotenoid pigments in the plastids of any of the tissues of the petal lobes. The anthocyanins are distributed in the vacuoles of some or of all of the petal tissues in intensities and concentrations that may differ. These combinations result in various shades ranging from clear pink to rose.

Five characters which involve color difference between *Mimulus cardinalis* and *M. lewisii* and whose inheritance has been studied are discussed below.

7. *Yellow upper epidermis in petal lobes*

The character "yellow upper" is expressed by plants having yellow carotenoid pigments in plastids surrounding the vacuole of upper epidermal cells of the petal lobes. This character was clearly described by Brožek (1932) and it is present in all races of *M. cardinalis, M. verbenaceus, M. eastwoodiae,* and *M. nelsonii.* The carotenoid chromoplasts are absent in the petal lobes of all races of *M. lewisii.* In *M. lewisii* they are localized and are only found in two narrow

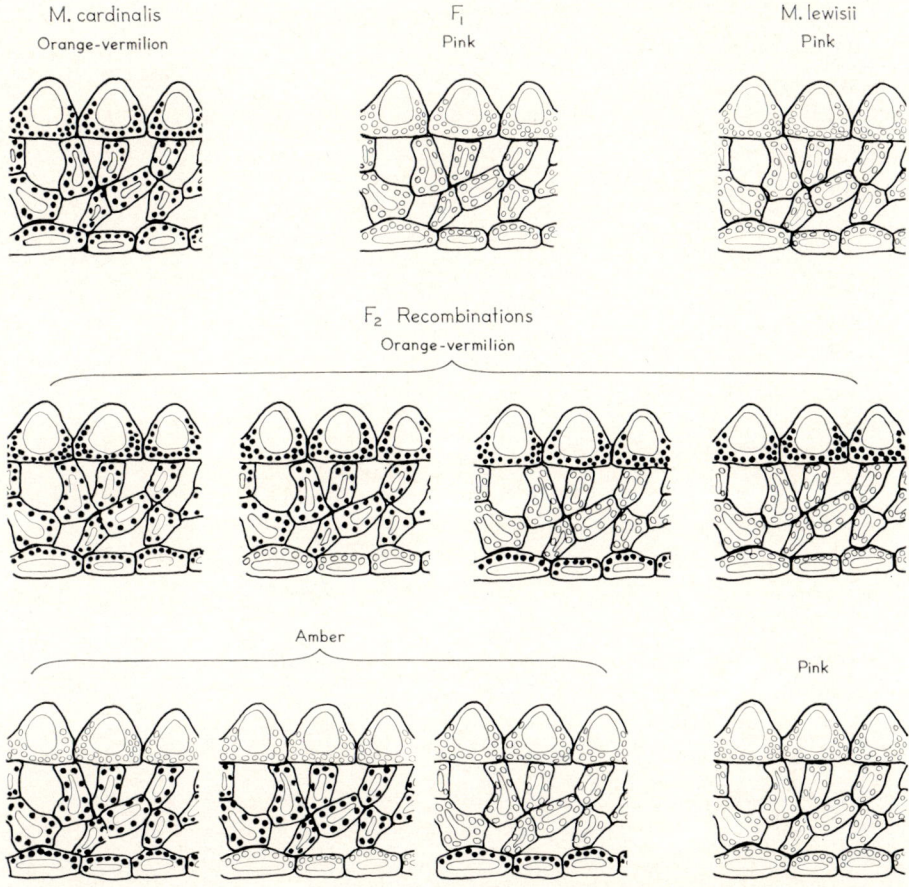

Figure 19. Diagrams showing different combinations of pigment distribution in the upper epidermis, mesoderm, and lower epidermis of petals of *Mimulus cardinalis, M. lewisii,* and their F_1 and F_2 progeny. Solid black plastids represent the presence of carotenoids; open plastids, their absence. See text.

bands along the inside ventral surface of the corolla tube, and in trichomes along the petal margins. Vickery and Olson (1956) studied the inheritance of this character in a hybrid between *M. cardinalis* and *M. lewisii* and reported a simple Mendelian 1:3 ratio, a conclusion supported by the data presented below.

"Yellow upper" is a character that is easily recognized and can be readily tabulated in hybrid populations growing in garden cultures in all environments. It is the most clear-cut genetic marker of any that we have studied.

It is likewise the only character among the 24 pursued in our studies whose inheritance follows a simple 1:3 Mendelian pattern. Apparently *M. lewisii* carries a simple dominant suppressor for the production of carotenoids in the plastids of the upper epidermis of the petal lobes, so that F_1 hybrids lack this character, and F_2 populations segregate in the ratio of 3 without "yellow upper" to 1 with carotenoid chromoplasts. Table 9 summarizes the data from parental, F_1, F_2, and F_3 populations from the cross *M. cardinalis* Los Trancos × *M. lewisii* Timberline.

SHIFTS IN F_2 SEGREGATION RATIOS OF "YELLOW UPPER" IN POPULATIONS ESTABLISHED AT STANFORD AND TIMBERLINE. A shift in class frequencies among surviving F_2 progeny germinated and established as seedlings at the Timberline transplant station as compared with a similar population germinated and established at Stanford has been observed in the "yellow upper" character. Surviving seedling plants of Timberline-established populations show a higher percentage of individuals lacking the yellow chromoplasts than among seedlings established at Stanford. Data summarizing these observations are shown in table 10.

There is also a marked shift in frequency distribution in sample F_2 populations established at Stanford during the winter as compared with seedlings established during the warm summer months (table 10). Normally, sowings of F_2 progenies at Stanford are made during the winter months when temperatures are cooler and more favorable for the establishment of seedlings. In summer sowings there is a higher mortality rate. The available data indicate strongly that summer conditions introduce a selective bias in favor of a higher percentage of survival of individuals resembling *M. cardinalis*, with yellow pigment in the upper epidermis.

The shift in frequency of Timberline-established plants favoring the survival of individuals without yellow chromoplasts in the upper epidermis of the flowers falls in the opposite direction. When, however, all of the data from the F_2 population of this cross are pooled, the final totals fit a 3:1 Mendelian ratio moderately well (table 9). Mather-established F_2 seedlings of the same origin did not depart strongly from the 3:1 ratio, being 2.5:1.0, as indicated in table 10.

From the above results one might question the validity of the conclusion that the character "yellow upper" is controlled by a simple Mendelian model fitting a 3:1 ratio. The data could be fortuitous in that the average observed frequencies of the various experiments working in different environments happen to coincide with this hypothesis. Our own doubts have been resolved largely on the basis of data from F_3 progenies, presented in table 9 which with one exception (culture 7566) are remarkably consistent with the 3:1 hypothesis.

TABLE 9
Inheritance of Yellow Upper Epidermis

Species or Combination	Culture Number	Generation	Number of Plants	Phenotype of Parent	Percentage Frequency of Progeny	
					Without Yellow Upper	With Yellow Upper
M. cardinalis (selfed).......	7113	parent	31	with	0.0	**100.0***
M. lewisii (selfed)..........	6634	parent	33	without	**100.0**	0.0
M. cardinalis × M. lewisii.. (and reciprocal)	6546 6547	F$_1$	17	...	**100.0**	0.0
M. cardinalis × M. lewisii.. (and reciprocals)	7111, 7112 7135, 6637 6699, 6638 6700	F$_2$ (pooled data)	748	without	**75.6**	24.4
M. cardinalis × M. lewisii..	7541	F$_3$	200	without	**100.0**	0.0
M. cardinalis × M. lewisii..	7429	F$_3$	291	without	**100.0**	0.0
M. cardinalis × M. lewisii..	7544	F$_3$	232	without	**100.0**	0.0
M. cardinalis × M. lewisii..	7542	F$_3$	324	without	**100.0**	0.0
M. cardinalis × M. lewisii..	7545	F$_3$	308	without	**100.0**	0.0
M. cardinalis × M. lewisii..	7566	F$_3$	171	without	**88.3**	11.7
M. cardinalis × M. lewisii..	7543	F$_3$	285	without	**75.8**	24.2
M. cardinalis × M. lewisii..	7430	F$_3$	277	without	**72.2**	27.8
M. cardinalis × M. lewisii..	7427	F$_3$	210	without	**74.7**	25.3
M. cardinalis × M. lewisii..	7426	F$_3$	300	with	0.0	**100.0**
M. cardinalis × M. lewisii..	7565	F$_3$	198	with	0.0	**100.0**

* Values in boldface are classes of highest frequency.

The differential selection observed among seedling populations for "yellow upper" at Stanford and at Timberline is similar to that observed for the character "corolla aperture" (cf. table 7).

8. *Yellow lower epidermis in petal lobes*

This character, "yellow lower," is expressed when yellow chromoplasts occur in the lower epidermis of corolla lobes, in the mesophyll, or in both tissues. The scoring of this character was done visually on a 1–9 scale using key plants which included the parents, F_1, and a series of F_2 reference individuals which had been previously studied histologically. The data are summarized in table 11. The most extreme contrast in the expression of the character is between *M. cardinalis* and *M. lewisii*. In *M. cardinalis*, the lower epidermis and mesophyll are densely packed with this carotenoid pigment, while in *M. lewisii*,

TABLE 10

Segregation among F_2 Progeny of *Mimulus cardinalis* × *M. lewisii* Germinated and Established at Three Altitudes

Conditions of Germination and Early Establishment	Percent Seedling Mortality	Number of Plants Maturing	Ratio of Pink-Flowered to Orange-Flowered Individuals
Stanford, summer sown	89	180	1.7:1.0
Stanford, winter sown (elevation 150 ft.)	71	463	4.4:1.0
Mather, summer sown (elevation 4600 ft.)	71	104	2.5:1.0
Timberline, summer sown (elevation 10,000 ft.)	78	242	8.7:1.0

this coloration is either lacking entirely, or present only in very dilute form, causing the under surface to be translucent.

The inheritance of this character differs from the preceding "yellow upper" in that segregation in the F_2 generation is not simple but complex, yielding an array of classes that range from one parental class to the other. The frequency distribution among classes (when plotted on a scale of 1 to 9) is somewhat bimodal and skewed towards *M. lewisii*. Third-generation progenies derived from various grades of phenotypic expression all segregate widely, with maximum class frequencies differing in the same general direction as the phenotype of the parent.

9. *Rose*

The character we designate as "rose" is based on a subjective visual interpretation of the overall intensity of the rose-colored anthocyanins in the cell sap of all the tissues in petal lobes.

These pigments are present in all species of the *Erythranthe* section of *Mimulus*. In all races of *M. lewisii* from the Sierra Nevada of California, and also in all

TABLE 11

INHERITANCE OF YELLOW LOWER EPIDERMIS

Species or Combination	Culture Number	Generation	Number of Plants	Phenotypic Class of Parents	Percentage Frequency of Progeny, by Class								
					1	2	3	4	5	6	7	8	9
M. cardinalis (selfed)	7113	parent	31	9									**64.5**
M. lewisii (selfed)	6634	parent	31	1	**83.9***	16.1							
M. cardinalis × M. lewisii (and reciprocal)	6546 6547	F₁	17	2	47.0	**53.0**							
M. cardinalis × M. lewisii	7111 7112 7135	F₂	306	...	22.9	**25.2**	3.9	12.7	17.3	3.9	4.6	5.2	4.2
M. cardinalis × M. lewisii	7541	F₃	200	1	**68.5**	28.0	2.5	0.5	0.5				
M. cardinalis × M. lewisii	7429	F₃	291	1	**34.7**	6.2	19.2	5.2	**34.7**				
M. cardinalis × M. lewisii	7544	F₃	232	1	**47.4**	19.4	3.4		29.8				
M. cardinalis × M. lewisii	7542	F₃	323	1	27.4	24.4	3.2		**44.4**				0.6
M. cardinalis × M. lewisii	7545	F₃	308	2	**36.0**	30.2	1.0		32.8				
M. cardinalis × M. lewisii	7566	F₃	190	2	8.9	**37.4**	25.3	11.6	7.4	3.7	3.2	1.0	1.6
M. cardinalis × M. lewisii	7543	F₃	284	1	17.0	21.9			**48.9**				9.2
M. cardinalis × M. lewisii	7430	F₃	277	2	17.7		17.0		**50.5**				14.8
M. cardinalis × M. lewisii	7427	F₃	281	5		0.4	22.1		**63.7**		0.7		13.2
M. cardinalis × M. lewisii	7426	F₃	272	8	1.1		5.1		**50.4**				43.4
M. cardinalis × M. lewisii	7465	F₃	197	7				1.0	8.6	6.7	11.7	14.2	**57.9**

* Values in boldface type are classes of highest frequency.

natural races of *M. cardinalis,* these anthocyanins are confined to the cells of the upper epidermis. In northern races of *M. lewisii,* and in some horticultural forms of *M. cardinalis* from European botanical gardens, the rose pigment is found in both the mesophyll and lower epidermis as well as in the upper epidermis.

From microscopic comparisons on the petal lobe tissues of parental, F_1, and F_2 hybrids of crosses between *M. cardinalis* × *M. lewisii* it is evident that the overall intensity of our visual impression of this color is dependent on two factors. The first is the intensity of color in the cell sap, which can range from very pale pink to intensely brilliant magenta. The second is the distribution pattern of the pigment from cell to cell. In examples studied, the pigment pattern was found to vary from a uniformly dense distribution of pigment in the vacuoles of all cells of all tissues to varying mosaic patterns of cells, ranging from colorless through different shades of pink to intense magenta.

In scoring this character in parental and hybrid populations, plants were classified on a scale from 1 to 9, as were the previous characters. The classes were established by histological study of key plants which covered the entire range of variability in the experimental populations, and these plants were retained as a reference scale throughout the experiments. The most densely pigmented northern strains of *M. lewisii* were assigned values of 8 or 9, and a value of 1 was assigned to a hypothetical class having no anthocyanin present (not in fact obtained in the experiments). The range of spread among hybrid derivatives of *Mimulus cardinalis* Los Trancos × *M. lewisii* Timberline was thereby compressed within the midrange of the scale (cf. table 12).

The inheritance of "rose" as evaluated in this manner shows a complex segregation. The progeny of both selfed parents show variability, indicating that neither parent is homozygous for all of the factors that control this complex system. The F_1 hybrid, however, is uniform, and falls in class 4, which lies in the area of overlap between populations derived from the self-pollinated parents. In second- and third-generation progenies this character segregates between the entire range of the parental values and transgresses the lower values of *M. lewisii* with less intense pigmentation. Obviously, no simple Mendelian interpretation suffices to account for the complex expression of this character. As Pollock, Vickery, and Wilson (1967) conclude from their chemical studies on the anthocyanin pigments of the *Erythranthe,* differences in intensity probably reflect quantitative differences in the amount of the various component anthocyanins that are present.

10. *Light areas*

The character "light areas" is used here specifically to describe an unpigmented band about 2mm wide at the base of petal lobes in forms of *Mimulus lewisii* from the Sierra Nevada (see figure 14). The bands represent a diminution of anthocyanin within the cells of all tissues in this segment. It is a useful

TABLE 12
Inheritance of Rose

Species or Combination	Culture Number	Generation	Number of Plants	Phenotypic Class of Parents	Percentage Frequency of Progeny, by Class								
					1	2	3	4	5	6	7	8	9
M. cardinalis (selfed)	7113	parent	31	6				3.2	3.2	**93.4***			
M. lewisii (selfed)	6634	parent	28	3			**71.4**	28.6					
M. cardinalis × *M. lewisii* (and reciprocal)	6546 7111	F_1	17	4				**100.0**					
M. cardinalis × *M. lewisii*	6547 7112 7135	F_2	306	...		9.2	**41.5**	38.9	10.1	0.3			
M. cardinalis × *M. lewisii*	7541	F_3	200	3		8.0	**86.0**	6.0					
M. cardinalis × *M. lewisii*	7429	F_3	295	3		17.6	**57.3**	23.4	1.7				
M. cardinalis × *M. lewisii*	7544	F_3	240	3		18.4	**62.9**	17.5	1.2				
M. cardinalis × *M. lewisii*	7542	F_3	331	3		26.0	**47.5**	22.0	4.5				
M. cardinalis × *M. lewisii*	7545	F_3	309	3		17.5	**45.3**	29.4	7.8				
M. cardinalis × *M. lewisii*	7566	F_3	192	5		2.1	18.2	**67.2**	12.5				
M. cardinalis × *M. lewisii*	7543	F_3	289	3		8.6	34.2	**39.8**	17.4				
M. cardinalis × *M. lewisii*	7430	F_3	273	3		8.8	30.8	**43.2**	16.1	1.1			
M. cardinalis × *M. lewisii*	7427	F_3	280	4			20.4	**47.1**	25.0	7.5			
M. cardinalis × *M. lewisii*	7426	F_3	299	4		6.7	27.4	**44.5**	19.7	1.7			
M. cardinalis × *M. lewisii*	7565	F_3	197	4		0.5	13.2	**56.8**	25.4	3.6	0.5		

* Values in boldface type are classes of highest frequency.

genetic marker in crosses between the Sierran forms of *M. lewisii* and other species, or in combination with northern forms of *M. lewisii* that lack this characteristic.

In segregating F_2 and F_3 progenies this character can be classed as being either present or absent, and seems to be governed by a relatively simple gene system. In F_1 hybrids between *M. cardinalis* and *M. lewisii* this character is dominant, and F_2 populations segregate in ratios approximating 3:1 although some marked deviations have been observed in F_3 progenies in which the ratios are closer to 2:1.

11. *Star*

The character "star" is a visual impression of a patterned arrangement of brilliant magenta to maroon-red anthocyanin pigments in the corolla throat. The pigments are confined to the cells of the upper epidermis of the corolla tube, and are arranged as a series of longitudinal stripes extending from the base of the corolla tube at the junction of the stamens up to just beyond the corolla aperture. The term "star" suggests the appearance of this arrangement when looking into the corolla (Plate I, *M. cardinalis,* also figures 2 and 14). This character was described and studied in 1931 by Brožek, who was unable to account for its inheritance in Mendelian terms. *Mimulus lewisii* lacks the character "star," although sometimes it is slightly evident as small elongate flecks or spots. In *Mimulus cardinalis, M. verbenaceus, M. nelsonii,* and *M. eastwoodiae,* this character is expressed, but it is most evident in *M. cardinalis.* Since *M. cardinalis, M. verbenaceus, M. eastwoodiae,* and *M. nelsonii* all have three pelargonidin anthocyanins in common that are lacking in all races of *M. lewisii* (Pollock, 1964; Pollock, Vickery and Wilson, 1967), it seems likely that these are the pigments responsible for the corolla tube and throat marking referred to as "star."

The inheritance of "star" is complex, and in F_2 progenies of crosses between *M. cardinalis* and *M. lewisii* this character segregates into classes ranging between the parental species. The progeny can be scored on a scale of 1 to 9, a value of 1 indicating complete absence of this character, and 9 its most intense expression. As can be seen from table 13, F_1 plants resemble *M. lewisii* more closely than do plants of *M. cardinalis,* and the frequency distribution in the F_2 generation is skewed in the direction of *M. lewisii*. In the F_3 progenies wide segregation is observed among offspring from divergent F_2 phenotypes. From the inheritance pattern in the F_2 and F_3 populations it is evident that this character is the resultant of many independently controlled heritable factors.

MODIFIABLE CHARACTERS AS EXPRESSED IN DIFFERENT ENVIRONMENTS. In a later section of this chapter differences between species and races and F_1, F_2, and F_3 derivatives that are expressed in development and growth at the altitudinal transplant stations at Stanford, Mather, and Timberline will be discussed.

TABLE 13
INHERITANCE OF STAR

Species or Combination	Culture Number	Generation	Number of Plants	Phenotypic Class of Parents	Percentage Frequency of Progeny, by Class								
					1	2	3	4	5	6	7	8	9
M. cardinalis (selfed).......	7113	parent	31	7						16.0	61.0*	23.0	
M. lewisii (selfed)...........	6634	parent	33	1	79.0	21.0							
M. cardinalis × M. lewisii (and reciprocal)	6546 6547	F_1	17	...			65.0	35.0					
M. cardinalis × M. lewisii...	7111 7112 7135	F_2	306	3	5.0	31.0	27.0	22.0	6.0	7.0	2.0		
M. cardinalis × M. lewisii...	7541	F_3	200	1	7.0	60.0	30.0	2.0	1.0				
M. cardinalis × M. lewisii...	7429	F_3	291	2	0.7	37.0	40.0	20.0	1.7				
M. cardinalis × M. lewisii...	7544	F_3	240	2	17.0	58.0	18.0	6.0	0.8				
M. cardinalis × M. lewisii...	7542	F_3	330	4	1.2	14.2	26.0	30.3	15.2	7.3	5.4	0.4	
M. cardinalis × M. lewisii...	7545	F_3	307	2	3.6	23.4	41.4	19.5	6.2	3.9	1.9		
M. cardinalis × M. lewisii...	7566	F_3	189	4		6.3	22.2	46.7	14.8	7.4	2.6		
M. cardinalis × M. lewisii...	7543	F_3	288	3	6.9	37.2	23.6	11.4	5.9	6.2	5.9	2.4	0.3
M. cardinalis × M. lewisii...	7430	F_3	278	3	3.2	26.6	24.8	18.0	10.8	8.6	5.8	1.4	0.7
M. cardinalis × M. lewisii...	7427	F_3	281	5		9.2	12.4	12.1	16.0	18.9	19.2	7.8	4.3
M. cardinalis × M. lewisii...	7426	F_3	300	6			1.3	5.3	20.0	34.7	28.0	10.3	0.3
M. cardinalis × M. lewisii...	7565	F_3	197	6			0.5	9.6	5.6	34.5	45.2	4.6	

* Values in boldface type are classes of highest frequency.

These characters are an important complement to the essentially nonmodifiable markers discussed above, and as shown in a later section of this chapter, are partially linked with them genetically.

INTRASPECIFIC COMBINATIONS. Table 14 lists cultures of intraspecific combinations made within the *Erythranthe* section. Most of these were carried only through the first generation for the purpose of comparing parental and different combinations of F_1 hybrids at the transplant stations. It will be noted that emphasis has been laid on crosses between ecological races within *M. cardinalis* and within *M. lewisii*.

TABLE 14

INTRASPECIFIC CROSSINGS IN *Mimulus*

Culture No.	Combination *
1. *Mimulus cardinalis* Dougl.	
6692	6543-111 Trancos × 6546-5 Trancos
6693	6546-5 Trancos × 6543-111 Trancos
6885	6875-2 Baja × 6546-5 Trancos
7257	6546-5 Trancos × 6694-105 Yosemite
7258	6694-105 Yosemite × 6546-5 Trancos
7259	6546-5 Trancos × 7119-16 Baja
7260	7119-16 Baja × 6546-5 Trancos
7261	6546-5 Trancos × 7120-15 San Antonio
7262	7120-15 San Antonio × 6546-5 Trancos
7263	6694-105 Yosemite × 7119-16 Baja
7264	7119-16 Baja × 6694-105 Yosemite
7265	6694-105 Yosemite × 7120-15 San Antonio
7266	7120-15 San Antonio × 6694-105 Yosemite
7267	7119-16 Baja × 7120-15 San Antonio
7268	7120-15 San Antonio × 7119-16 Baja
7437	6546-5 Trancos × 7210-1 Priests
7438	7210-1 Priests × 6546-5 Trancos
7439	6546-5 Trancos × 7244-2 Marshall
7440	7244-2 Marshall × 6546-5 Trancos
7441	6694-105 Yosemite × 7210-1 Priests
7442	7210-1 Priests × 6694-105 Yosemite
7443	6694-105 Yosemite × 7244-2 Marshall
7444	7244-2 Marshall × 6694-105 Yosemite
7445	7119-16 Baja × 7210-1 Priests
7446	7210-1 Priests × 7119-16 Baja
7447	7119-16 Baja × 7422-2 Marshall
7448	7244-2 Marshall × 7119-16 Baja
7449	7244-2 Marshall × 7210-1 Priests
7450	7210-1 Priests × 7244-2 Marshall
2. *Mimulus lewisii* Pursh	
6687	6632-1 Stevens × 6541-1 Timberline
6688	6541-1 Timberline × 6632-1 Stevens

* The numbers refer to clones that were crossed. Origins indicated by localities shown under "reference code" in Table 2.

(*Continued on following page*)

TABLE 14—Continued

Culture No.	Combination *
7269	7121-5 Yosemite × 7122-13 Tamarack
7270	7122-13 Tamarack × 7121-5 Yosemite
7271	7121-5 Yosemite × 7208-3 Timberline
7272	7208-13 Timberline × 7121-5 Yosemite
7273	7122-13 Tamarack × 7208-13 Timberline
7274	7208-13 Timberline × 7122-13 Tamarack
7275	7124-18 Porcupine × 7121-5 Yosemite
7276	7124-18 Porcupine × 7122-13 Tamarack
7277	7124-18 Porcupine × 7208-13 Timberline
7451	7411-1 Stevens × 7413-2 Rainier
7452	7413-2 Rainier × 7411-1 Stevens
7453	7411-1 Stevens × 7415-1 Logan
7454	7415-1 Logan × 7411-2 Stevens
7455	7411-2 Stevens × 7410-2 Warner
7456	7413-1 Rainier × 7415-1 Logan
7457	7415-1 Logan × 7413-1 Rainier
7458	7413-1 Rainier × 7424-3 Timberline
7459	7424-3 Timberline × 7413-1 Rainier
7460	7415-2 Logan × 7424-3 Timberline
7461	7424-2 Timberline × 7415-2 Logan
7462	7424-2 Timberline × 7410-1 Warner
7595	7424-3 Timberline × 7461-1 Logan

* The numbers refer to clones that were crossed. Origins indicated by localities shown under "reference code" in Table 2.

As explained in Chapter I, the intraspecific crosses revealed the existence of partial genetic barriers between northern forms of *M. lewisii* having dark purplish flowers and the forms from the Sierra Nevada of California with lighter colored lavender-pink to whitish flowers, and a similar barrier between forms of *M. cardinalis* from the Santa Catalina Mountains in Arizona and the Pacific coast forms.

Another result from the intraspecific crossing experiments is the finding that heterosis is evident in all intraspecific combinations that have been investigated. The degree of expression of heterosis is dependent both upon the genetic constitution of the parental forms, and the environment in which the parents and their F_1 progeny are being compared. An example of heterosis as expressed in the Stanford garden between combinations of *M. cardinalis* races is shown in table 15 in which the dry weight yields of the tops of plants are compared. The dry weights provide a crude measure of total seasonal productivity. Associated with higher rates of bulk production of dry matter are the usual manifestations of enhanced growth, including more numerous and longer flowering stems per plant, larger numbers of flowers per inflorescence, and proportional increases in the growth in underground portions of the plants. The large standard errors shown in table 15 reflect the high degree of individual variations among both parental and hybrid plants in garden-grown cultures. That the degree of enhancement of vigor in F_1

TABLE 15

Dry Weight Yields of Intra-*cardinalis* F_1 Hybrids and Parents at Stanford

	Combination	Mean Dry Weights of Above-Ground Parts*			Percent Increase in F_1 over Mean of Parents
		P_1	F_1	P_2	
7257	Los Trancos × Yosemite	54.8 ± 5.07	166.5 ± 10.6	142.8 ± 34.79	59.0
7258	Reciprocal		167.5 ± 25.8		
7259	Los Trancos × Baja California	54.8 ± 5.07	373.5 ± 62.5	126.2 ± 26.93	89.0
7260	Reciprocal		242.2 ± 45.8		
7261	Los Trancos × San Antonio	54.8 ± 5.07	183.1 ± 29.5	107.9 ± 28.30	83.3
7262	Reciprocal		115.0 ± 22.7		
7263	Yosemite × Baja California	143.8 ± 34.79	290.8 ± 86.8	126.2 ± 26.93	114.0
7264	Reciprocal		285.0 ± 25.1		
7267	Baja California × San Antonio	126.2 ± 26.93	270.0 ± 32.6	107.9 ± 28.30	100.0
7268	Reciprocal		199.7 ± 23.7		
					89.06 = Mean

*Values are means for 10 to 15 space-planted ramets of parental clones and an equal number of F_1 seedling progeny obtained during 1963–1965.

progenies differs significantly with different parental combinations is also evident from table 15.

RESPONSES OF PARENTAL AND HYBRID COMBINATIONS AT THE TRANSPLANT STATIONS

Much effort has been devoted to the comparative study of the performance of species, ecological races, and first-, second-, and third-generation progenies at the contrasting altitudinal stations at Stanford, Mather, and Timberline. The principal objective was to gain a reasonably comprehensive overall understanding of the various degrees of tolerance of the ecologically diverse members of the *Erythranthe* section to extremes in climate, and to study the inheritance of morphological marker characters in relation to responses at the altitudinal transplant stations.

From these studies significant facts have emerged which it may be helpful to summarize before presenting details:

1. There are striking differences in capacity to survive at the three altitudinal transplant stations. Most contrasting are forms of *M. cardinalis* from lower altitudes and latitudes as compared with all forms of *M. lewisii*, especially forms from the north.

2. Ecological races from different altitudes and latitudes within *M. cardinalis* and within *M. lewisii* differ from each other in their ranges of tolerance to a demonstrable degree.

3. Interspecific first-generation hybrids between *M. cardinalis* and *M. lewisii* that include combinations between altitudinal races of both species invariably show marked enhancement in vigor of growth at all three altitudinal stations as compared with the parental forms, and also a much greater range of tolerance for survival in contrasting climates than the parents.

4. Intraspecific first-generation hybrids within *M. cardinalis* and within *M. lewisii* show hybrid vigor as compared with the parental races at one or two of the altitudinal stations, but usually not at all three altitudes.

5. Second-generation progeny of hybrids between *M. cardinalis* and *M. lewisii* that segregate widely in morphological characters also segregate widely in their vigor of growth responses and survival at the three transplant stations. The interstation responses with respect to growth and survival are clearly associated with combinations of morphological markers that distinguish the original parents.

6. Third-generation progenies derived from second-generation individuals having different combinations of characters respond to transplanting in markedly different ways that are likewise associated with the morphological markers they inherit.

GROWTH AND SURVIVAL OF SPECIES AND RACES AND F_1 HYBRIDS AT STANFORD, MATHER, AND TIMBERLINE. The response-patterns of the species and races of the

TABLE 16

Growth* and Survival† of Species, Races, and Hybrids of *Mimulus* at Stanford, Mather, and Timberline

Culture	Stanford (30 m)		Mather (1400 m)		Meadow Garden Timberline (3050–3100 m)		Slope Garden	
	Growth	Survival	Growth	Survival	Growth	Survival	Growth	Survival
Mimulus cardinalis								
Los Trancos	152	100	14	0	0	0	4.0	0
Jacksonville	80	90	28	0	1.6	20	1.8	100.0
Priests Grade	84	84	18	20	0	0	.2	40.0
Grass Valley	184	80	30	0	...	...	3.5	.7
Crane Creek	147	77	33	0	...	...	.5	1.3
Yosemite	230	97	29	0	0	0	5.0	2.0
Middle Fork	211	87	35	0	0	0	3.4	3.3
Woodfords	166	66	40	13	0	0	.7	20.0
Baja	137	87	26	0	0	0	6.4	3.3
San Antonio	134	79	66	27	2.4	60	5.0	60.0
Marshall Gulch	30	80	11	20	1.7	40	3.1	100.0
Bear Wallow	30	60	0	0	.2	60	2.8	100.0
Mimulus lewisii								
Yosemite	9.4	0	0	0	22.1	100	4.0	100.0
Tamarack	8.4	20	24	20	16.8	100	4.8	100.0
Porcupine	15.7	40	6	0	14.4	100	2.4	100.0
Timberline	4.4	0	0	0	14.9	100	4.2	100.0
Stevens Pass	0	0	...	...	...	...	...	...
Logan Pass	0	0	0	0	4.6	100	1.8	100.0
Mt. Rainier	0	0	0	0	3.4	100	6.5	100.0
Mimulus verbenaceus								
Grand Canyon	32.0	50	0	0	0	0	0	0
Mimulus eastwoodiae								
Arches	4.0	0	0	0	0	0	0	0
Mimulus nelsonii								
El Salto	58.0	100	0	0	0	0	0	0
Intra-*cardinalis* F₁ hybrids								
Trancos × Yosemite	167	95	31	20	0.6	0	5.3	78
Trancos × San Antonio	149	70	44	20	0.5	20	9.9	100
Trancos × Baja	308	90	39	0	1.8	10	8.7	50
Yosemite × Baja	288	90	36	10	1.6	10	10.6	100
Yosemite × San Antonio	175	90	23	30	2.0	60	10.5	100
San Antonio × Baja	234	100	54	50	2.6	80	16.0	100
Intra-*lewisii* F₁ hybrids								
Yosemite × Tamarack	3.8	0	31	0	8.8	100	10.2	100

Hybrid	Yield* (g)	Survival† (%)	Yield* (g)	Survival† (%)	Yield* (g)	Survival† (%)	Yield* (g)	Survival† (%)
Yosemite × Porcupine	3.2	0	7	0	8.7	100	2.0	100
Yosemite × Timberline	5.9	0	15	0	9.3	100	4.3	100
Tamarack × Porcupine	6.0	0	34	0	11.8	100	9.0	100
Tamarack × Timberline	7.7	0	13	0	10.2	100	5.3	100
Porcupine × Timberline	6.2	0	7	0	14.9	100	5.6	100
Mimulus cardinalis × *lewisii* F₁ hybrids								
Trancos × Yosemite	76	90	217	40	12	100	22.6	100
Trancos × Tamarack	82	100	80	60	11	100	16.3	100
Trancos × Smoky Jack	204	100	172	40	…	100	19.3	100
Trancos × Porcupine	84	80	150	60	13	100	15.0	100
Trancos × Timberline	72	100	96	50	8	100	17.3	100
Yosemite × Yosemite	76	80	102	80	8	100	14.3	100
Yosemite × Tamarack	69	90	64	40	15	90	11.7	100
Yosemite × Smoky Jack	164	100	137	40	…	100	20.6	80
Yosemite × Porcupine	77	100	110	80	15	100	14.3	100
Yosemite × Timberline	75	100	70	80	10	100	9.1	100
Baja × Yosemite	100	90	86	40	12	100	12.4	100
Baja × Tamarack	100	90	142	50	14	100	14.6	100
Baja × Porcupine	92	80	132	60	10	100	10.3	100
Baja × Timberline	97	90	106	50	7	100	7.3	100
San Antonio × Yosemite	76	80	60	60	8	100	9.8	100
San Antonio × Tamarack	40	60	62	50	8	100	7.4	100
San Antonio × Timberline	30	70	32	20	5	80	2.8	90
San Antonio × Logan Pass	32	0	43	15	5	100	6.7	100
cardinalis × *verbenaceus* F₁ hybrids								
San Antonio × Grand Canyon	99	67	37	89	0	0	2.0	33
cardinalis × *eastwoodiae* F₁ hybrids								
Yosemite × Arches	29	50	12	0	0	0	1.6	0
Baja × Arches	48	93	24	60	0	0	2.1	0
San Antonio × Arches	33	33	10	83	0	0	0.5	17
lewisii × *eastwoodiae* F₁ hybrids								
Yosemite × Arches	30	40	24	40	0	0	1.4	100
Tamarack × Arches	31	40	36	40	1.4	40	2.3	60
Timberline × Arches	16	83	19	66	0	20	1.7	100
verbenaceus × *eastwoodiae* F₁ hybrids								
Grand Canyon	34	73	13	53	0	0	0.4	36

* Growth expressed as mean dry weight yield per plant (grams) of above-ground material per growing season of cloned transplants. Values are means over a three- to five-year period at each station.

† Survival of cloned transplants expressed in percentage over the same period.

Erythranthe section and of their hybrid derivatives cannot be fully described by means of simple tables and graphs, or even by more elaborate statistical means. It will suffice, however, to review some features that are of particular interest in relation to mechanisms of natural selection. Table 16 presents a comparative evaluation of growth and survival of some of the principal cultures that have been tested at the three altitudinal transplant stations.

The striking reversal in growth and survival of races of *M. cardinalis* as a whole as compared with races of *M. lewisii* at the Stanford and Timberline transplant stations is clearly evident from table 16. These results are in accord with the distinct regional and ecological distribution of the two species in their respective natural habitats as outlined in Chapter I (pp. 4–7).

Within *M. cardinalis* there are notable differences in response between ecological races from the more extreme natural habitats within the range of the species, especially among races from different altitudes. The coastal Los Trancos race of this species survives only at the low altitude station at Stanford in contrast with the mid-Sierran races, from Carlin, Middle Fork, and Yosemite, that tolerate both the Stanford and Mather climates, but not the Timberline. Races from the higher altitudes at San Antonio Peak and Marshall Gulch are capable of surviving at all three stations, although they are not vigorous at any of them. At Timberline they develop only to vegetative or early flowering states, and are unable to attain full maturity. The extent of ecotypic differentiation within *M. cardinalis* falls short of that which occurs in such species as *Potentilla glandulosa* and *Achillea lanulosa* which have wider geographical ranges, as described in earlier volumes of this series.

The present-day center of distribution of *Mimulus cardinalis* appears to be in the vicinity of the San Gabriel Mountains in Southern California. Extensions northward along the Pacific coast to Oregon, inland to middle altitudes of the Sierra Nevada, and eastward to the Santa Catalina Mountains of Arizona may have evolved from this center.

Within *M. lewisii,* apart from the morphologically distinct forms from the northern part of the range of the species frequent in Washington and in the mountainous parts of Idaho, Montana, and Utah, as contrasted with the components from the Sierra Nevada of California, our evidence for differentiation into ecological races is less clear. Plants of *M. lewisii* from lower elevations in the Sierra Nevada at Tamarack Flat at 1800 m are taller and somewhat larger than plants from near Timberline at 3200 m when grown at the three transplant stations. Likewise, as can be seen in table 16, the Tamarack population survives somewhat better at Stanford and at Mather than does the Timberline race. The northern forms of *M. lewisii* are even more difficult to maintain in culture at Stanford or Mather than the Sierran Timberline form. Only at Timberline is it possible to maintain any of the races of *M. lewisii* over extended periods of time. A difficulty experienced in our studies has been our inability to propagate cloned transplants of *M. lewisii* at Stanford with sufficient reserve strength to become established in garden plantings, even at Timberline.

There is evidence that altitudinal races exist in *M. eastwoodiae* and in *M. verbenaceus*. The culture 7421 or *M. eastwoodiae* from Rainbow Bridge (table 2), originally from 1000 m elevation, has longer stems with more widely spreading stolons than 7144 from Arches National Monument at 1300 m elevation. In *M. verbenaceus,* culture 7143 from Bright Angel Trail at 610 m elevation in Arizona differs from 7548 from Zion National Park at 1500 m elevation in Utah, as do also the more southern forms from Mexico, 7639 from Surotato at 920 m elevation and 7638 from Sinaloa at 1550 m. *M. nelsonii* is apparently of more restricted distribution and appears to lack ecological races, but there is herbarium evidence for the existence of intermediates between *M. nelsonii* and *M. verbenaceus.*

Mimulus eastwoodiae is essentially a nonsurvivor at all three transplant stations. *M. verbenaceus* grows successfully at Stanford but does not survive at either Mather or Timberline, while *M. nelsonii,* like races of *M. cardinalis* from the higher elevations, is barely able to live at Timberline but grows well at both Stanford and Mather.

VIGOR OF INTRASPECIFIC F_1 HYBRIDS AS EXPRESSED AT STANFORD, MATHER, AND TIMBERLINE. The heterosis expressed in F_1 hybrids between different races of *Mimulus cardinalis* as reflected by dry weight yields shown in table 15 is not so evident when clones of the same individuals are grown at the Mather and Timberline transplant stations. The bar diagram shown in figure 20 depicts the relationship between the average dry weight yields for four interracial crosses of *M. cardinalis* grown at the three altitudinal stations over a three-year period. Since the plants grown at the three stations are clones of the same individuals, identical genotypes were sampled at each station. The examples shown in figure 20 are representative of the 10 interracial combinations of crosses that have been compared at the three transplant stations.

At Mather and Timberline there is a much smaller absolute gain in total dry weight of the F_1 hybrids than at Stanford. This is represented graphically in figure 20. When the gains of the F_1 hybrids are computed as percentage increase over the means of the parents, however, they are more impressive, as shown in Part A of table 17. The marked diminution in total yield at Timberline is undoubtedly due to the very short growing season at the subalpine station.

Although the individual variability within each F_1 progeny is large at each station, it is nevertheless evident from figure 20 and table 17 that statistically some parental combinations show markedly greater growth enhancement at one of the transplant stations than at any of the others. The Baja parent, for example (clone 7119-16), in combination with other races yields F_1 hybrids at Stanford that display greater hybrid vigor than do progeny of San Antonio Peak (clone 7120-15). At Mather and at Timberline, however, these relationships may be reversed (table 17). It is to be noted that the Los Trancos race, a consistent nonsurvivor at both Mather and Timberline, when combined in an F_1 hybrid with Yosemite, San Antonio Peak, or Baja, yields progeny that are able to survive at Mather and even to some extent at Timberline. At the high-altitude station neither the Los Trancos nor the Yosemite races are capable of surviving, yet their F_1 hybrids are able to persist to a surprising degree.

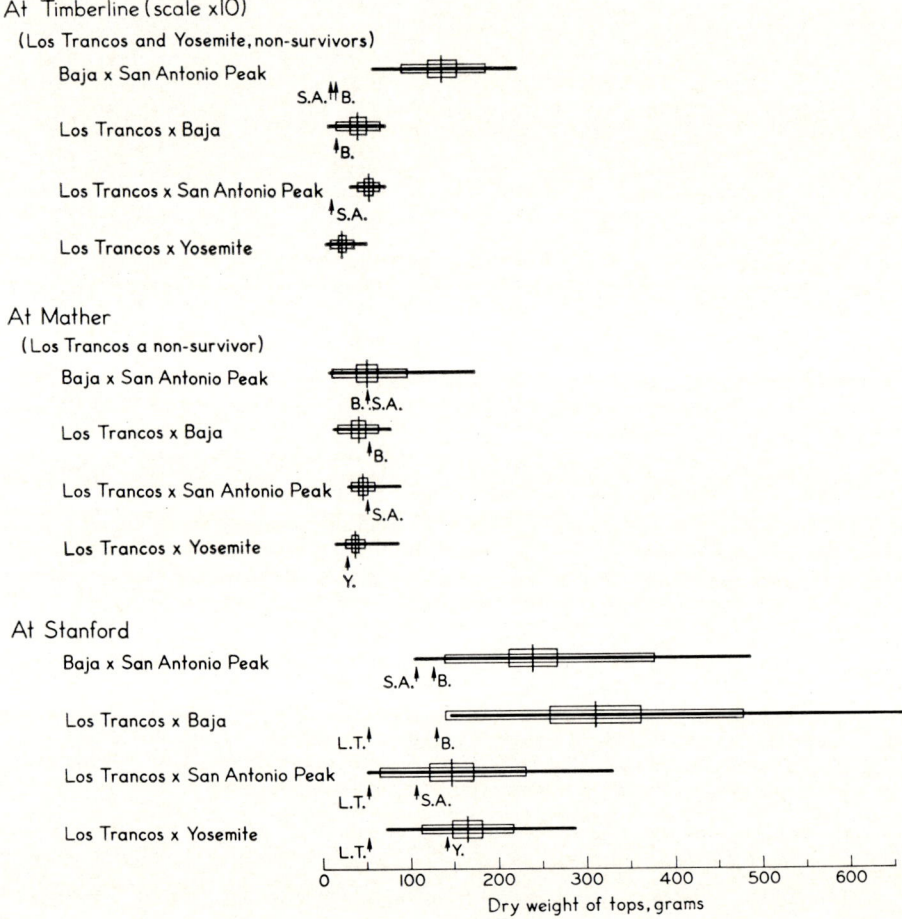

Figure 20. Dry weight yields of cloned transplants of F_1 hybrids between different intraspecific combinations of *Mimulus cardinalis* races when grown in gardens at the different altitudes of the Stanford (30 m), Mather (1400 m), and Timberline (3050 m) stations. For explanation of bar diagrams, see figure 14. Arrows point to mean values for parental forms. Note that the values in the graphs for the Timberline cultures have been expanded by a factor of 10.

Although considerable effort has been devoted to determining to what extent, if any, hybrid vigor is expressed in intraspecific combinations within *M. lewisii*, our data are very fragmentary and provide only tentative answers to some of the questions originally posed. The failure of our efforts is due mostly to the inability of all forms of *M. lewisii* to grow successfully in the Stanford and Mather environments, and their slow establishment even at Timberline when brought as cloned transplants from Stanford in a weak condition. The few

TABLE 17

Percent Increase in Dry Weight of F_1 Hybrids over Means of Parents

Combinations	Stanford	Mather	Timberline
A. Intra-*cardinalis* F_1's			
Los Trancos × Yosemite	59.0	114.0	219.0
Los Trancos × Baja	89.0	203.0	278.0
Los Trancos × San Antonio	83.3	32.8	264.8
Yosemite × Baja	114.0	30.6	111.4
Baja × San Antonio	100.0	18.0	235.0
Totals	445.3	398.4	1,108.2
Means	89.0	79.6	221.6
B. Intra-*lewisii* F_1's			
Yosemite × Tamarack	1.5	77.0	48.5
Yosemite × Timberline	214.0	27.3	3.2
Tamarack × Timberline	263.0	−23.4	35.9
Porcupine × Yosemite	26.7	−29.1	9.9
Porcupine × Tamarack	165.0	89.3	65.5
Porcupine × Timberline	...	148.0	86.9
Totals	670.2	289.1	249.9
Means	134.0	48.2	41.6
C. *cardinalis–lewisii* F_1's			
Los Trancos × Yosemite	190.2	2,500.0	372.5
Los Trancos × Tamarack	264.0	565.0	401.0
Los Trancos × Porcupine	159.2	5,000.0	535.5
Los Trancos × Timberline	119.0	2,110.0	522.0
Yosemite × Yosemite	−1.3	425.0	189.5
Yosemite × Tamarack	−8.3	138.5	188.0
Porcupine × Yosemite	0.0	465.0	342.0
Yosemite × Timberline	−8.6	267.0	261.0
Yosemite × Baja	39.6	375.0	731.5
Baja × Tamarack	48.8	554.0	373.5
Porcupine × Baja	34.8	620.0	320.0
Baja × Timberline	41.8	512.0	224.0
San Antonio × Yosemite	29.8	126.0	154.5
San Antonio × Tamarack	−31.5	36.2	163.5
San Antonio × Timberline	−48.5	−16.3	79.4
San Antonio × Logan Pass	−48.9	30.0	250.0
Totals	780.1	13,707.4	5,107.9
Means	48.7	856.7	319.2

data that are available, however, do indicate that F_1 progeny display about the same relative vigor with respect to the parents as in intraracial crosses within *M. cardinalis*. Part B of table 17 summarizes the available data from representative intra-*lewisii* combinations.

VIGOR OF INTERSPECIFIC HYBRIDS AT THE TRANSPLANT STATIONS. Most interspecific F_1 hybrids between various combinations of *M. cardinalis* and *M. lewisii* show spectacular gains in both vigor and survival at all three altitudinal stations as compared with their parents. These gains are especially evident at the Mather station, where only a few of the parental races of *M. cardinalis* and none of *M. lewisii* survive, yet most F_1 hybrid combinations are conspicuously successful

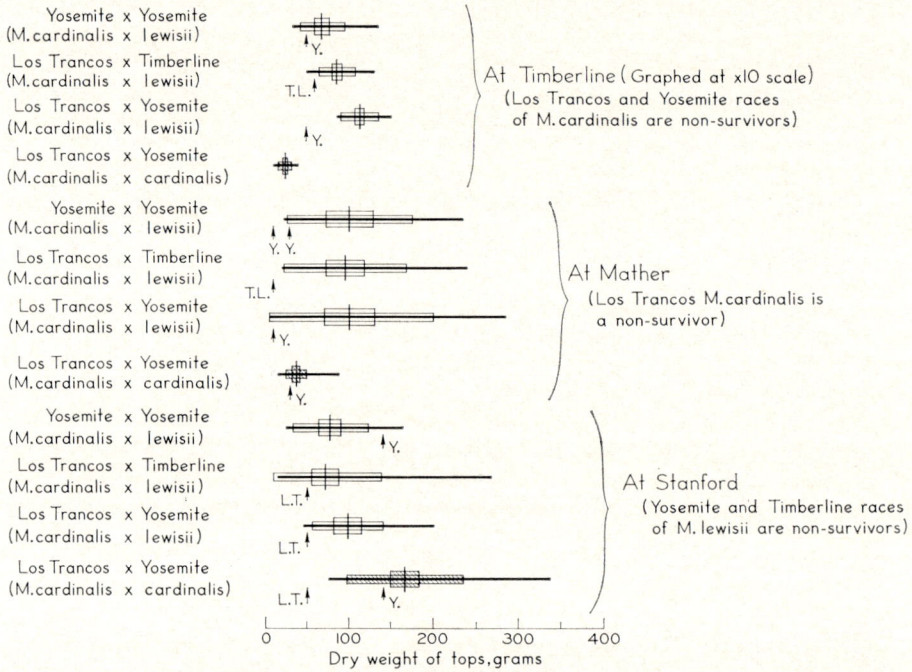

Figure 21. Dry weight yields of cloned transplants of F_1 hybrids between different interspecific combinations of *Mimulus lewisii* and *M. cardinalis* when grown in gardens at the different altitudes of the Stanford (30 m), Mather (1400 m), and Timberline (3050 m) stations. Data for the intra-*cardinalis* combination Los Trancos × Yosemite shown in figure 20 are also included here for comparison (the cross-hatched bar diagrams). For explanation of bar diagrams, see figure 14. Arrows point to mean values for parental plants.

there. The dry weight yield of tops of F_1 hybrid populations from three representative combinations of *M. cardinalis* × *M. lewisii* at Stanford, Mather, and Timberline are shown in figure 21 in comparison with one of a typical intra-*cardinalis* combination (Los Trancos × Yosemite) represented by the shaded bar diagram.

At Stanford the total seasonal dry weight yields of intra-*cardinalis* hybrids are mostly higher than those of interspecific combinations between *M. cardinalis* and *M. lewisii*. Since the *M. lewisii* parents entering into these hybrids are nonsurvivors at Stanford, the percentage increase in dry weight yield of the F_1 progeny over the means of the parents is, nevertheless, often greater than in intra-*cardinalis* hybrids, as shown in table 17.

At Mather, where the intra-*cardinalis* F_1 hybrids make only modest growth, *cardinalis–lewisii* F_1's greatly exceed them in both relative and absolute dry weight yields in all but a few combinations. At Timberline, likewise, F_1 hybrids between *M. cardinalis* and *M. lewisii* display marked heterosis even in combinations in which the *cardinalis* parent is a nonsurvivor at the subalpine station. A comparison of the percentage increase in dry weights of F_1 hybrids in intra-*cardinalis* in contrast with *cardinalis–lewisii* hybrids at the three transplant stations is shown in table 17. Figure 22 illustrates the responses of subalpine *M. lewisii*, coastal *M. cardinalis*, their F_1 hybrid and F_3 progenies originating from contrasting F_2 individuals at Timberline.

Among the *cardinalis–lewisii* F_1 progenies, some well-marked differences occur. Combinations between the Los Trancos race of *M. cardinalis* originally from near sea level when combined with various strains of Sierran *M. lewisii* (i.e., Yosemite, Tamarack, Timberline) show extreme heterosis at Mather, in contrast with the F_1 derivatives of the San Antonio Peak race of *M. cardinalis* in combination with some races of *M. lewisii* (cf. table 17, Part C). The Baja race of *M. cardinalis* in combination with various races of *M. lewisii* likewise yields F_1 progenies displaying marked vigor at all three altitudinal stations.

One might expect that either inter- or intraspecific F_1 combinations between races from high altitudes would perform better at Timberline than combinations from low altitudes. Our data, however, do not support this conclusion. The high degree of variability among the various parental populations from different altitudes overshadows data that might seem to support this hypothesis. Possibly, more extensive studies including additional races of both *M. cardinalis* and *M. lewisii* would substantiate such a trend.

Expression of phenological characteristics at Stanford, Mather, and Timberline. The interaction between genotypes represented by the altitudinal and latitudinal races of *Mimulus cardinalis* and *M. lewisii* and their seasonal responses at the altitudinal stations reveal physiological differences that are important in natural selection.

The date of first flowering is a phenological character that differs considerably between altitudinal races of both *M. cardinalis* and *M. lewisii*. The study of seasonal initiation of flowering and its inheritance as expressed at the three transplant stations reveals some significant relationships between highly modifiable phenological characters and the relatively nonmodifiable markers described on pages 32 to 58.

The histograms in figure 23 show the seasonal spread in flowering for the Los Trancos race of *M. cardinalis* as compared with subalpine *M. lewisii* from Timberline and their F_1 and F_2 progenies when grown as cloned transplants at

Stanford, Mather, and Timberline. Points of interest that are revealed by these diagrams may be summarized as follows:

1. At Stanford the Los Trancos race of *M. cardinalis* is the first to flower during the spring, subalpine *M. lewisii* being significantly later. This race of *M. cardinalis* is winter active at this lowland station in spite of winter frosts, and flowers in early May. In contrast, subalpine *M. lewisii* is winter dormant at Stanford and develops weak flower stems that start to emerge in mid-April. This weakened condition appears to be due to a depletion of food reserves during the relatively warm Stanford winters. As a consequence, *M. lewisii* flowers late, poorly and irregularly during June and July.

First-generation hybrids are clearly intermediate between parental *M. cardinalis* and *M. lewisii* with respect to time of flowering at Stanford. They are also intermediate with respect to their degree of winter activity at Stanford. The F_2 progeny display wide segregation that encompasses both of the parental ranges, as they do also with respect to many of the nonmodifiable characters as described in pages 32 to 58.

2. At Mather coastal *M. cardinalis* is forced to winter dormancy by the cold weather, like *M. lewisii*. Both emerge in spring growth at about the same time and with greatly reduced vigor. If they survive sufficiently long, both species will flower at approximately the same time with completely overlapping ranges for individuals of the two species. The much more vigorous F_1 plants also

Figure 22. (A) Parental *Mimulus lewisii*, clone 7405-4 from Timberline (*left*), the F_1 hybrid between *M. lewisii* and *M. cardinalis* 6546-3 (vigorous plant in *center*), and the vacancy of the nonsurviving *M. cardinalis* parent, 6546-5, marked by the tape (*right*) at Timberline, September, 1967, following an early autumn snowfall.

Figure 22. (B) Three third-generation progenies from the above cross in the same garden during the summer of 1967. *Row 1*, F_3 progeny of the *M. lewisii*-like F_2 plant 7111-16; *row 2*, F_3 progeny of the F_1-like F_2 plant 7111-17; *row 3*, F_3 progeny of the *M. cardinalis*-like F_2 plant 7135-35.

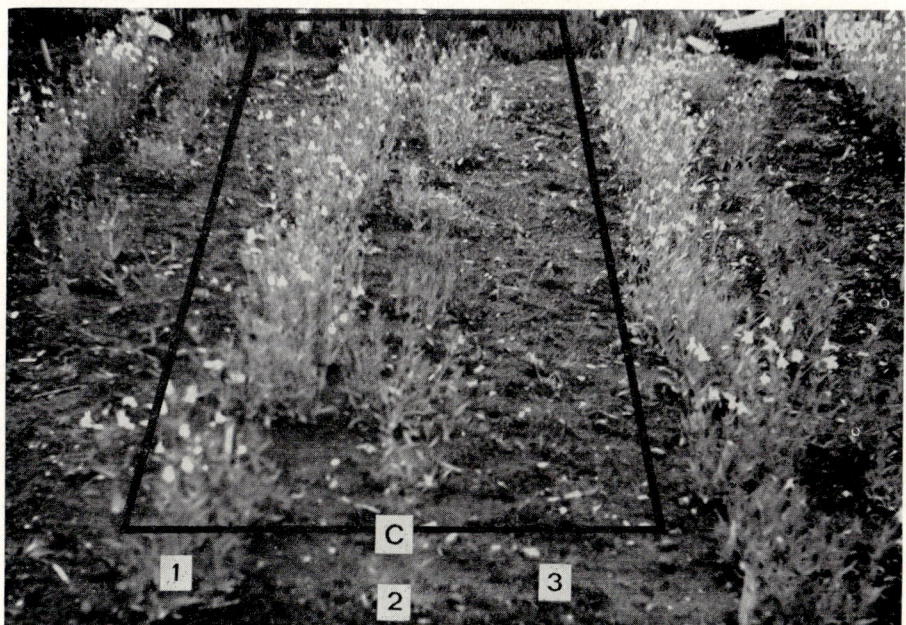

Figure 22. (C) The same rows in 1968, all plants in row 3 having been winter-killed in contrast with the vigorous plants in row 1. The progeny in row 2 show variable vigor and survival.

flower at about the same time as the parental species, and segregation in the F_2 progeny extends far beyond the parental ranges in both directions towards earliness and lateness.

3. At Timberline *M. lewisii* flowers during the latter part of July, whereas coastal *M. cardinalis,* which at best barely manages to survive one or sometimes two winters before being eliminated, may occasionally produce one or two flowers before killing frosts begin in early September. As at Stanford, Mather, and Timberline, the F_1 hybrids are intermediate with respect to the

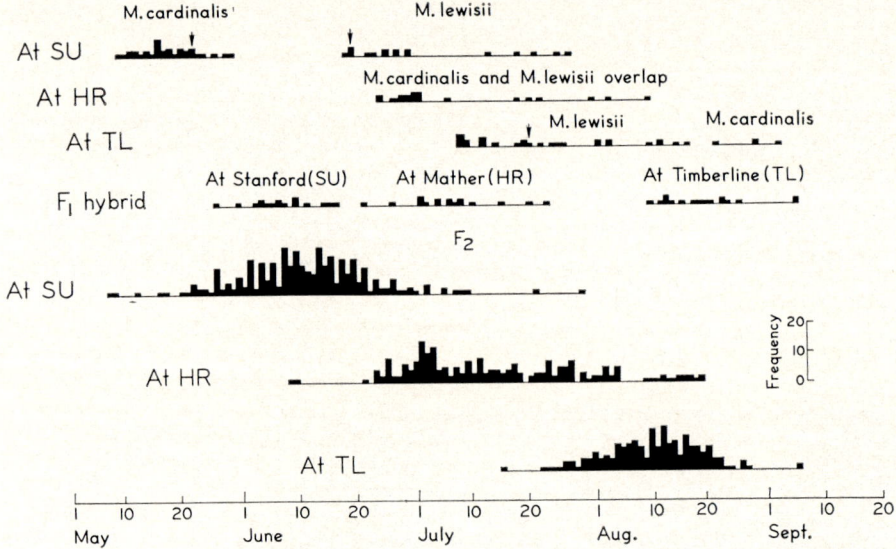

Figure 23. Dates of first flowers of parental populations of *Mimulus cardinalis* and *M. lewisii* derived by selfing the parents, and of their F_1 and F_2 progeny transplanted as clones at the altitudinal stations of Stanford (30 m), Mather (1400 m), and Timberline (3050 m). At Mather the flowering dates of the parental populations overlap. See text.

parents in time of flowering, and the F_2 progeny segregate over the range between the parental extremes.

It is clearly evident that different degrees of earliness in different ecological races are genetically controlled, yet the expression of this character may be so modified by environment that their relative order of flowering may be reversed at one station as compared with another.

The segregation of three F_3 populations at the transplant stations with respect to flowering is shown in figure 24. The three progenies differ both in the range of variation among individual plants at any one station and in the frequency distribution among different classes.

The most interesting attribute of these F_3 cultures is that although they all have a wide range of variation that overlaps from one culture to another in the extreme classes, each progeny reacts essentially as an independent entity. At Stanford there is a reversal in onset of first flowering as compared with that found in the parental *M. cardinalis* and *M. lewisii* populations. Population 7541,

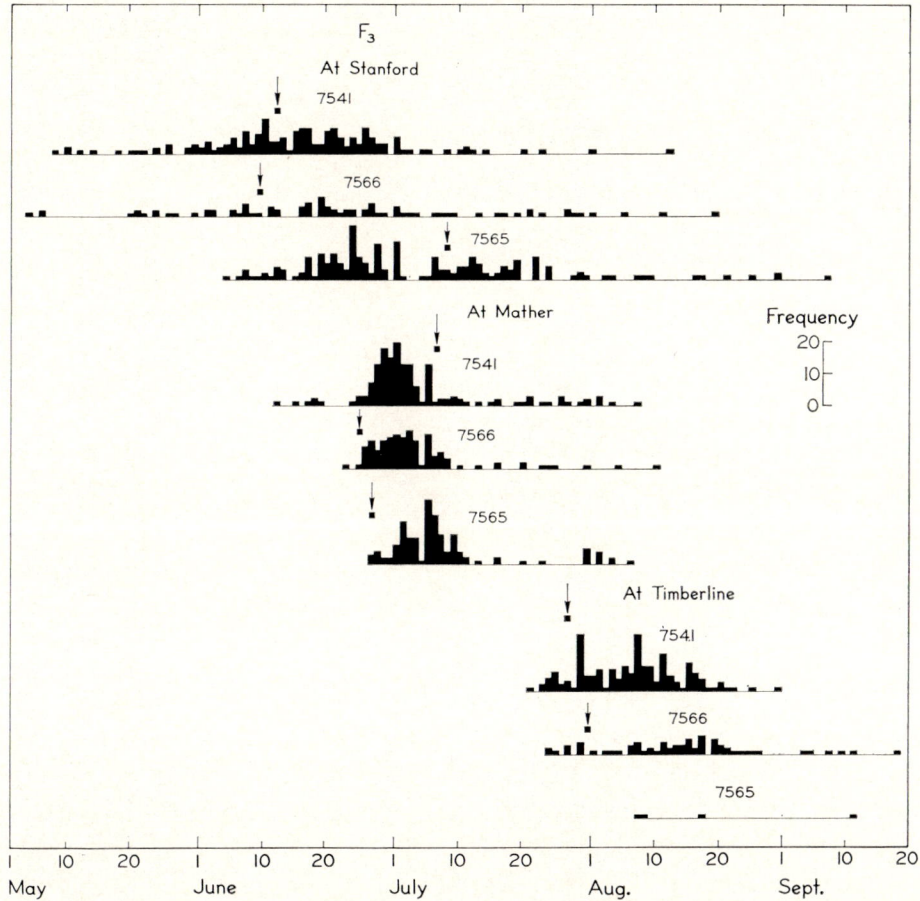

Figure 24. Dates of first flowering of F_3 progenies derived from selfing three F_2 plants from the cross *M. lewisii* Timberline × *M. cardinalis* Los Trancos grown as cloned transplants at the altitudinal stations of Stanford (30 m), Mather (1400 m), and Timberline (3050 m).

Culture 7541 was derived from the *M. lewisii*-like F_2 plant 7111-16, 7566 from the F_1-like F_2 plant 7111-17, and 7565 from the *M. cardinalis*-like F_2 plant 7135-35. The data from cultures 7566 and 7565 at Timberline are incomplete because of the limited number of individuals capable of flowering there.

stemming from the F_2 individual 7111-16, which closely resembles *M. lewisii,* unlike the parental population of late-flowering *M. lewisii,* is predominantly early flowering at Stanford. This is in contrast with the late-flowering *cardinalis*-like F_3 population 7565 derived from a late-flowering F_2 individual 7135-35. Population 7566, originating from the F_1-like F_2 individual 7111-17, segregates over an even greater range than the original F_2 population.

At Mather the three F_3 populations are essentially alike with respect to date of onset of flowering. At Timberline the flowering pattern of the same three cloned F_3 progenies follows the same sequence as in the original parental populations of *M. cardinalis* and *M. lewisii*. The *M. lewisii*-like population 7541 responds like subalpine *M. lewisii* in being early, whereas 7565, the *cardinalis*-like population, is extremely late, like lowland *M. cardinalis*. It is so late in its flowering response that, during the three-year experimental period, only four plants were able to flower before the occurrence of killing frosts in September. The population 7566 from the F_1-like F_2 plant 7111-17 resembles the original F_2 population in its responses at Timberline station.

WINTER ACTIVITY AT STANFORD. Another phenological character that has been studied is the degree of winter activity at Stanford. At this lowland station the winters are mild, but frosts occur approximately 80 days per year.[1] Table 18 describes the relative degree of winter activity of growth by different races and species of the *Erythranthe* at Stanford. Alpine and subalpine races and species are in general winter dormant at Stanford, whereas lowland races of the same or related species are usually winter active. The degree of winter activity in intermediate races varies from year to year depending upon the severity of frosts.

Differences in degree of winter activity as expressed at Stanford are inherited by F_1, F_2, and F_3 progenies in much the same pattern as are differences in earliness of flowering. The most extensively studied hybrid combinations include crosses between *M. cardinalis* and *M. lewisii*. For example, F_1 hybrids between winter-active *M. cardinalis* Los Trancos × winter-dormant *M. lewisii* Timberline are semidormant for a short period, and the F_2 progeny segregate over the entire range from winter-active to winter-dormant individuals, following essentially a normal frequency distribution curve. Third-generation progenies range over differing frequency patterns: those most resembling the *M. cardinalis* parent have higher frequencies of winter-active types, and those from *M. lewisii*-like F_2 plants tend to be more winter dormant. Intermediate expressions can be observed at Stanford through varying degrees of winter activity or inactivity. Individual plants of progenies grown in the field have been scored on a scale of 1 to 9 during the periods of most severe frost in the Stanford garden. These data have been incorporated in the statistical analysis for the study of correlations, as explained in pages that follow.

FROST SUSCEPTIBILITY AT TIMBERLINE. A phenological character related to winter activity at Stanford is the degree of frost susceptibility of vegetative parts of plants on cloned transplants at Timberline towards the end of the growing

---

[1] U.S. Weather Bureau data.

season. This character is best observed after moderately heavy freezing weather when minimum night temperatures drop within the range of $-8°$ to $-5°$ C for several days following the season's active growth period. Temperatures colder than these cause all plants of *Mimulus* to freeze to the ground level so that no differences can be observed. At somewhat warmer temperatures there is less effect except in especially frost-susceptible individuals among F_2 and F_3 progenies from *cardinalis–lewisii* hybrids, or in races of *M. verbenaceus, M. eastwoodiae,* and *M. nelsonii.*

Our principal interest in the study of frost susceptibility at Timberline is in

TABLE 18

Degree of Winter Activity of Species and Races of the *Erythranthe* Section at Stanford

Species	Degree of Winter Activity
Mimulus cardinalis	
Los Trancos	highly winter-active
Jacksonville	highly winter-active
Priests Grade	highly winter-active
Yosemite	moderately winter-active
Baja California	moderately winter-active
Woodfords	partially winter-dormant
San Antonio Peak	winter-dormant
Marshall Gulch	winter-dormant
Mimulus lewisii	
All races	winter-dormant
Mimulus verbenaceus	
Grand Canyon, Arizona	highly winter-active
Zion Canyon, Utah	partially winter-dormant
Surotado, Mexico	highly winter-active
Sinaloa, Mexico	highly winter-active
Mimulus eastwoodiae	
Arches, Utah	winter-dormant
Rainbow Bridge, Utah	winter-dormant
Mystery Canyon, Utah	winter-dormant
Mimulus nelsonii	
El Salto, Mexico	highly winter-active

connection with comparisons between parental races in both intra- and interspecific hybrids and their F_1, F_2, and F_3 progenies. With moderately heavy frosts at Timberline the tops of lowland forms of *M. cardinalis* are killed, whereas local *M. lewisii* continues to retain green leaves and stems although the flowers may be frozen.

First-generation hybrids between Los Trancos *M. cardinalis* and subalpine *M. lewisii* show a degree of frost resistance at Timberline even higher than that of the parental *M. lewisii,* as can be seen in figure 22. Second-generation progenies segregate widely, ranging from highly frost susceptible to individuals which are more frost resistant than the F_1 hybrids.

The three F_3 progenies 7141, 7565, and 7566 tested as cloned transplants differ markedly from each other (cf. figure 22). The more *lewisii*-like plants of 7141 have a much higher frequency of frost-resistant individuals than the *cardinalis*-like derivative of 7565. The intermediate culture 7566 displays a wider range of segregation than either of the other F_3's. Scoring of individual cloned transplants of F_1, F_2, and F_3 progenies on a scale of 1 to 9, as described for previous characters, was made at Timberline over several years. The average data were incorporated in computations of correlations, as described in later pages of this chapter.

MODIFIABLE CHARACTERS. The usual characters found to become highly modified when clones of the same individuals of various races and species are transplanted to the altitudinal transplant stations (Clausen, Keck, and Hiesey, 1940) are also similarly modifiable in transplants of *Mimulus*. The length of inflorescences of the Yosemite race of *Mimulus cardinalis,* for example, may range between 70 and 90 cm at Stanford, and may be reduced to 8 or 10 cm at Mather; at Timberline it is not likely to flower at all, but in favorable years may bear a blossom or two in an inflorescence 2 or 3 cm long. The number of flowers borne on a single stem may range up to a hundred at Stanford, up to 20 at Mather, and from zero to 1 at Timberline. Leaf sizes may also be modified to a high degree, but leaf shape (i.e., leaf ratio, as explained on p. 48) is relatively constant. *M. lewisii* shows similar modifications, but in an opposite direction: plants in their natural environment near Timberline may have numerous stems up to 70 cm in height and bear up to 18 or 20 flowers per stem, but when transplanted to the Stanford garden become weak, with only a few stems, rarely over 25 cm in length, and seldom bearing more than 6 flowers per inflorescence. *Mimulus verbenaceus* grows vigorously at Stanford with well-developed inflorescences, but these become much reduced at Mather. The thickness, size, texture, and color of leaves can be modified on any particular clone of any of the species by differences in light intensity, the effect of temperature, and gaseous composition (CO_2 and O_2 concentration) of the atmosphere surrounding the leaves, as described more fully in Chapter III.

GENETIC COHERENCE. Genetic coherence may be defined as the tendency of F_2 and later generation progeny to inherit combinations of characters of the parents more frequently than would be predicted on the basis of free random recombination. Evidence pointing to genetic coherence as a general principle governing the inheritance of characters in interspecific and interracial hybrids among plants has been slowly accumulating during the last thirty years. Detailed study of genetic coherence and its significance in natural selection and the evolution of races and species are matters that have come to general attention only in relatively recent years.

The pioneer contributions of Edgar Anderson (1939a, 1939b) and Kenneth Mather (1941, 1942, 1943) provided both experimental evidence and helpful

F$_2$ plants over a period of 3 to 5 years in garden cultures grown as cloned transplants and studied at all three transplant stations.

Partial linkages between most of the pairs of character combinations are clearly evident in figure 25. Of the 120 possible pairs of character combinations between the 16 characters represented, 28, or 23.3 percent (table 19), have r values ranging between 0.000 and 0.148, indicating little or no genetic coherence below the 5 percent level. The remaining 92, or 76.7 percent, have r values above the 5 percent level. The r values of highest frequency lie in the range between 0.251 and 0.350, indicating a high degree of character association. All of the morphological markers show strong linkage, including such unrelated characters as the degree of petal reflexing and the number of dentations on leaves.

Most characters involving responses at the transplant stations, such as the degree of winter activity at Stanford and of frost resistance at Timberline, are also strongly associated with morphological characters, although dry weight yield at Mather is conspicuously independent of the morphological markers. In this connection it will be recalled that neither of the parental species is a survivor at Mather. Dry weight yield at Timberline is likewise associated with very few morphological markers.

If one excludes from consideration the dry weight yields at the Stanford, Mather, and Timberline transplant stations in studying the partial linkage relations of the characters represented in figure 25, there remain 78 possible pairs of character combinations among the 13 remaining characters. Of these 74, or 94.8 percent, show significant partial correlation. The comparison between the percentage of nonsignificant correlations whether or not dry weight responses are included suggests that, as a whole, transplant-response characteristics are not as highly linked with morphological characters as are the marker characters to each other.

The breakdown of frequencies of different degrees of correlation between the characters shown in table 19 reveals a fairly symmetrical distribution with the highest frequencies in the r range between 0.251 and 0.350. This is a considerably higher mean value than was found in *Potentilla glandulosa* Upper Monarch Lake × Santa Barbara by Clausen and Hiesey (1958, p. 116) where the correlations of highest frequency fell in the range between 0.09 and 0.20. The stronger degree of correlation found in *Mimulus* may be due in part to a more accurate scoring of individual character expression in F$_2$ progenies in *Mimulus* made possible by the more distinctive contrasts in marker characters.

It is noteworthy that Anderson (1939) estimated on theoretical grounds that an organism with 10 pairs of chromosomes, each having one chiasma and bearing 10 gene differences in a polygenic system would yield an F$_2$ progeny showing less than one in 10^{19} of the possible number of recombinations if the distribution of the genes were purely at random. This enormous restriction would be imposed by linkage alone, excluding additional possible mechanisms such as pleiotropy, or gametic or zygotic elimination. The data from *Potentilla glandulosa* and from *Mimulus* appear to come closest to providing actual experimental information on the idealized situation postulated by Anderson where there are adequate numbers of morphological markers distinguishing the parents combined with high interfertility. Anderson's own classic studies on linkage between floral characters of the cross *Nicotiana alata* × *N. langsdorfii* were complicated by the existence of quite strong genetic barriers.

Of special interest is the extent of overall correlation between morphological characters of the F_2 progeny and their capacity to survive at the Stanford,

TABLE 19

Frequency Distribution of Correlation Values between Character Combinations in F_2 Progeny of *Mimulus cardinalis* Los Trancos × *M. lewisii* Timberline

Classes of r Values	14 Characters		16 Characters	
	Frequency	Total Combinations, Percent	Frequency	Total Combinations, Percent
0.000–0.113 *	4	5.2	28	23.3
0.114–0.148 †	4	5.2	6	5.0
0.149–0.250	14	18.0	22	18.3
0.251–0.350	**20** ‡	**25.6**	**26**	**21.6**
0.351–0.450	18	23.1	21	17.5
0.451–0.550	9	12.5	8	6.7
0.551–0.650	4	5.2	5	4.2
0.651–0.750	4	5.2	4	3.4
0.751–0.850	0	0.0	0	0.0
0.851–0.999	0	0.0	0	0.0
Totals	77	100.0	120	100.0

* Correlation values not significant, indicating free recombination.
† Values significant between 5% and 1% levels. Higher values are significant above the 1% level.
‡ Values in boldface type are the classes of highest frequency.

Mather, and Timberline transplant stations. This may be evaluated, in terms of r between index values, determined as explained on page 30, and survival ratings of cloned transplants at the altitudinal stations. The r values are as follows:

Index values vs. survival

    at Stanford .... +0.1466 (significant at the 1% level)
    at Mather .... +0.0104 (not significant)
    at Timberline .... −0.1671 (significant above 1% level)

The positive significant correlation at Stanford indicates that for the F_2 population as a whole, the higher the index value, the better the survival record at the lowland station, i.e., plants having characters approaching *M.*

cardinalis are favored. Conversely, at Timberline the negative correlation indicates that plants with low index values approaching *M. lewisii* are the better survivors. The insignificant correlation at Mather can be interpreted to mean that statistically there is no relationship between morphological characters and survival at the mid-altitude station. Alternately, it could mean that plants having index values in the intermediate range of index values are favored. In view of the strong heterosis of F_1-like plants that is expressed at Mather, as explained on pages 70–71, the second interpretation is obviously the correct one.

The fact that the degree of correlation at none of these stations is very high implies that, although the correlations may be significant, a considerable number of recombination types are capable of surviving with reasonable success at at least one of the three contrasting altitudes. This conclusion has been amply substantiated at the three altitudinal stations.

An analysis of the correlation coefficients of F_2 progeny from the reciprocal cross, *M. lewisii* Timberline $\times$ *M. cardinalis* Los Trancos (culture No. 6700) was likewise made on a population of 200 individuals grown only at Stanford. In this population 12 character combinations that were the same as in the reciprocal *M. cardinalis* Los Trancos $\times$ *M. lewisii* Timberline were compared. The computed correlation coefficients between morphological marker characters are in close agreement with those depicted in figure 25 for the same pairs of character combinations.[1] The extent and patterns of segregation in the two reciprocal F_2 progenies as observed at Stanford are so similar that a presentation of detailed data from culture No. 6700 would be redundant.

When partial genetic incompatibility exists between the parental forms, as for example when northern forms of *M. lewisii* are crossed with *M. cardinalis* from the Pacific coast, coherence is expressed even more strongly than that in the F_2 progeny from *M. cardinalis* Los Trancos $\times$ *M. lewisii* Timberline. Figure 26 is a graphic summary of the degrees of correlation between 10 differentiating characters of the cross *M. lewisii* Warner $\times$ *M. cardinalis* Los Trancos which was studied only at Stanford. The male *M. cardinalis* parent was the same individual in both this and the previous crosses. The reduced genetic compatibility is evident through a reduction in percentage of viable pollen, lower seed fertility, and irregularities in meiosis (cf. table 1).

That this reduced fertility is related to a stronger expression of genetic coherence is evident when the F_2 progenies between the fully interfertile combination *M. lewisii* Timberline $\times$ *M. cardinalis* Los Trancos and the partially sterile combination *M. lewisii* Warner $\times$ *M. cardinalis* Los Trancos are compared with respect to the same ten character combinations. As shown in table 20, the correlation coefficients r having the highest frequency for the interfertile combination Timberline $\times$ Los Trancos lie between 0.251 and 0.350 in contrast with 0.651 and 0.750 for the partially intersterile Warner $\times$ Los Trancos

---

[1] These include petal reflexing, star, light areas, yellow upper, yellow lower, aperture, petal width, pistil length, number of dentations in leaves, leaf ratio, rose, and winter activity at Stanford.

F₂ progeny. Evidently in the combination Warner×Los Trancos a significant elimination of zygotes and gametes differing rather widely in genic composition from the original parental combination took place. In the F₂ progeny of *Nicotiana alata*×*N. langsdorfii* studied by Anderson (1939) the sterility barriers were undoubtedly of even greater magnitude than those here described for *M. lewisii* Warner×*M. cardinalis* Los Trancos.

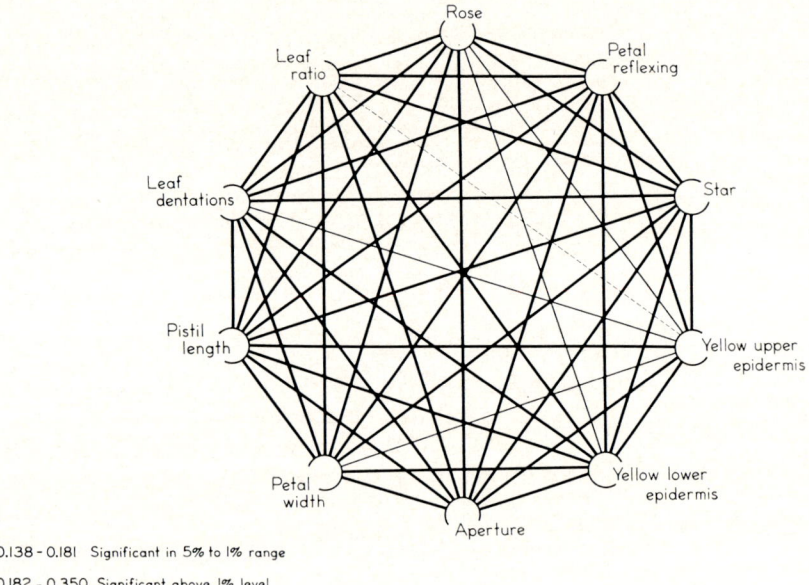

Figure 26. Degrees of correlation in the inheritance of characters distinguishing *Mimulus lewisii* Warner and *M. cardinalis* Los Trancos in F₂ progeny in a combination between which a partial sterility barrier exists. Values of the correlation coefficient *r* are computed as explained in figure 25.

In this combination with impairment in fertility the relative frequency of paired characters inherited purely at random is even less than in the highly interfertile combination shown in figure 25.

COHERENCE AS EXPRESSED IN F₃ PROGENIES. From a population of 310 cloned F₂ plants of the cross *M. cardinalis* Los Trancos×*M. lewisii* Timberline that were tested over a four-year period at Stanford, Mather, and Timberline, 52 individuals were selected for further study. These included plants representing the entire range of both morphological diversity and response patterns at the three altitudinal stations. Eleven of the F₂ plants showing particularly interesting character combinations were, in turn, self-pollinated, and from these, third-generation progenies consisting of 200 to 300 individuals each were obtained. The inheritance of the morphological characters described on pages 32–58 as expressed in these F_3 populations was then studied in considerable detail at Stanford.

Marked differences in the phenotypic composition of the various F_2 progenies were observed. In general, the progenies derived from F_2 plants approaching *M. cardinalis* consisted primarily of plants tending to resemble *M. cardinalis*, and conversely, those from *lewisii*-like F_2 individuals clustered in the direction of *M. lewisii*. Second-generation plants resembling F_1 hybrids always yielded

TABLE 20

Degrees of Correlation * in F_2 Progenies of Interfertile and Partially Intersterile Combinations of *Mimulus lewisii* × *M. cardinalis*

	Frequency of r Values	
Classes of r Values †	Timberline × Los Trancos, Interfertile Combination	Warner Mts. × Los Trancos, Partially Intersterile Combination
0.000–0.137 (insignificant correlation)	9	0
0.138–0.181 (significant in 5%–1% range)	4	1
0.182–0.250 †	9	9
0.251–0.350	**10** ‡	3
0.351–0.450	7	2
0.451–0.550	4	7
0.551–0.650	2	10
0.651–0.750	0	**11**
0.751–0.850	0	9
0.851–0.950	0	1
0.951–0.999	0	0
Number of Combinations	45	45

* Data from combinations of the same ten characters for both F_2 progenies of 200 individuals each. (cf. figures 25, 26)
† Significant above 1% level, unless otherwise noted.
‡ Values in boldface type are the classes of highest frequency.

F_3's having a wide range of segregation that approached that of the original F_2 population.

Examples of segregation among F_3 progenies derived from F_2 plants with divergent recombinations of characters are shown in figure 28 as frequency histograms plotted according to index values, as described on page 30. The most extreme progenies, 7541 and 7565, do not overlap; 7541 segregates plants favoring *M. lewisii*, in contrast with 7565, which segregates combinations favoring *M. cardinalis*. The populations 7566 and 7543, derived from F_2 plants falling within the range of F_1 progeny, segregate over a wide range. Plate II shows typical arrays of flowers that include the extreme and intermediate segregants within the populations 7541, 7565, and 7566.

Responses of cloned F_3 progenies at Stanford, Mather, and Timberline. The responses of the three F_3 progenies Nos. 7541, 7565, and 7566 were followed at the Stanford, Mather, and Timberline stations over a period of four years from 1964 to 1968. In this study 200 individuals of each of the F_3 populations were propagated as clones and transplanted at the altitudinal stations. Detailed notes were taken over a three-year period and the dry weights of harvested tops determined at the end of each year. Propagules that failed at a given station were replaced whenever possible, sometimes as many as four or five times during the experimental period.

The three F_3 progenies differed markedly from one another in their relative performance at Stanford, Mather, and Timberline. The *lewisii*-like population 7541 was conspicuously more successful at the Timberline station than the *cardinalis*-like population 7565 which, for the most part, failed to survive at this high altitude (figure 22). At Stanford, on the other hand, the F_3 population 7565 was conspicuously vigorous whereas 7541 showed weakness and rapid decline. At both Stanford and Mather, however, the plants of 7541 performed better than any of the original races of *M. lewisii* at these same stations. This *lewisii*-like F_3 progeny apparently inherited genetic factors from the *M. cardinalis* grandparent that extended its tolerance for growth at lower altitudes. The intermediate highly segregating F_3 population 7566 showed much higher variability among its members at all three stations than either of the other two F_3 progenies. At Stanford the more *cardinalis*-like individuals of the 7566 population displayed good vigor and high survival capacity but at Mather most of the plants were weak and unsuccessful. They had a considerably lower percentage of surviving individuals than the original F_2 population in which the F_1-like plants were conspicuously more vigorous than the recombinations resembling the *M. cardinalis* or *M. lewisii* parents. At Timberline, likewise, the 7566 F_3 progeny displayed greater variability in vigor and survival capacity than either *lewisii*-like 7541 or *cardinalis*-like 7565. The relative differences in growth between the three F_3 populations at the transplant stations are reflected in the mean dry weights of the tops, as shown in bar graphs in figure 27.

The coherence between morphological characters and physiological responses at the transplant stations as expressed by the F_2 cloned populations at Stanford, Mather, and Timberline thus also is clearly expressed in third-generation progenies. The correlation values of r between combinations of characters similar to those presented in figure 25 were also computed for each of the F_3 progenies grown as cloned transplants at the three altitudinal stations. The network of partial linkages for each of the three F_3 populations strongly resembles those depicted in figure 25 for the original F_2 populations.

Genetic composition of transplant garden "weedlings." In the cultivated transplant gardens at Stanford, Mather, and Timberline where the widely segregating cloned F_2 individuals of *M. cardinalis* Los Trancos × *M. lewisii*

Timberline were being grown between the years 1960 to 1965, large numbers of seedling progeny germinated and had to be continually weeded to avoid contamination of the cloned garden transplants. In 1966 samples of such volunteer "weedings" were transplanted from gardens at each station to flats and grown to maturity in the nursery at Stanford. The morphological characters of the seedlings that were able to germinate and establish spontaneously at each

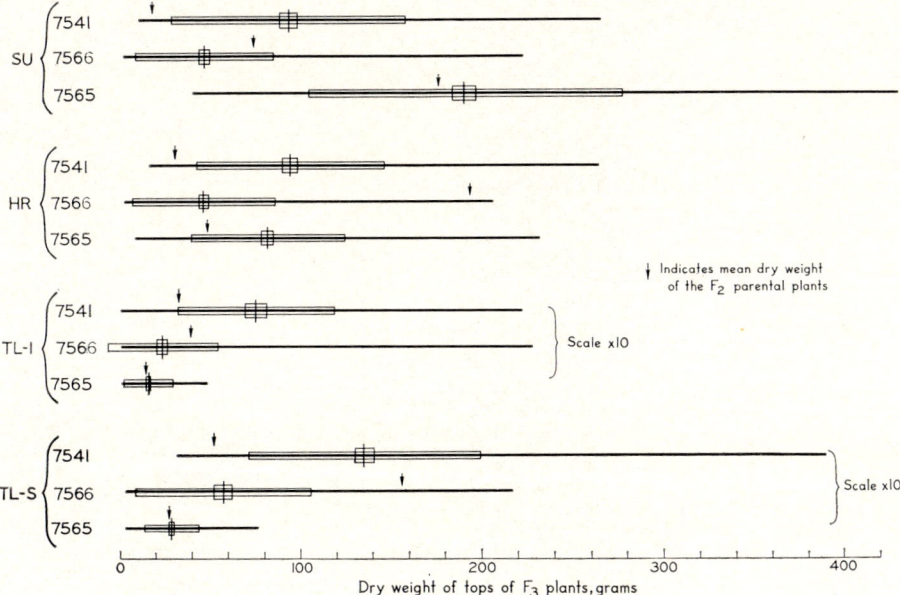

Figure 27. Dry weight yields of cloned F_3 progenies from the cross *Mimulus lewisii* Timberline × *M. cardinalis* Los Trancos grown at the altitudinal transplant stations— SU, grown at Stanford (30 m); HR, grown at Mather (1400 m); TL-I, grown at the Timberline main interstation garden (3050 m), scale × 10; TL-S, grown in the Timberline slope garden (3100 m), scale × 10.

Culture 7541, F_3 progeny of the *M. lewisii*-like F_2 plant 7111-16; culture 7565, F_3 progeny of the *M. cardinalis*-like F_2 plant 7135-35; culture 7566, F_3 progeny of the F_1-like F_2 plant 7111-17. Values are means over a 3-year period. Note the reversal in yield patterns between the Stanford and Timberline gardens.

of the altitudinal stations were tabulated to determine which classes of phenotypes are in highest frequency among the seedlings. The distributional spread of the sampled "weedling" populations is shown in terms of index values at the bottom of figure 28.

The striking contrasts in composition of the "weedling" populations at the Stanford, Mather, and Timberline stations lend support to the conclusion that the morphological markers used in determining the index values are highly correlated with the capacity for self-perpetuation in these environments. The

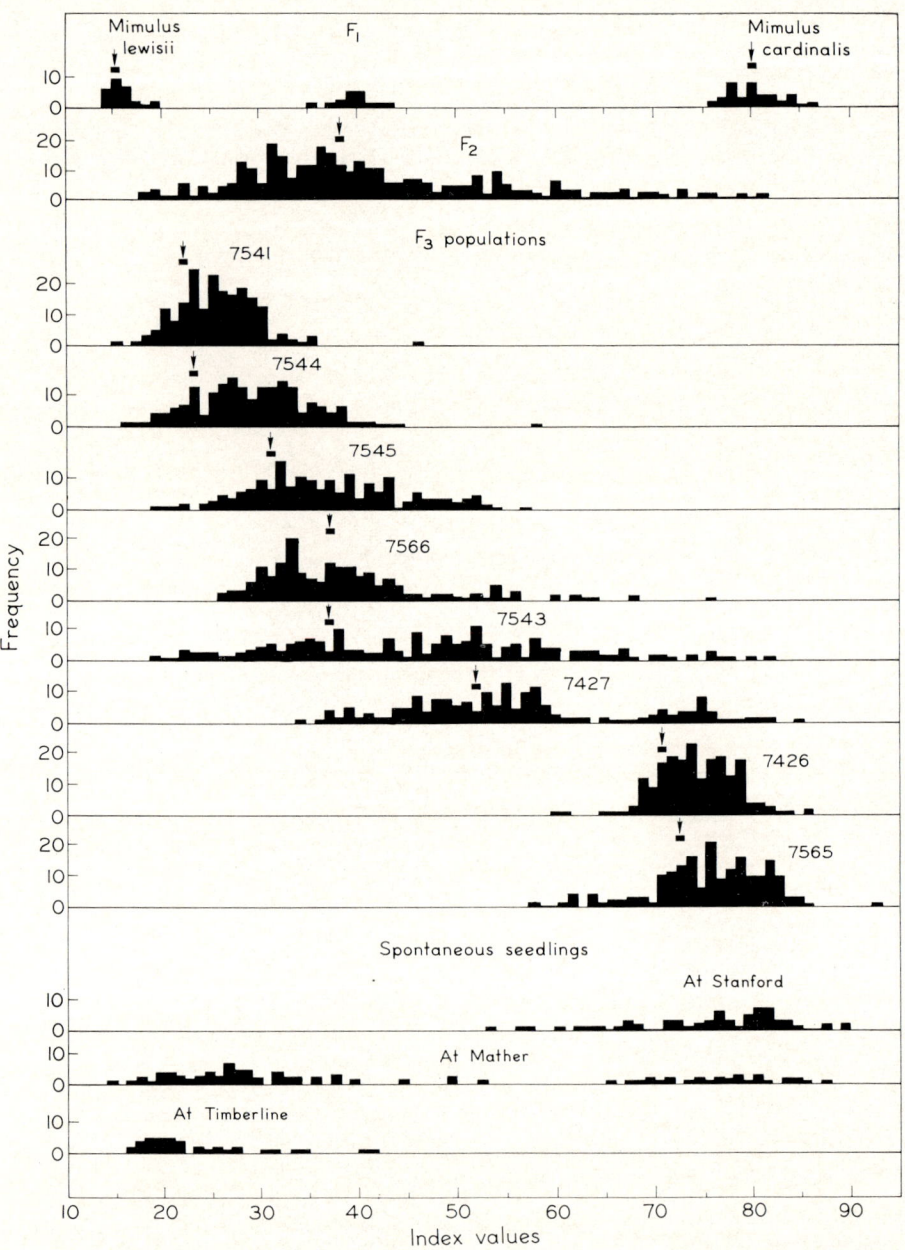

Figure 28. Histograms indicating frequencies of individuals in progenies of self-pollinated parental, F_1, and F_2 plants of the cross *Mimulus lewisii* Timberline × *M. cardinalis* Los Trancos, showing morphological classes of characters in which they fall in terms of the characters distinguishing the parents. Low index value (11 to 20) include characters falling within the range of *M. lewisii*; values between 75 and 90, those of *M. cardinalis*. For method of scoring individuals to obtain their index values, see page 30.

The three graphs at the bottom indicate the distribution of characters among spontaneous seedlings originating from open pollination between highly segregating F_2 transplants at the Stanford, Mather, and Timberline transplant stations.

clustering of *lewisii*-like types of seedlings from Timberline in the low range of index values, and of *cardinalis*-like types from Stanford in the high index range, is highly significant.

At Mather there is a suggestion of bimodal segregation favoring parental types in both directions rather than a normal frequency distribution having F_1-like types in highest number. Since F_1 hybrid transplants of this combination show extreme heterosis at Mather (see pp. 70–71), the bimodal distribution of the "weedling" plants appears to support the hypothesis advanced by Kenneth Mather (1943) that heterosis represents an unstable genetic balance that through selection in subsequent generations is replaced by more stable genic recombinations.

SUMMARY OF THE GENETIC STRUCTURE OF THE ERYTHRANTHE SECTION

It seems appropriate to summarize some of the major features pertaining to the genetic structure of the *Erythranthe*, as follows:

1. All members of the *Erythranthe* section of the five species studied (*Mimulus cardinalis, M. lewisii, M. verbenaceus, M. eastwoodiae,* and *M. nelsonii*) are diploid with 8 pairs of chromosomes. It has been possible to obtain vigorous F_1 hybrids in all possible combinations, but fertility tests on these F_1 hybrids indicate that the section has become differentiated into two major divisions. The first includes *M. lewisii* and *M. cardinalis,* and the second the remaining species, including, perhaps, *M. rupestris,* which has not been included in these studies. Strong sterility barriers are present between these two major cyto-taxonomic groups. A vigorous, fertile amphiploid was, however, obtained from one of the most sterile combinations, demonstrating that the section as a whole is composed of taxa of common genetic ancestry.

2. In interfertile combinations the inheritance of nearly all of the morphological markers that distinguish species and races is governed by multiple series of genes rather than by a single gene. The resultant segregations with respect to any one character in F_2 and F_3 progenies are, accordingly, complex and of a quantitative type. An exception is a single character (yellow upper epidermis) whose presence or absence appears to be determined by a single recessive gene that yields 3:1 Mendelian ratios in F_2 and F_3 progenies.

3. Heterosis, or hybrid vigor, is evident when races of species are crossed. The degree of heterosis expressed in relation to the parents is highly dependent both upon the genetic composition of the parent individuals and upon the environment in which the parents and F_1 progeny are compared. Parental forms that are incapable of surviving at a given altitude may give rise to hybrids that display a high degree of vigor and survival capacity in that same environment. The degree of heterosis displayed by F_1's from interspecific crosses between *M. cardinalis* × *M. lewisii* is, in general, much greater than that displayed by interracial crosses within either *M. cardinalis* or *M. lewisii.*

4. Transgressive segregation is observed in some characters governed by polygenic systems in both the second and third generations. Other characters segregate within a narrower range. On the whole, F_2 progenies resulting from interspecific combinations fall within the ranges of the parents, with most peak frequencies in the intermediate ranges.

5. Between characters differentiating species and races of the *Erythranthe* section there is a strong genetic coherence that is expressed in both the F_2 and F_3 generations. The network of partial genetic linkages includes both morphological marker characters and such physiological attributes as capacity to survive in contrasting environments. The correlations between morphological characters and physiological traits are strong enough to make possible reasonably accurate predictions of the performance of a given individual when transplanted to the Stanford, Mather, and Timberline altitudinal stations.

III

COMPARATIVE PHYSIOLOGICAL STUDIES ON ECOLOGICAL RACES AND SPECIES

The striking differences in inherited capacity for growth and survival in contrasting natural environments by ecologically diverse but closely related species or races of the same species lead logically to inquiries regarding the nature of their underlying physiological characteristics. Analysis of functional variation among such races or species is probably the chief means by which a substantially increased understanding of natural selection and speciation can be achieved. This area of investigation, nevertheless, has remained largely unexplored.

Undoubtedly an important obstacle has been the lack of adequate techniques for comparative studies of physiological functions and of facilities for growing experimental plant materials under controlled, reproducible environments. The marked progress made within recent years in the development of new instruments and methods, and in the extensive use of controlled growth facilities, has greatly diminished this problem. Another difficulty, still unresolved, is that of linking a particular physiological response to a given environmental factor, or combination of factors, when it is realized that the observed response is actually the resultant of the interaction between the genotype as a whole and an entire complex of environmental variables.

The present chapter will be devoted both to a discussion of working principles and to a presentation of experimental results with *Mimulus* and other plant groups. It should be emphasized that this is only a beginning in an extensive field of inquiry of basic theoretical and of much potential practical significance.

UNSCRAMBLING THE VARIABLES. The complexity of the interacting variables that must necessarily be resolved in studies on the comparative physiology and biochemistry of ecologic races and species make essential the adoption of clear working principles for guiding experiments. Three major sets of factors need to be taken into account: (1) the genetic, (2) the ecologic, and (3) the physiologic. The genetic includes the entire biosystematic structure of the species and races under investigation; the ecologic, the innumerable external environmental influences that interreact throughout the range of distribution of the species and races; and physiologic, the intricate functioning of the internal physiological and biochemical processes that take place in every living individual in its habitat. Since each of these three major sets of variables is a universe of complexity within itself, the experimentalist, of necessity, must exercise extreme care in (1) the choice of his experimental material, (2) in the selection of external environmental factors to be controlled, and (3) the selection of physiological processes to be studied.

The selection of experimental material becomes easier when based on background information obtained from biosystematic, genetic, and transplant investigations. Among the many plants that might be chosen for study, one can select clones of genotypes known to differ significantly in their capacity to survive in extreme environments. Since a great deal of time, effort, and expense is involved in controlled laboratory investigations, such studies must, of necessity, be limited to a few individual clones. Among the many divergent forms of *Mimulus* of the *Erythranthe* section described in the preceding chapters it has been possible to include only a very few of the most contrasting members of this group for physiological investigation.

The problem of dealing with external environmental factors is admittedly a difficult one for which no ideal solution seems to be in sight. It is common knowledge that the influence of such external variables as light, temperature, mineral nutrition, and composition of the atmosphere on physiological functions of plants is of great importance, but to study the interaction between any one of these variables and any specific physiological function on a particular individual in a specified environment is a complex problem requiring a high degree of sophistication in experimental design and technique.

That natural diurnal or seasonal fluctuations of external environmental factors in contrasting climates are of great importance in differentiating ecological races and species has been amply demonstrated by investigators who have studied this problem experimentally. In the present stage of our studies, however, meaningful additional physiological information can be gained only by utilizing much simpler and readily reproducible environments having but a single controlled component varied in any given experiment. The selection of the variable to be controlled in any experiment necessarily depends to a large degree on the physiological process being studied. Essentially, it is the interaction between a given variable on the functioning of a specific measured physiological process that is useful in comparing the performance of one genotype with another. Such information provides the basic bits of data on which interpretative conclusions must rely. Eventually, when more information has been collected, it may become possible to conduct experiments to investigate the simultaneous effect of two or more interacting variables on one or more processes. Measurements under field conditions, currently only exploratory and qualitative, may become to a greater extent quantifiable.

The choice of physiologic function to be investigated is a matter of prime importance and determines the techniques that need to be developed for its effective study. By "physiologic function" we include not only the study of the function itself but also biochemical processes directly related to it, such as the capacity of specific enzyme steps known to be of key importance in a particular physiological process. We are not concerned, however, with differences in molecular composition per se. As pointed out by Prosser (1967), analyses of proteins and nucleic acids may be valuable for establishing relationships, but they tell us little about the mechanism of natural selection and speciation unless it is clear how the micromolecular differences influence the adaptedness of the organism.

For reasons explained more fully below, we have chosen to focus our studies on the comparative photosynthetic performance of contrasting ecological races and species. Comparative studies on such other physiological functions as respiration, translocation, and ion absorption might have resulted in additional informative data, but the necessity for concentrating our efforts on the study of one function will be evident to the reader.

From the above discussion it follows that the investigator must be content at first with small bits of information which accumulate from experiment to experiment. The results of a number of experiments may be needed before a satisfactory answer may be realized on what might seem to be a relatively simple problem. To compare, for example, the physiological capacity of two genotypes over a range of environments, their performance over a wide range of controlled conditions must be known. Fortunately, as basic information accumulates, progress accelerates exponentially when based on reproducible, cross-referable experimental results. Evidence for the beginning of such an accelerating growth period in the area of physiological ecology is already at hand.

MEASUREMENTS OF PHYSICAL PARAMETERS IN NATURAL ENVIRONMENTS. In comparative physiological studies of species and races from diverse natural habitats it is essential that basic information is available on the physical environments themselves. A meaningful description of a habitat requires an evaluation of energy load—sunlight and thermal radiation—imposed on the organisms by the environment. Unfortunately, it is only very rarely that adequate information on these parameters is available, and lack of confirmation of anticipated correlations in plant growth or in the response of physiological processes may, in many instances, be the result of incomplete knowledge regarding these factors.

In our current work it has not been possible to include adequate studies of the diverse natural environments in which members of the *Erythranthe* section of *Mimulus* grow. Fortunately, however, with the kind help of Dr. David Gates (Gates *et al.*, 1964) a beginning has been made centering along the transect of the Stanford, Mather, and Timberline transplant stations.

During the summer of 1963 Dr. David M. Gates worked with our group for approximately one month during which a number of critical measurements on temperature and light intensity were made. One of the primary objectives was to evaluate the energy exchange between the plants and their environments, especially on leaves of *Mimulus*.

Figure 29 shows temperature measurements on leaves of *Mimulus cardinalis, M. lewisii,* and other species made directly at several natural habitats and in the experimental gardens at the Mather and Timberline transplant stations. Leaf temperatures were measured with a Stoll-Hardy infrared radiometer, and ambient air temperatures with a mercury thermometer. The measurements were made from August 12 through August 15, 1963, during mostly clear weather between 10:00 A.M. and 3:00 P.M., PST.

Several points of interest are revealed by the data presented in figure 29. Of special significance is the departure of leaf temperatures of different species (indicated by various symbols) from the ambient air temperatures (indicated by the horizontal lines) at the different sites along the transect. At the Sierran foothill site at Priests Grade at 300 meters elevation, where ambient air temperatures exceeded 35° C, measured leaf temperatures of *Mimulus cardinalis* (the

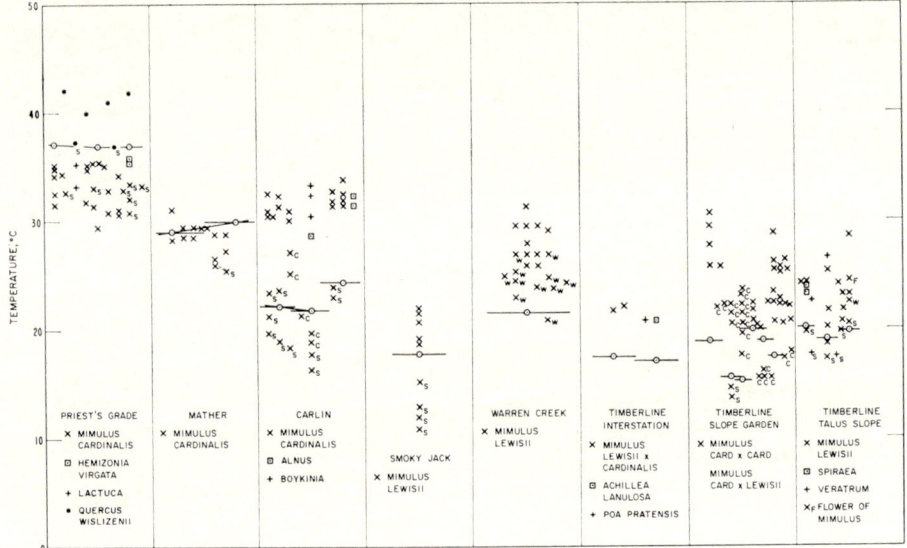

Figure 29. Leaf temperatures of various species at sites along the Sierran transect on clear days, August 12–15, 1963.

Altitudes of sites as follows: Priests Grade, 400 m; Mather, 1400 m; Carlin, 1400 m; Smoky Jack, 2300 m; Warren Creek, 2800 m; Timberline interstation, 3050 m; Timberline slope garden, 3100 m; Timberline talus slope, 3200 m.

Horizontal lines indicate ambient air temperatures; points indicate observations on fully sunlit leaves except where noted: C, cloudy; S, shade. W indicates wind.

original collection site of culture No. 7210, table 2) may be up to 10° C cooler than the ambient air temperatures. In contrast, at the Timberline talus slope site at 3500 m elevation mature leaves of *M. lewisii* (the original collection site of culture No. 7405, table 2) may be up to 10° warmer than the ambient air temperature. At both sites leaf temperatures vary over a considerable range depending on whether the leaves are in full sun or in shade, and upon wind movements. An overall interpretation of these data leads to the unexpected conclusion that although the ambient midday air temperatures at these contrasting sites differ by approximately 20° C, the actual leaf temperatures of the two *Mimulus* species differ considerably less, and, in fact, may overlap.

Another point of interest shown in figure 29 is that at Priests Grade leaves of *Quercus wislizenii A.* DC, a tree with typically sclerophyllous leaves, growing on an arid slope, and confined in distribution to warm foothill regions in California, have temperatures several degrees above that of the ambient air at around 40° C. These are in contrast with leaves of closely adjacent *M. cardinalis*, which are 5° to 7° cooler than the ambient. The highly mesophytic leaves of *M. cardinalis* undoubtedly are cooled by transpiration. At the Priests Grade

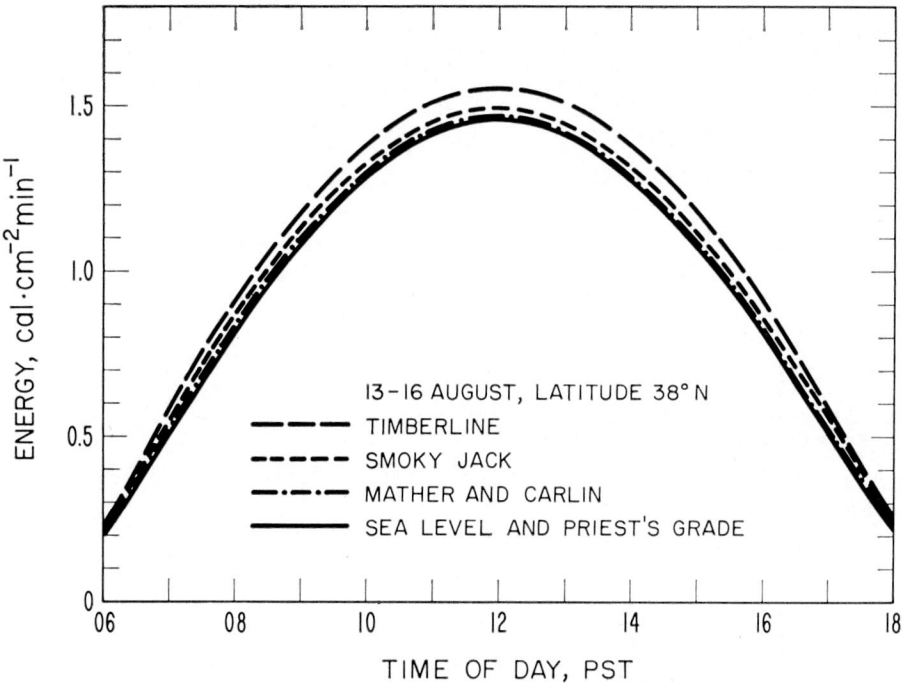

Figure 30. Estimated incident solar radiation of a horizontal surface as a function of time of day for sites in the Sierra Nevada of California. Elevation of sites as in figure 29.

site *Mimulus cardinalis* is confined to a wet area near a spring where many of the plants grow in standing water. The leaf structure of the Priests Grade race of *M. cardinalis* is essentially the same as that for the nearby Jacksonville race, illustrated by leaf cross sections in figure 42. The contrast in temperature of leaves of *Quercus* and *Mimulus* exemplifies differences between divergent species in their energy balance with their surroundings in a natural environment that is the same except with respect to water supply. A final point of interest is that among the other herbaceous species associated with *Mimulus* in its moist habitat, all have leaf temperatures within the range of those measured on *Mimulus*.

The total diurnal radiant energy impinging on a horizontal surface at different altitudes along the Sierran transect at 38° N. latitude is very much the same at all altitudes, as determined by measurements made by Dr. Gates. These are graphed in figure 30. The radiant solar energy received at Timberline is slightly higher than at sea level because the thinner atmosphere contains fewer obscuring suspended particles.

A plant exchanges energy with its environment by radiation from the sun and from surrounding surfaces, including the ground and other objects, from the atmosphere by convection to and from the air, and by moisture exchange, mostly through transpiration. The lower part of figure 31 shows the ambient air temperatures and measured leaf temperatures of *Mimulus cardinalis* and *M. lewisii* at sites along the altitudinal transect. The upper half of the same figure shows measured or computed values made by Dr. Gates [1] of the overall energy balance between *Mimulus* leaves and their surrounding natural environments at the sites indicated at the bottom of the figure. More than half of absorbed energy is re-radiated to the surroundings, but a very significant fraction is used in evaporating water through transpiration. A very small fraction is absorbed or lost to convection air currents. Of special interest in this connection is that the total radiant energy absorbed by the leaf for phyotosynthesis is too small a fraction of the total (about 2%) to be of importance when considering the overall parameters determining energy exchange equilibria that we are considering in the present discussion.

TRANSPIRATION MEASUREMENTS IN CONTROLLED CABINETS. The importance of transpiration in affecting temperatures of *Mimulus* leaves suggested by the field measurements were confirmed by experiments in controlled cabinets. The rates of transpiration were determined by sealing leafy shoots of *Mimulus* and of other species into potometers and placing them in controlled cabinets under a constant light intensity. Controlled temperatures were varied over the range between 9° to 60° C. Leaf temperatures were measured by a thermocouple

---

[1] Dr. Gates' computations are based on the equation:
$$a\frac{(1+r)(S+s)}{2} + e\frac{(R_a + R_g)}{2} + e\sigma T_1^4 + C + P + E = 0$$
where

$a =$ absorptivity of the leaf to sunlight (0.50)
$r =$ reflectivity of the ground to sunlight (varies between 0.10 and 0.20 for different sites)
$S =$ direct solar radiation (measured)
$s =$ scattered sunlight (derived from physical equations)
$e =$ the long-wave emissivity and absorptivity of the leaf (0.96)
R_a and $R_g =$ thermal radiation downward from the air and upward from the ground (measured data)
$\sigma =$ Stefan-Boltzman constant
$T_1 =$ leaf temperature in degrees Kelvin (measured)
$C =$ energy exchanged by convection (determined from the leaf-air temperature differential and the leaf dimensions)
$E =$ energy exchanged by transpiration (determined by computation)
$P =$ energy consumed in photosynthesis (in terms of the parameters here discussed, the value of P is negligible).

(Cf. Gates, 1965.)

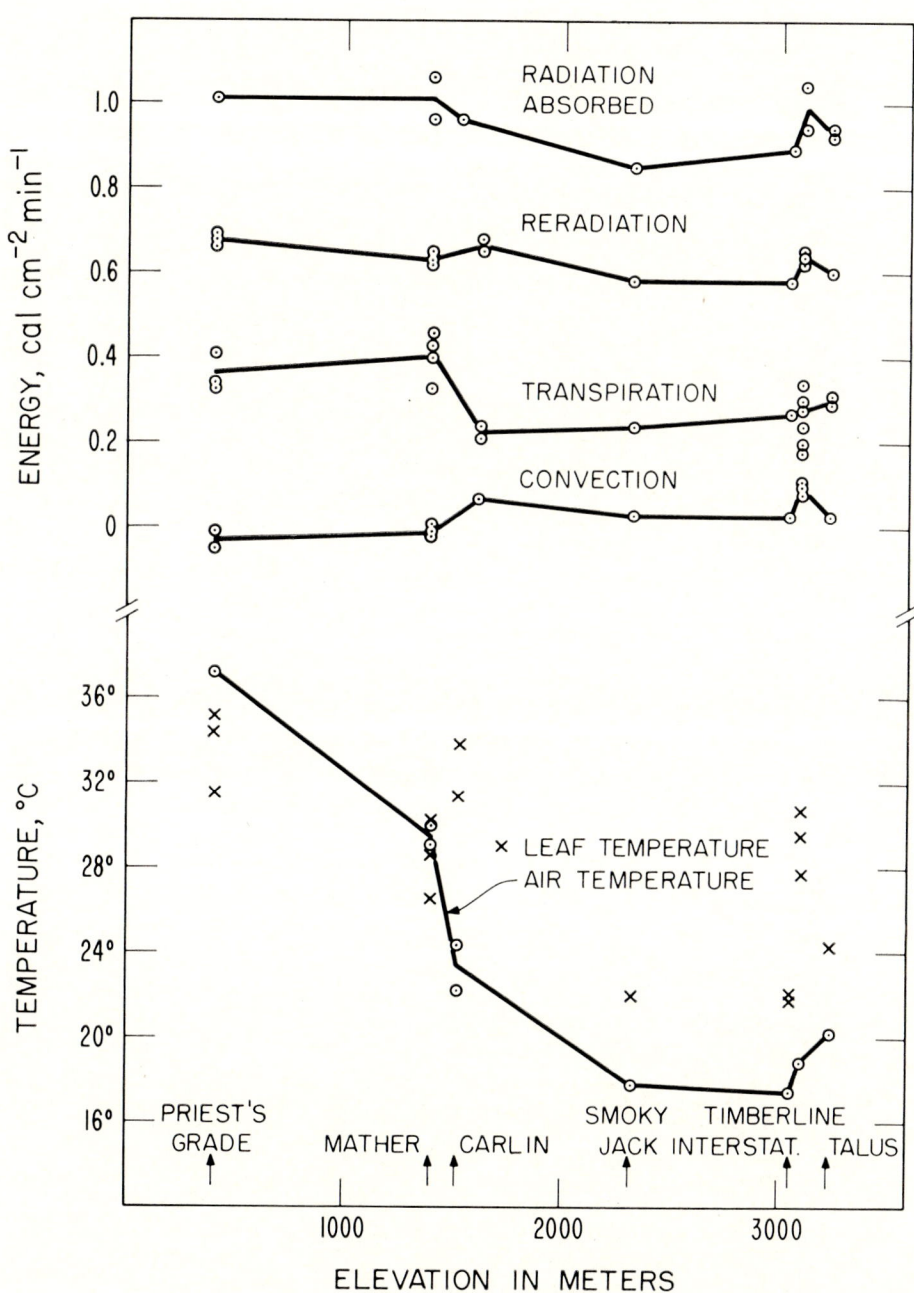

Figure 31. Total radiation absorbed by a horizontal leaf during clear days, August 12–15, 1963, in the Sierra Nevada of California. The energy lost by reradiation (measured), transpiration (calculated), and convection (calculated) is shown. Measured leaf and air temperatures are also indicated.

junction threaded into the leaf, the other junction being in ice water outside the chamber. Experiments were run at three different light intensities.

Figure 32 shows the observed rates of transpiration of two clones of *Mimulus cardinalis* and one of *M. lewisii* as a function of temperature under different constant light intensities. Between 10° and 30° C there is a nearly linear in-

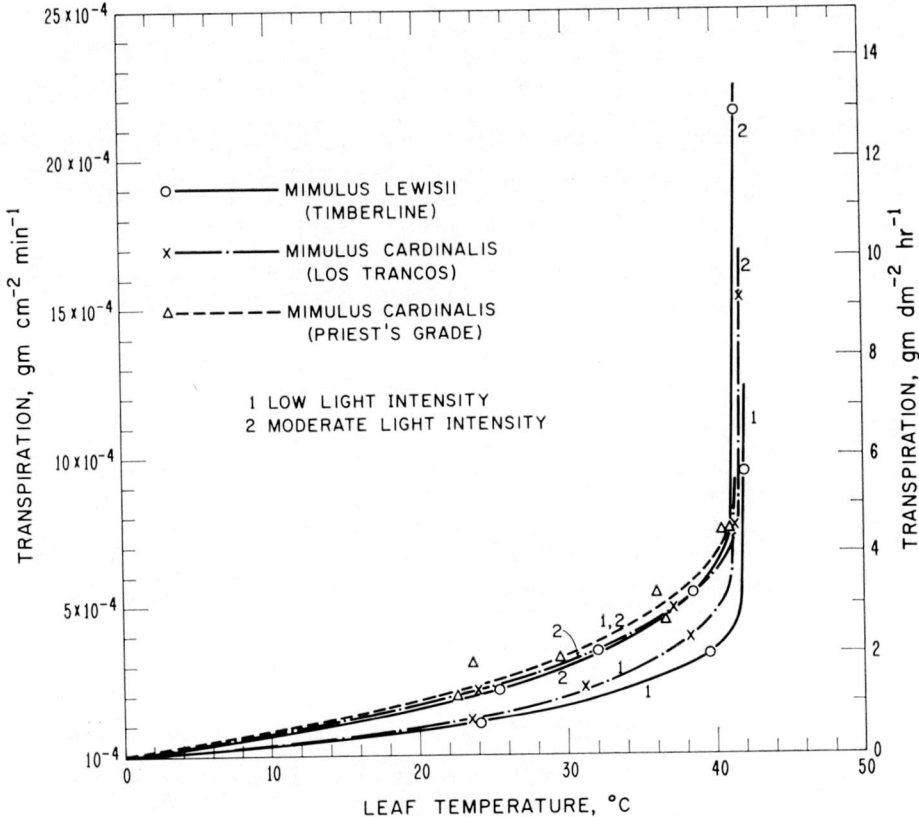

Figure 32. Transpiration rate of *Mimulus* as a function of leaf temperature for low (50,000 erg cm^{-2} sec^{-1}) moderate (68,000 erg cm^{-2} sec^{-1}) illumination.

crease in transpiration rate as the temperature rises (Gates, 1968). At 40° C there is a sudden breakdown of the leaf tissues in both *Mimulus* species that results in essentially free evaporation of water from these tissues. There are no significant differences between *M. cardinalis* and *M. lewisii* in these respects.

The departure of the leaf temperatures of *Mimulus* from ambient air temperatures is shown in figure 33. Below 20° C the leaves in all instances are warmer than in the ambient air, whereas above 30° C they are cooler except under conditions of very high illumination, where the crossover point is at approximately 40° C. Similar differences between leaf and air temperature were observed with other species of higher plants, as, for example, in such divergent species as *Nerium oleander* L., *Raphiolepis ovata* Briot. and a horticultural hybrid of *Rhododendron indicum* L. Obviously these effects of transpiration on leaf temperature are not peculiar to *Mimulus*.

From these field and laboratory data it is clear that in leaves of *Mimulus cardinalis* and *M. lewisii* the cooling effect of transpiration at warm temperatures and low altitudes and the warming effect of absorbed incident radiation at high altitudes and cool temperatures tend to offset each other, so that the physiologi-

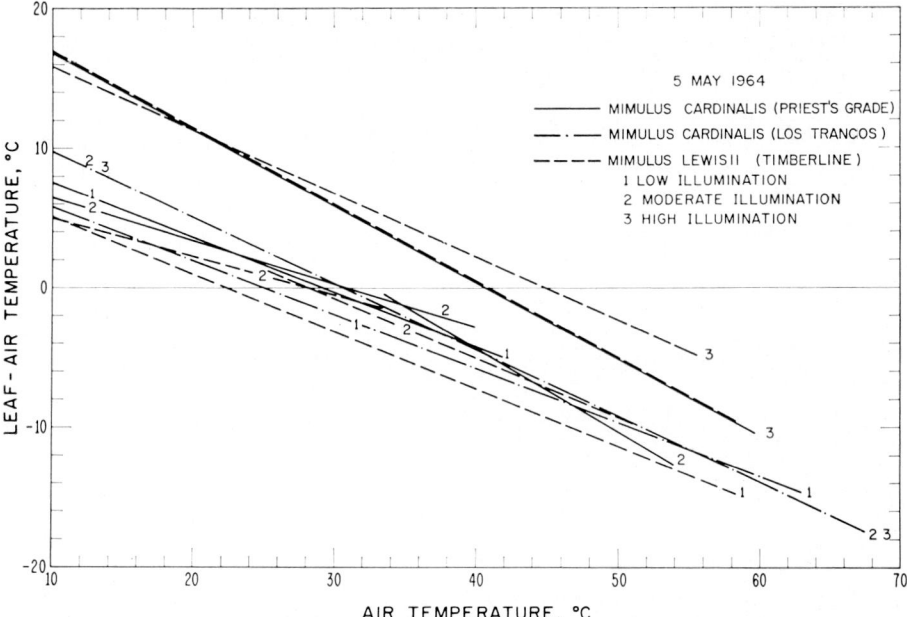

Figure 33. Departure of leaf temperature from air temperature for three clones of *Mimulus* at low (50,000 erg cm^{-2} sec^{-1}), moderate (68,000 erg cm^{-2} sec^{-1}), and high (85,000 erg cm^{-2} sec^{-1}) illumination.

cal effects of the wide differences between ambient air temperatures at such contrasting altitudinal sites as Priests Grade and the Timberline talus slope are minimized.

It should be remembered, however, that over the entire active seasonal growing period at such diverse sites there are nevertheless wide contrasts between the extremes in temperature with which the plants must cope if they are to survive. From the standpoint of comparative physiological studies it is therefore essential to explore the entire ranges of tolerance of such contrasting ecologic races.

There are three equally important experimental approaches to comparative physiological studies of ecological species and races. The first is the comparison of growth responses under controlled conditions using a single external variable. The second is the quantitative measurement of the physiological processes selected for study. The third is the biochemical study of compounds known or thought to be closely linked with these physiological processes.

Technically, each approach presents different sets of problems, requiring different skills for their solution. In the present work each of the three approaches was developed singly over a 10-year period. The experience gained through trial and error and the continuous inflow of new technical improvements in measurement and assay techniques during this period have made it possible to relate experimental results from the three approaches.

In the presentation that follows we will attempt to present as fully integrated an account as the available incomplete data allow. We will not attempt to describe details of technique because these can for the most part be found in other publications and, moreover, such details often become rapidly outmoded by continuing improvements.

Use of controlled growth facilities. Comparisons of growth between contrasting ecological races and species by using a single controlled variable can reveal much about their physiological capabilities that cannot be found in the cruder but more encompassing transplant experiments at the altitudinal transplant stations described in Chapter II. Such studies in controlled environments are invaluable in planning experiments involving quantitative measurements of physiological functions and, as will become evident in later pages, are a necessity for obtaining valid comparative information. Moreover, controlled growth facilities are indispensable for maintaining stock clones of races and species from extreme environments that are only able to survive for a short period of time under uncontrolled conditions in a climate unfavorable to them. None of the forms of *Mimulus lewisii,* for example, can be maintained successfully for more than one season at Stanford, whether in the field, the nursery, or the greenhouse. We have had to depend on plants propagated and maintained in growth cabinets for all our comparative physiological work.

A pair of cabinets used in the present investigations is illustrated in figure 34. The units illustrated were designed for the control of temperature and light intensity, as well as of CO_2 and O_2 concentration in the air surrounding the experimental plants. Relative humidity is not precisely controlled, but is held constant within known limits, depending upon the adjustment of the temperature controlling device. Details of construction of the cabinets have previously been described[1] and the system used for the regulation of the gaseous composition of the atmosphere is described on pages 131–132. A simplified block diagram of the gas control system is shown in figure 35.

[1] See Hiesey and Milner (1962) for details of frame construction and assembly, and Björkman, Hiesey, Nobs, Nicholson, and Hart (1967) for a description of controls for CO_2 and O_2 concentration.

Each cabinet unit is independent and can be used either singly or in combination with other units. The two cabinets illustrated in figure 34, for example, were often used as a working pair. The six units employed in the present investigations have proven to be reasonably adequate. Modifications in design dictated by particular experimental requirements are possible and are an important feature in the operation and use of such growth cabinets.

During the years 1962 through 1969 comparative growth experiments on various races of *Mimulus cardinalis* and *M. lewisii* have been made in growth cabinets, with temperature, light intensity, day length, and CO_2 and O_2 con-

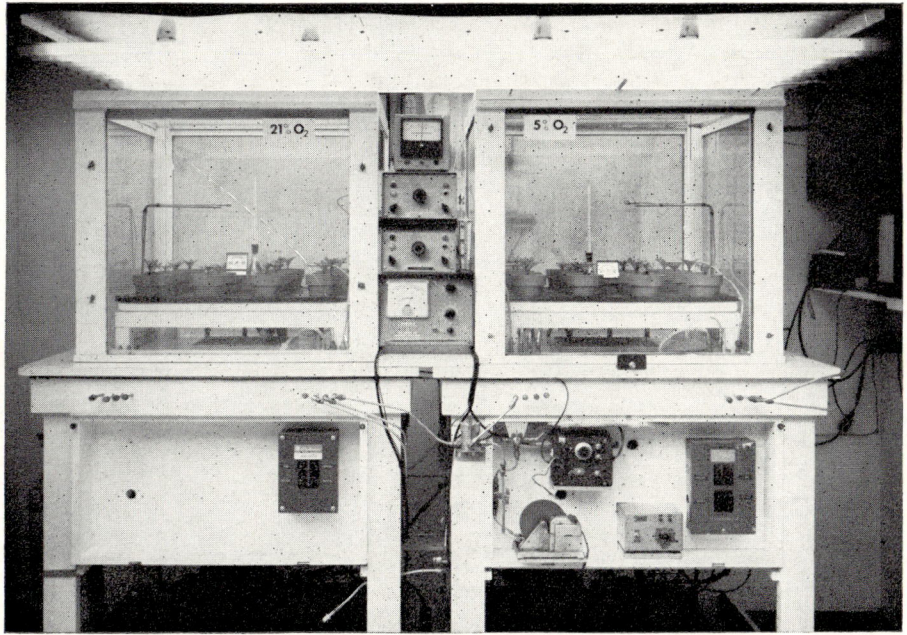

Figure 34. A pair of controlled growth cabinets used in various experiments. See text.

centration as variables. From these experiments considerable information about the growth characteristics of *Mimulus* under known conditions has been obtained. The data, however, are by no means exhaustive, and many questions remain unanswered.

The original problem was to find controlled conditions under which both races of *M. cardinalis* and *M. lewisii* can be grown successfully (in equally healthy condition) in order that subsequent laboratory measurements could be made on plants previously subjected to identical treatment. Success in this effort was realized only after several years of trial-and-error experimentation.

Comparative growth responses under controlled conditions can at best only provide clues regarding underlying functional differences between given clones. Studies of specific physiological processes are needed to analyze mechanisms that may or may not prove to be of importance in natural selection.

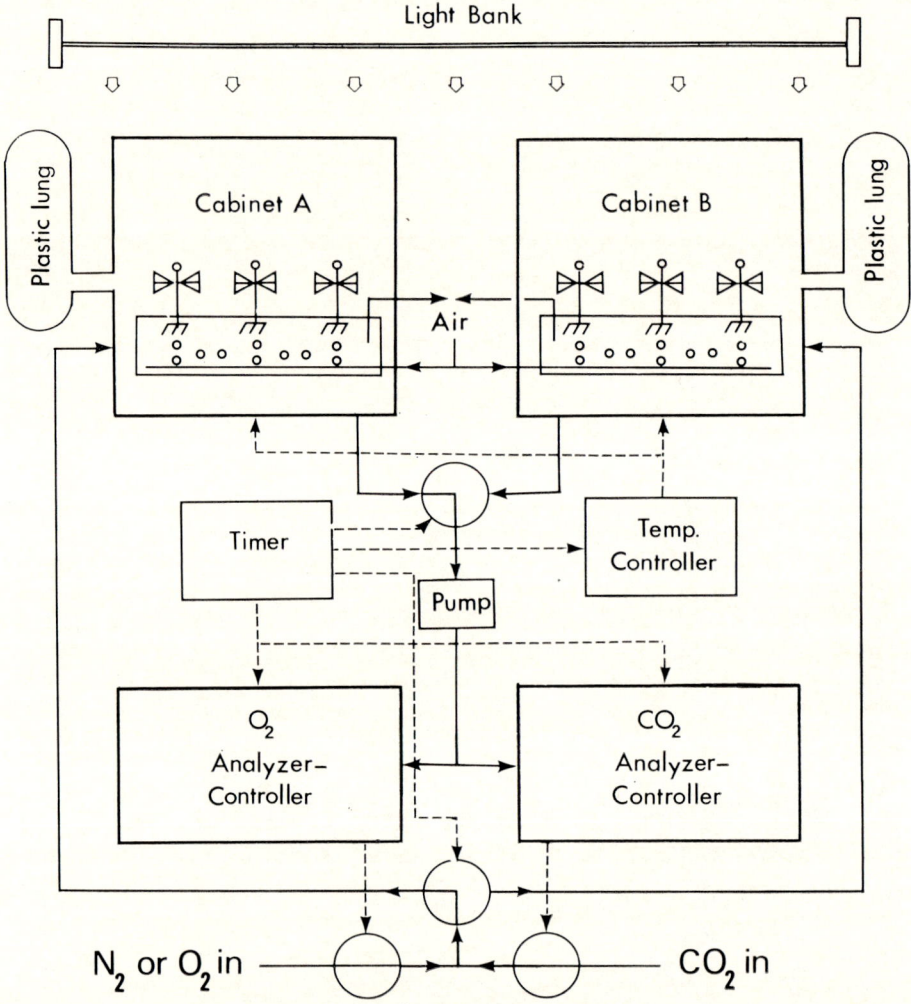

Figure 35. Block diagram of gas control system.

PHOTOSYNTHETIC PERFORMANCE AS A MEANS OF COMPARING ECOLOGIC RACES AND SPECIES. In all green plants photosynthesis provides the sources of chemical energy and the primary substrates to drive all other biosyntheses, and one can assume that adequate functioning of photosynthesis in natural habitats is basic for the survival and success of any species or race. Consequently, only after investigating the photosynthetic performance of contrasting climatic races over known ranges of external variables can one logically embark on comparative studies of other physiological processes. Because of the complexity of the photosynthetic process, a review of the major elements involved in its study will help in interpreting the significance of experimental results.

The photosynthetic response of a leaf to controlled variation under any one of the major external variables, such as the intensity and quality of light, temperature, and gaseous composition of the atmosphere, will depend on the genetic constitution of the plant and the environment to which it has been exposed. The limits within which the individual is capable of adjusting phenotypically are set by the genotype.

The photosynthetic rate that a leaf can sustain under a given set of external factors is dependent on a number of properties of the leaf at different levels of organizational complexity. We must first take into account a number of physical characteristics. They include (1) the orientation of the leaf, which influences light interception; (2) leaf size and shape, which influence the movement of air at the leaf surface, thus affecting the boundary-layer resistance to the diffusion of CO_2 into the leaf, and of O_2 and water vapor from it; (3) the size and frequency of the stomata, which strongly affect the resistance to gas exchange between the interior of the leaf and its immediate surroundings; and (4) the thickness and other physical properties of the mesophyll, which influence the transport both of gas and of dissolved compounds inside the leaf.

Besides these physical factors important internal factors that must be taken into account include: (1) quality and quantity of photosynthetic pigments, which determine the efficiency with which light quanta of different wavelengths are trapped, and also the efficiency with which absorbed light is converted into early photoproducts in the primary steps of photosynthesis; (2) the conversion of these early photoproducts to stable compounds; and (3) the reduction of carbon dioxide to the level of carbohydrates. The processes involved in (2) and (3) are governed by many temperature dependent enzymatically controlled steps whose capacity may be expected to influence both the total photosynthetic rate of the leaf, and the relative amounts of the various products of photosynthesis. A very simplified outline of how green plant photosynthesis is currently believed to operate is depicted in figure 36.

The photosynthetic capacities of leaves may differ greatly under different constellations of external variables even if it is assumed that the photosynthetic pathways are identical. For example, at low light intensities, such as those prevailing on shaded forest floors, the overall rate of photosynthesis is limited mainly by the capacity of the light-harvesting network of chlorophyll molecules, or by the capacity of steps concerned with the primary conversion of light quanta into early photoproducts. These early steps are thought to be effected through the complementary action of photosystem I and photosystem II (cf. figure 36). Under high light intensities, on the other hand, enzymatic steps, both those preceding and those following the fixation of CO_2 (as well as the carboxylation step itself) would be expected to be limiting, particularly

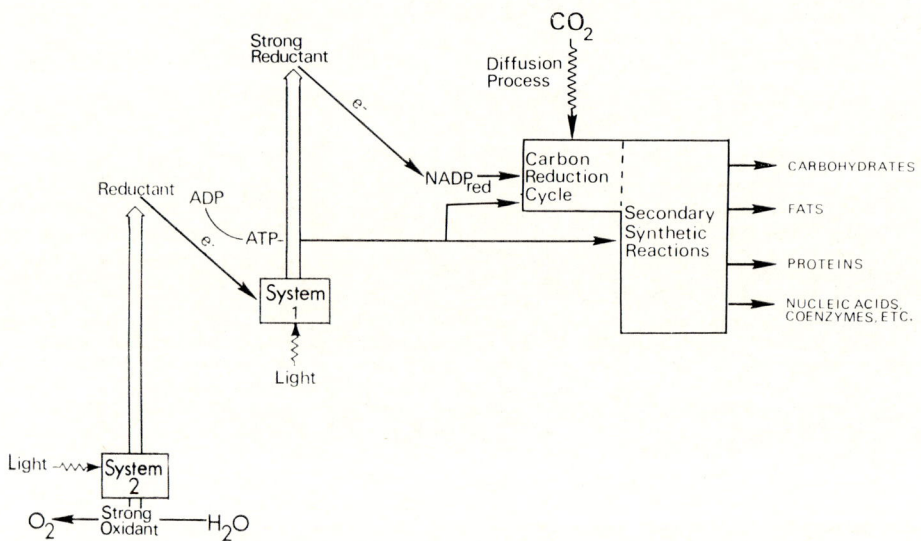

Figure 36. Photosynthesis takes place in two stages: a light-dependent stage, the "light" reactions, and a light-independent stage, the "dark" reactions.

During the first step in photosynthesis, light is absorbed by a chlorophyll molecule producing an excited state. This excited molecule then transfers its absorbed energy into chemical energy.

Two separate light reactions, called I and II, each one with its own pigment system, operate in photosynthesis. These two light reactions cooperate to produce an oxidant strong enough to oxidize water to oxygen gas, and a reductant capable of reducing carbon dioxide to the level of carbohydrates. In addition, ATP is formed from ADP and inorganic phosphate in a process known as photosynthetic phosphorylation.

Several steps of photosynthesis, the "dark" reactions, can take place in the absence of light, provided that compounds normally produced in the previous light reactions are supplied. One such dark reaction is the link between the two light reactions; others operate in the oxygen evolution step itself and in the electron transport from the primary reductant, formed in the light reactions, to $NADP_{ox}$ and other electron acceptors. A very important series of "dark" reactions is the Calvin cycle in which atmospheric carbon dioxide is reduced to carbohydrates, proteins, lipids, etc. This reduction uses $NADP_{red}$ and ATP, both of which are formed in previous steps of photosynthesis.

In most higher plants, including *Mimulus,* carbon dioxide diffusing from the ambient air through the stomata and the mesophyll to the reaction sites in the chloroplasts reacts with ribulose-1,5-diphosphate (RuDP) to form two molecules of phosphoglyceric acid. This reaction is catalyzed by the enzyme RuDP carboxylase (carboxydismutase). In some other species, notably grasses of tropical origin but also in some dicotyledonous species, CO_2 reacts with phospho-enol-pyruvate (PEP) to form oxalacetic acid. This reaction is catalyzed by the enzyme PEP carboxylase.

at low temperatures. With air of low CO_2 content, such as normally occurs, the capacity of the carboxylation step in addition to the physical barriers to CO_2 diffusion may limit the overall rate of CO_2 uptake. One can infer on this basis that the relative capacities of the different component processes of photosynthesis may differ among plants from ecologically diverse habitats in such a manner as to enable each race to perform efficiently under the conditions prevailing in its particular environment.

Methods for measuring photosynthetic properties of leaves. Much information on photosynthetic characteristics of different races and species can be obtained from measurements of responses in gas exchange by single attached leaves to controlled variation in light quality and intensity, temperature, and to CO_2 and O_2 concentration. By appropriate experimental design, the effect of leaf shape and size on the rate of gas exchange can be diminished. Until very recently measurements of photosynthetic gas exchange by leaves had been limited almost exclusively to CO_2. Such measurements are readily made with infrared gas analyzers or techniques based upon the incorporation of $^{14}CO_2$. The very recent development of sufficiently sensitive O_2 analyzers appears to have great promise for photosynthesis measurements in leaves. One of these is a paramagnetic analyzer with greatly improved sensitivity (Schaub et al., 1969). Another is based on the electromotive force created when oxygen diffuses through a zirconium oxide cell at high temperatures (Björkman and Gauhl, 1969). Most of the results on photosynthetic gas exchange reported here have been obtained with infrared CO_2 analyzers modified for differential measurements, but in some experiments the zirconium cell O_2 analyzer was used as well.

Simultaneous measurements of the exchange of CO_2 (or O_2) and of water vapor on attached leaves make it possible to estimate the effects of stomatal resistance to gas diffusion on the rate of photosynthesis. In our measurements we have employed the microwave hygrometer described by Falk (1966).

Other methods for determining the capacity of different component processes of photosynthesis include measurement of the light-harvesting capacity of intact leaves at different wavelengths, by devices employing integrating spheres, and of the amount of photosynthetic pigments and enzymes in leaf extracts. Of particular significance in this connection have been studies of the activities of the enzyme RuDP carboxylase (carboxydismutase) in leaves of clones of different races subjected to different growing conditions in connection with the study of light-saturated photosynthetic rates. This enzyme is responsible for the fixation of CO_2 in *Mimulus* and there is evidence that its activity is of great importance in determining the rate of photosynthesis under conditions of strong irradiance in many higher plants (Björkman 1968a, b).

EFFECTS OF LIGHT INTENSITY

Since light is the driving force in the photosynthetic process, the relationship between its intensity and the rate of photosynthesis is of great importance in evaluations of photosynthetic capacity. This relationship is depicted in figure 37. At low light intensities the rate of photosynthesis is a linear function of

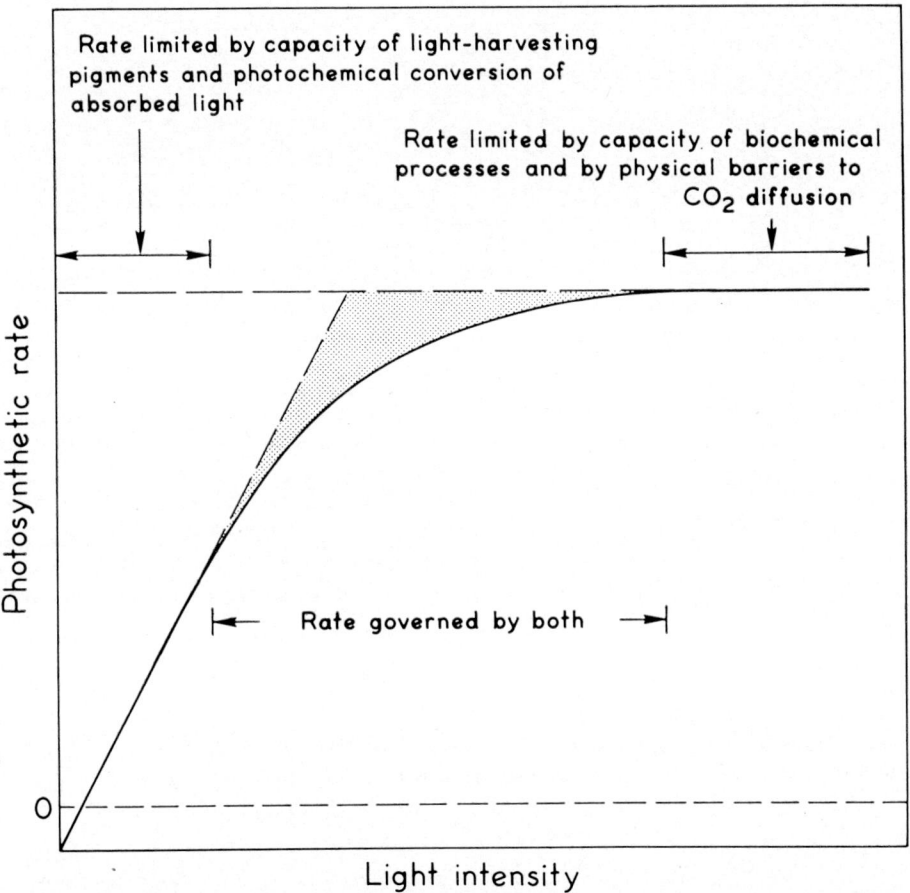

Figure 37. Diagram showing general relationship between light intensity and photosynthetic rate. See text.

intensity, and the efficiency of light conversion is constant and maximal. Internal leaf factors that limit photosynthesis under these conditions are the efficiency with which light quanta are trapped by the light-harvesting system of chlorophyll molecules, and the efficiency with which the absorbed light quanta are converted to early photoproducts.

As light intensity is further increased photosynthesis becomes progressively less dependent on it, and at sufficiently high intensities the curve reaches a plateau, i.e., photosynthesis is light saturated. In its light-saturated state photosynthesis no longer is limited by the capacity of the light-harvesting pigment system, or by primary photoacts, but by the capacity of enzyme-controlled steps. At the low carbon dioxide concentrations of normal air it is also limited by physical barriers to gas diffusion.

It is well established (see Björkman and Holmgren, 1963, 1966) that light intensity during leaf development may strongly influence the light-saturated rate of which a leaf is capable. In plants occupying sunny habitats in nature, high light intensity for growth generally results in a higher light-saturated rate of photosynthesis. This ability of phenotypic adjustment of the photosynthetic apparatus to high light intensity is often lacking in plants that are native to shaded natural habitats. Such plants often fail to yield higher light-saturated rates when they are grown in strong light than in weak light, and in many cases exposure to high light intensities is detrimental and results in damage to the photosynthetic apparatus (see Björkman, 1968).

Light intensity during leaf development also affects the anatomical characteristics of leaves. Strong light during growth generally results in thicker leaves and increased number of cell layers in the palisade parenchyma. This situation is found both in "shade" and "sun" plants.

In the following paragraphs we will report on the response of photosynthesis to light intensity, and on the extent of modification of photosynthetic properties caused by variation of the intensity of the light under which the different *Mimulus* clones were grown. We will also report on the relationship between light intensity and the rate of dry matter production during growth.

It should be pointed out that there are no great differences in light intensity in the habitats in which most races and species of the *Erythranthe* section of *Mimulus* grow. From this consideration one may not anticipate photosynthetic differentiation to be a result of genetic selection to different light intensities in this group of plants. Nevertheless, responses of photosynthesis to light intensity, and the extent of phenotypic plasticity of the photosynthetic apparatus with respect to this factor, are of basic interest and essential for evaluating their photosynthetic responses to other major parameters such as temperature. Moreover, it is of importance to determine whether or not different races and species of *Mimulus* to differ genetically with respect to their capacity to respond to differences in light intensity.

EFFECT OF LIGHT INTENSITY DURING GROWTH ON SUBSEQUENT PHOTOSYNTHETIC EFFICIENCY AS MEASURED UNDER LOW LIGHT INTENSITIES. The rate of CO_2 uptake (i.e., apparent rate of photosynthesis) can be measured as a function of wavelength, thus providing action spectra in which the number of moles of CO_2 per absorbed mole quantum of light can be plotted as a function of wavelength. In these measurements monochromatic light was used. The intensity of the light was so adjusted that at each wavelength 2×10^{15} quanta cm^{-2} sec^{-1} were incident upon the leaf. At this intensity the steady state of CO_2 uptake is a linear function of light intensity at all wavelengths. The rate of CO_2 uptake

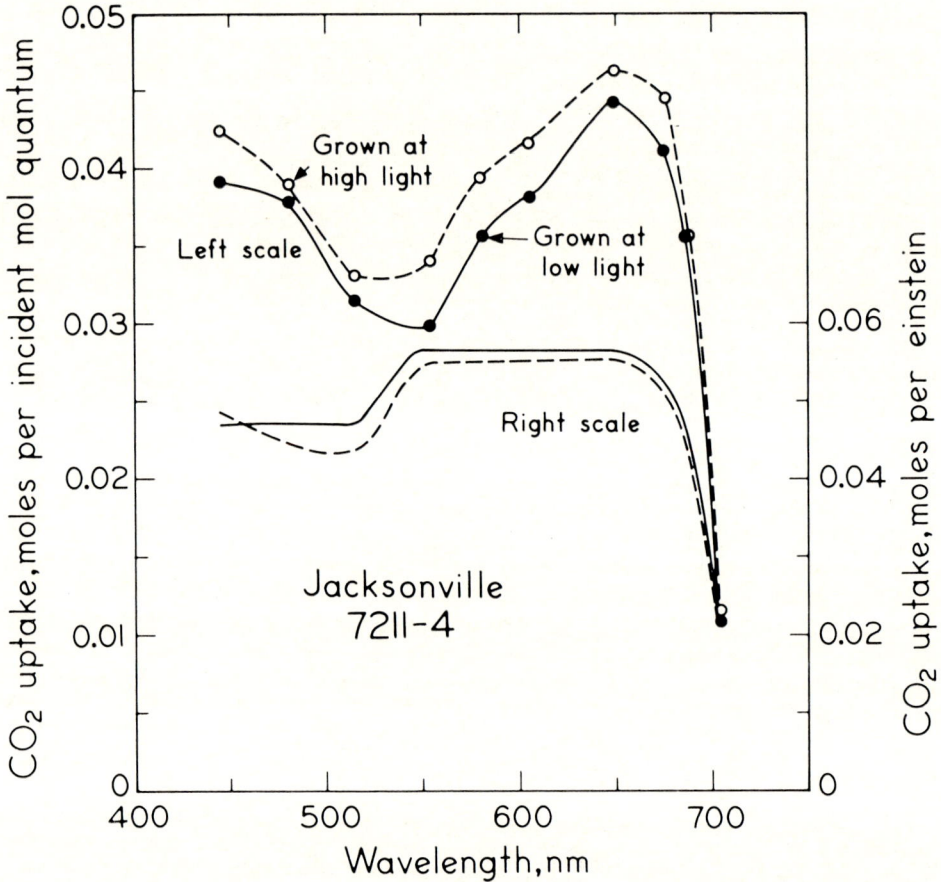

Figure 38. *Upper curves:* Action spectra of CO_2 uptake of leaves of a clone of *Mimulus cardinalis* from Jacksonville as a function of wavelength under a constant incident light energy input of 2×10^{15} quanta cm^{-2} sec^{-1}. The solid line with dark circles shows values for a leaf previously grown under light of low intensity (3×10^4 erg cm^{-2} sec^{-1}); the dotted line with open circles, values for a leaf previously grown under a high light intensity (1.5×10^5 erg cm^{-2} sec^{-1}). Use scale at the left.
Lower curves: Quantum yields of the same leaves as a function of wavelength. Use scale at the right.

at all wavelengths was measured to obtain action spectra. These values were checked by adjusting the number of incident quanta so that the same CO_2 uptake was obtained at all wavelengths.

Action spectra made with this technique on leaves of clones of the Jacksonville and San Antonio Peak clones of *M. cardinalis* grown at low and at high light intensity are shown in figures 38 and 39, respectively. The measurements were made at 22° C at a CO_2 concentration range between 280 and 330 ppm. All the curves have a maximum close to 650 nm, and a minimum range

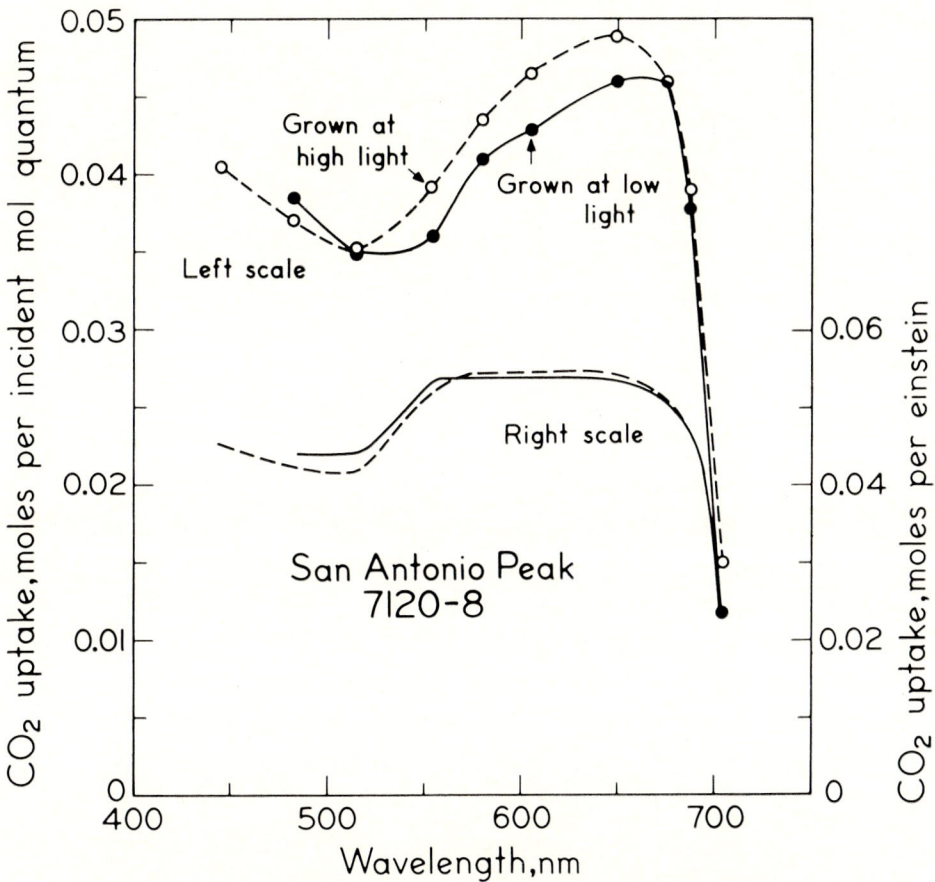

Figure 39. Action spectra of CO_2 uptake and quantum yields of leaves of a clone of *Mimulus cardinalis* from San Antonio Peak. See figure 38 for explanation of curves.

between 520 and 550 nm. Within each clone the efficiency in utilizing incident light energy is higher in the leaves developed under the high light intensity.

Such differences in the efficiency of utilization of weak light for photosynthesis could be caused either by differences in the absorption of incident light, or in the conversion of the absorbed light. To distinguish between these alternatives, the light-absorbing capacities of the leaves used for photosynthesis measurements were measured in an Ulbricht integrating sphere over the spectral range from

450 to 790 nm. The absorptance A_λ at each wavelength was obtained from the expression

$$A_\lambda = 1 - (T_\lambda - R_\lambda)$$

where λ is the wavelength, T_λ is the spectral transmittance and R_λ is the spectral reflectance of the leaf. The leaf absorptance is influenced primarily by its pigment content (chlorophylls and carotenoids) on the basis of leaf area as well as the thickness and other anatomical characteristics. The relation between absorptance and pigment content can be roughly expressed as

$$A_\lambda = 1 - e^{K_\lambda c}$$

where e is the base of the natural system of logarithms, K_λ is a constant at wavelength λ, and c is the amount of pigment per leaf area. An increase either in the concentration of pigments per leaf volume or in the thickness of the leaf will thus increase the absorptance.

The absorption characteristics of the two *Mimulus cardinalis* clones grown under high and low light intensities are shown in figures 40 and 41, while cross sections of the leaves are shown in figure 42.

The two clones differ considerably in leaf thickness. The thinner-leaved clone, 7211-4 from Jacksonville, shown at the bottom of figure 42, becomes thicker when grown under a higher light intensity, but so also do the leaves of clone 7120-8 from San Antonio Peak when grown under the same light, as shown in the upper part of the same figure. The thicker-leaved San Antonio Peak clone has a higher efficiency of incident light utilization than the Jacksonville clone. Also, in both clones the modified thicker leaves developed under high light intensity (1.5×10^5 ergs cm^{-2} sec^{-1} or about 5000 foot-candles) absorb somewhat more light than those developed under low intensity (3×10^4 ergs cm^{-2} sec^{-1}, or about 1000 foot-candles).

The differences in the percentage of the incident light absorbed by the genetically distinct Jacksonville and San Antonio clones, while measurable, are not as large as one might anticipate in view of the considerable differences in the thickness of their leaves as shown in figure 42. The principal difference between the two clones lies in the greater percentage of absorption of green light by the San Antonio Peak clone in the 500–600-nm wavelength region. Likewise, the modification in leaf thickness within both clones when grown under low and high light intensities amounts to only about 5 percent of the total light absorbed over the visible spectral range.

When the curves for the efficiency of CO_2 uptake per absorbed light quantum (quantum yield) are plotted for the two clones grown under low and high light intensities, as shown in figures 38 and 39, it is seen that they are all identical within the limits of experimental error.

It is evident that the difference in efficiency between these two clones, and between propagules of the same clone grown at low and high light intensities in utilizing incident light, can be attributed entirely to differences in absorptance of the leaves. Both the wavelength dependence and the absolute values of the quantum yields in both races are essentially the same, and are not significantly influenced by the light intensity under which the leaves are grown.

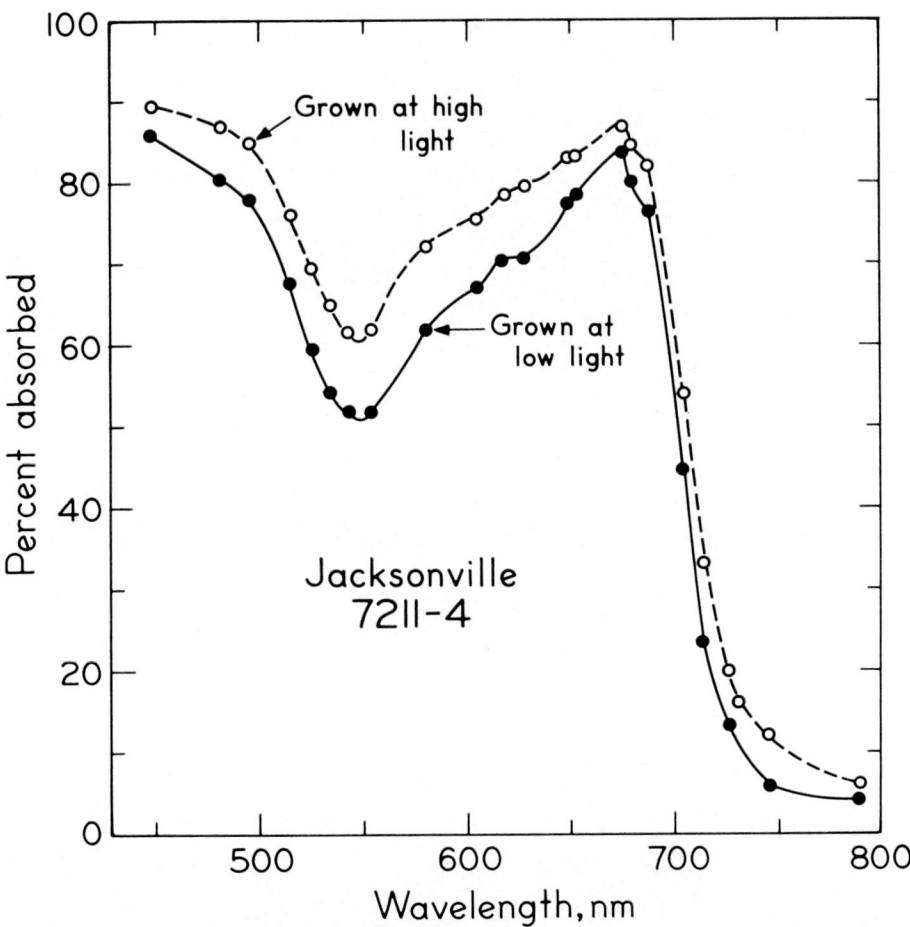

Figure 40. Percentage absorption of incident light by leaves of a clone of *Mimulus cardinalis* from Jacksonville as a function of wavelength when previously grown under a low light intensity (3×10^4 erg cm^{-2} sec^{-1}, solid line) and under a high intensity (1.5×10^5 erg cm^{-2} sec^{-1}, broken line), as measured with an Ulbricht integrating sphere.

From these data it is clear that, under conditions of low *incident* light intensities, differences in efficiency in utilizing the available light among the different *Mimulus* leaves depends on the light-intercepting capacity, or absorptance, of the leaves. The relatively thick-leaved San Antonio clone fixes a greater number of molecules of CO_2 per incident quantum of light than does the

Jacksonville clone. In both clones the propagules grown at high light intensity are likewise more efficient than the thinner-leaved modifications grown under low light intensity. The quantum yield, or efficiency of CO_2 uptake per *absorbed* light quantum is, within the limits of experimental error, the same in both clones whether grown at low or high light intensity.

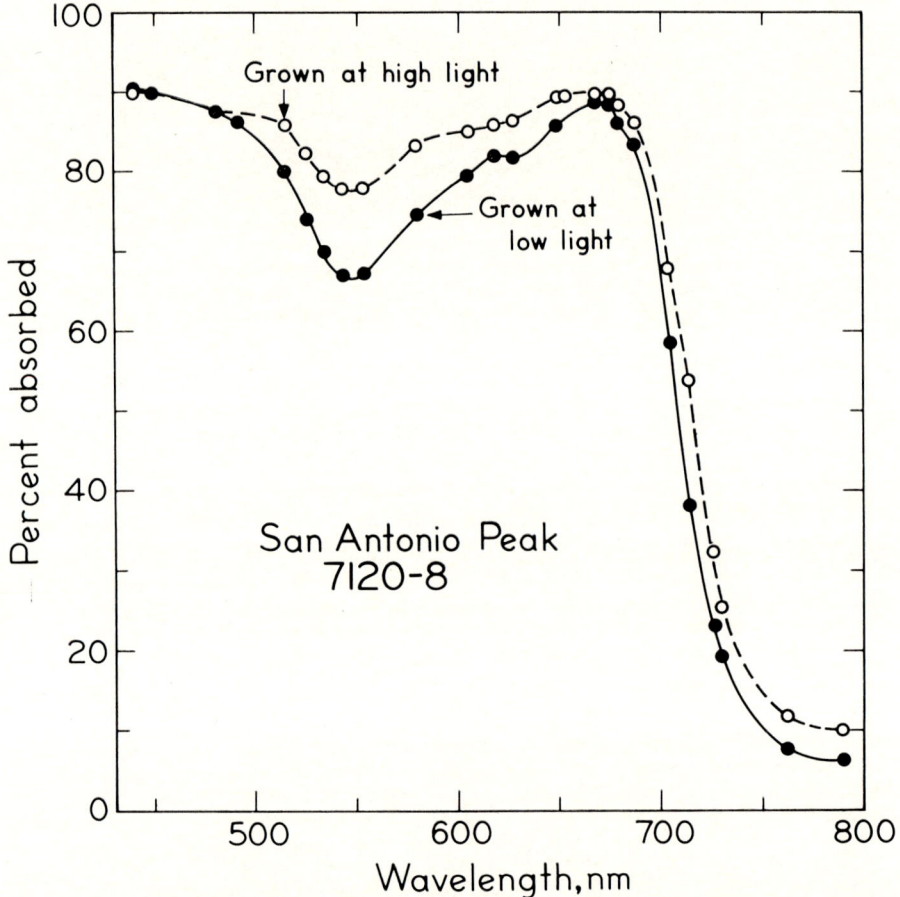

Figure 41. Percentage absorption of incident light by leaves of a clone of *Mimulus cardinalis* from San Antonio Peak as a function of wavelength when previously grown under a low, and under a high, light intensity. See figure 40 for explanation.

EFFECT OF LIGHT INTENSITY DURING GROWTH ON SUBSEQUENT PHOTOSYNTHETIC CAPACITY AS MEASURED UNDER HIGH LIGHT INTENSITIES. Under conditions of high light intensity, i.e., intensities above which the rate of CO_2 uptake is no longer linearly proportional to increases in light intensity, a very different set of factors comes into play in influencing photosynthetic performance. When temperature is kept constant and light intensity is varied from darkness to light saturation, the leaves of both the Jacksonville and San Antonio Peak clones grown under the high light intensity have a much higher light-saturated photosynthetic rate than leaves of the same clones grown under low

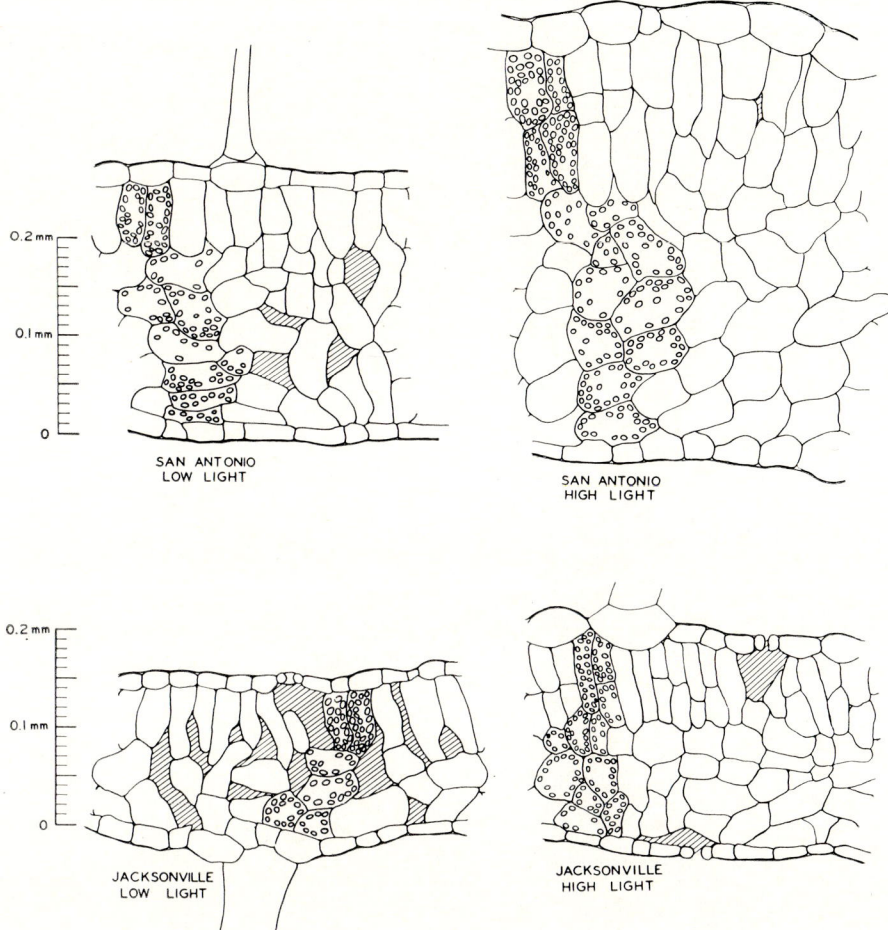

Figure 42. Sections of fully expanded leaves of Jacksonville and San Antonio Peak clones of *Mimulus cardinalis* grown under low and under high light intensities. Cross-hatched areas indicate intercellular spaces. Cf. figures 40, 41.

light intensity. Curves showing photosynthetic rates of the two clones grown under the two intensities are shown in figure 43.

Such reductions in light-saturated photosynthetic rate of clones grown under low light intensity as compared with high light occur in all races and species of *Mimulus* that we have studied, as well as in hybrid derivatives. This is shown in table 21, which lists ratios between photosynthetic rates of diverse

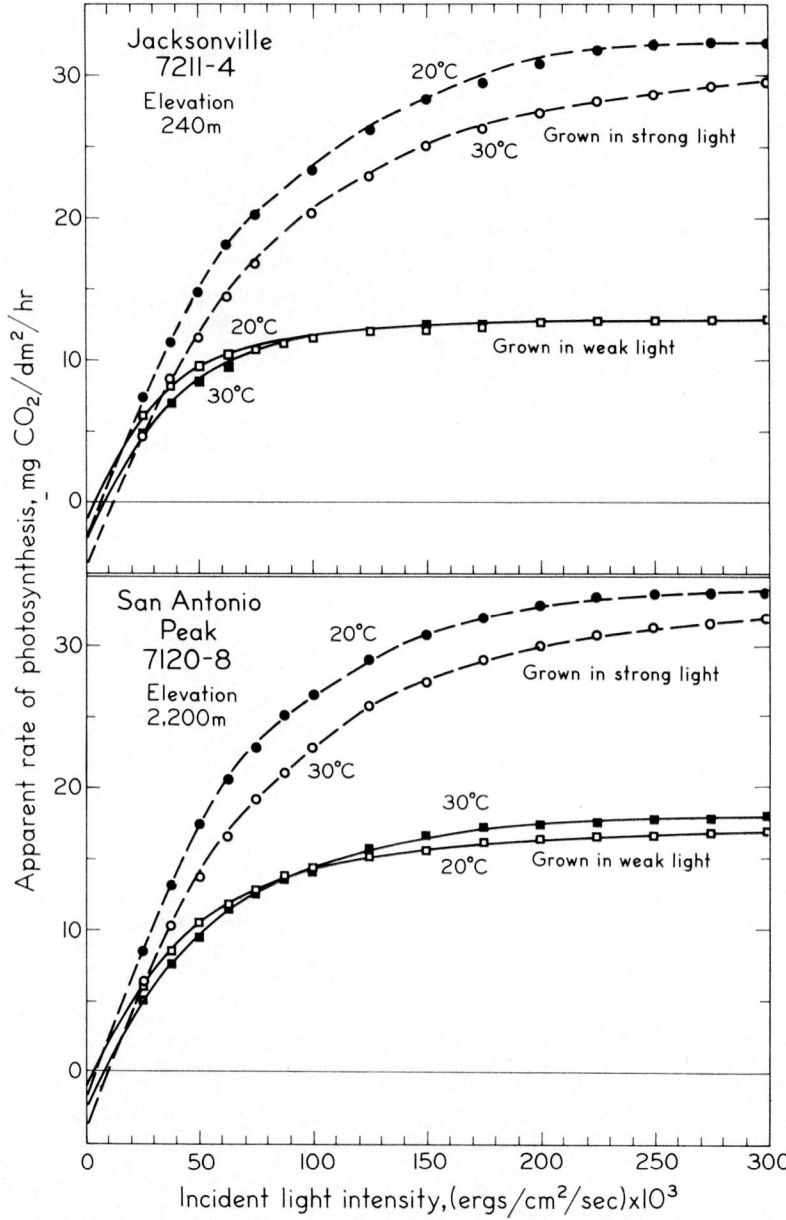

Figure 43. Apparent photosynthetic rates of *Mimulus cardinalis* as a function of light intensity on propagules of the same clones grown under strong light (100,000 erg cm^{-2} sec^{-1}) and under weak light (25,000 erg cm^{-2} sec^{-1}) when measured at 20° and 30°C.

clones grown under high:low light intensities. The values of all these ratios are greater than 1.00, a response that is characteristic of plants occurring naturally in sunny habitats. In strictly shade races or species this response may be reversed, as shown by Björkman and Holmgren (1963, 1966). It is also evident that the numerical values of the ratios for different clones listed in table 21 vary over a considerable range, a topic that will be discussed in more detail in later pages.

TABLE 21

Ratios between Light-Saturated Photosynthetic Rates of *Mimulus* Propagules Grown under High Light Intensities and Propagules Grown under Low Light Intensities *

M. cardinalis:		
Los Trancos, 6546-5		2.40
Jacksonville, 7211-4		2.50
San Antonio Peak, 7120-8		2.02
M. lewisii:		
Tamarack Flat, 7399-3		1.64
Timberline, 7405-4		1.26
Logan Pass, 7635-2		1.82
M. nelsonii:		
El Salto, 7422-12		1.87
Hybrids:		
cardinalis Los Trancos × *lewisii* Timberline, F$_1$:	6536-3	1.82
cardinalis Los Trancos × *lewisii* Timberline, F$_2$:	7135-35	1.88
cardinalis Los Trancos × *lewisii* Timberline, F$_2$:	7111-16	1.85
cardinalis Los Trancos × *lewisii* Timberline, F$_2$:	7111-17	1.66
lewisii Timberline × *nelsonii* El Salto, F$_1$:	7540-2-2x (diploid)	2.05
lewisii Timberline × *nelsonii* El Salto, F$_1$:	7540-2-4x (tetraploid)	2.38
lewisii Timberline × *nelsonii* El Salto, F$_2$:	7606-B (tetraploid)	1.93

* The high-light propagules were grown at 125,000 erg cm^{-2} sec^{-1} intensity, the low-light propagules, mostly at 25,000 erg cm^{-2} sec^{-1}. Photosynthetic measurements were made at 20° C in air with an average CO$_2$ concentration of approximately 0.030%.

Comparisons between clones of M. cardinalis and M. lewisii grown under different light intensities. A more detailed study of the effect of light intensity during growth on the capacity for light-saturated photosynthesis was made by comparing the *M. cardinalis* clone 7211-4 from Jacksonville with the *M. lewisii* clone 7635-2 from Logan Pass. In these experiments cloned individuals were grown under three different light intensities. In addition to photosynthesis, the leaf anatomy, leaf content of chorophyll and protein, and the activity of the carboxylation enzyme, RuDP carboxylase, were determined.

As is evident from table 22, the light-saturated rate of photosynthesis on the basis of unit leaf area approximately doubles when the light intensity during growth is increased from 18,000 to 53,000 erg cm^{-2} sec^{-1} (i.e., 75% higher in Logan Pass, 125% higher in Jacksonville). When the intensity during growth is further increased to 106,000 erg cm^{-2} sec^{-1}, the light-saturated rate

TABLE 22

Effect of Light Intensity during Growth on the Subsequent
Light-Saturated Photosynthetic Rate of *Mimulus* Clones *

Light Intensity during Growth, erg cm^{-2} sec^{-1}	Photosynthetic rate,* μ mol CO$_2$ $\times$ dm^{-2} $\times$ min^{-1}	
	M. lewisii Logan Pass (7635-2)	*M. cardinalis* Jacksonville (7211-4)
18,000	7.2	4.5
53,000	12.5	10.2
106,000	13.6	14.4

* Propagules grown at a constant temperature of 20° C with a 16-hour photoperiod, 300 ppm CO$_2$ concentration, and 21% O$_2$ concentration. Photosynthetic rates were measured at 20° C with 300 ppm CO$_2$ and 21% O$_2$ under saturating white light from a high-pressure xenon arc.

again increases, but in this step the increase in photosynthetic rate is less marked (abut 10% in Logan Pass, 40% in Jacksonville).

Figure 44 shows the effect of these three light intensities on the leaf anatomy of the two clones. Leaf thickness increases greatly with increasing light intensity in both, the thickness at the highest light intensity being about twice that of the lowest. When the clones grown under the same light intensities

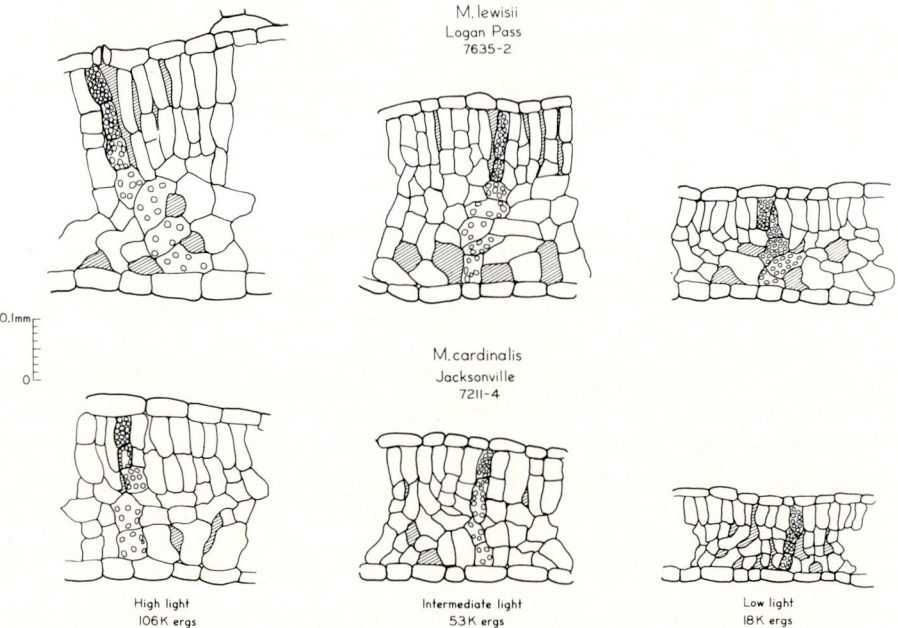

Figure 44. Sections of leaves of propagules of *M. lewisii* and *M. cardinalis* clones grown under low, intermediate, and high light intensities.

are compared, *M. lewisii* from Logan Pass invariably has the greater leaf thickness. As shown in figure 44, the increase is attributable to a greater number of cell layers in the palisade and spongy parenchyma as well as to an increase in the size of the cells. The modifications in leaf structure in the two clones due to differences in incident light intensity therefore appear to be parallel. They also result in differences in light absorption as shown in figures 45 and 46.

One might assume that the composition and the content (on the basis of unit leaf volume, or fresh weight) of photosynthetic components that determine the capacity for light-saturated photosynthesis do not change as leaf thickness increases. If this assumption were correct, one would predict that the light-saturated rate on the basis of unit leaf area would increase with increasing leaf thickness. The increase would be expected to be essentially directly proportional to the increase in leaf thickness, assuming that the leaf is saturated with respect to CO_2 concentration. Under normal CO_2 concentrations, however, the photosynthetic rate is at least partially limited by CO_2, and the longer diffusion pathways that result from increased leaf thickness would tend to counteract the effect of increased leaf mass in relation to area. From these considerations, the relationship between the light-saturated rate of photosynthesis in normal air and leaf thickness would be estimated to approximate the rates shown by curve C in figure 47.

From curves A and B of figure 47, which are based on experimental data from the two *Mimulus* clones, it is obvious that the observed results deviate strongly from the above prediction. The increase in photosynthetic rate with a given increase in leaf thickness is much greater than expected. This finding invalidates our original assumption that the composition and content of the components inside the leaves that determine the capacity for light-saturated photosynthesis remain constant. The activity (or amount) of these components on the basis of unit leaf volume must, therefore, increase with increasing light intensity for growth. Experimental data supporting the latter conclusion are shown in tables 23 and 24.

The activity of the carboxylation enzyme, RuDP carboxylase, on the basis of unit leaf fresh weight, approximately doubles when light intensity during growth is increased from 18,000 to 53,000 erg cm^{-2} sec^{-1} in both clones. When light intensity is further increased to 106,000 erg cm^{-2} sec^{-1}, the enzyme activity again increases, but the increase is considerably greater in the Jacksonville than in the Logan Pass clone (table 23). These results show that the level of at least one key enzyme that can be expected to influence the capacity of the light-saturated rate of photosynthesis increases with increasing light intensity during growth.

We have not assayed for the activities of photosynthetic enzymes other than the carboxylation enzyme. It seems likely, however, that since the level of soluble cell protein (table 24) roughly parallels that of RuDP carboxylase, the

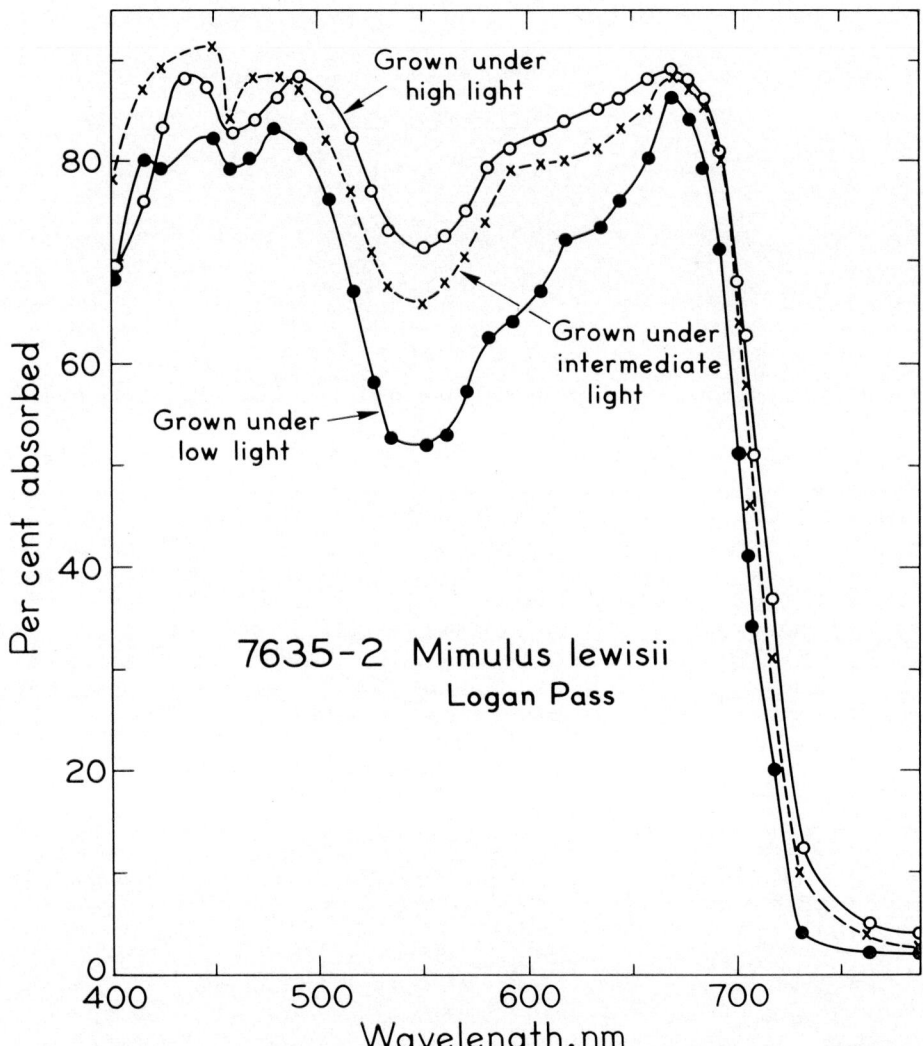

Figure 45. Percentage absorption of incident light by leaves of *Mimulus lewisii* Logan previously grown under low (18,000 erg cm^{-2} sec^{-1}), intermediate (53,000 erg cm^{-2} sec^{-1}), and high (106,000 erg cm^{-2} sec^{-1}) light intensities as a function of wavelength. See figure 44 (upper row) for anatomical cross sections of the same leaves.

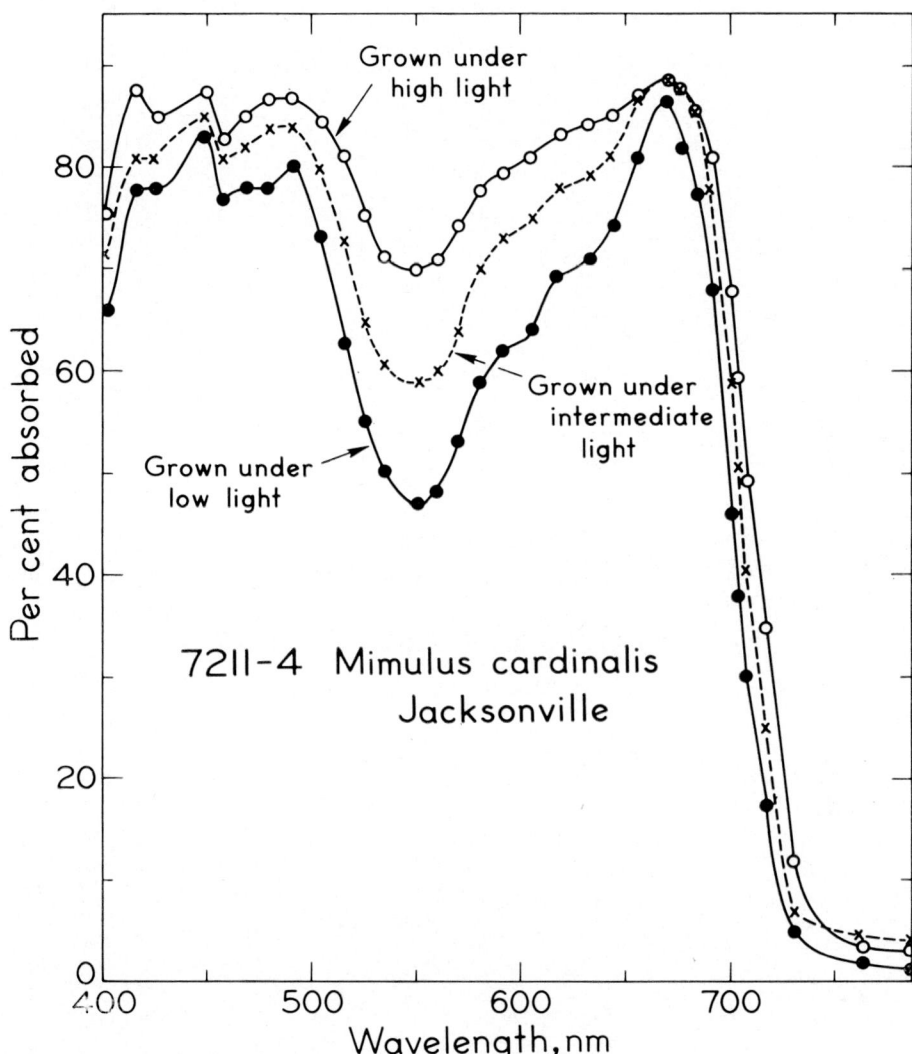

Figure 46. Percentage absorption of incident light of *Mimulus cardinalis* Jacksonville previously grown under low (18,000 erg cm^{-2} sec^{-1}), intermediate (53,000 erg cm^{-2} sec^{-1}), and high (106,000 erg cm^{-2} sec^{-1}) light intensities as a function of wavelength. See figure 44 (lower row) for anatomical cross sections of the same leaves.

level of other photosynthetic enzymes also increases as the light intensity during growth becomes greater. Although the content of chlorophyll on a fresh weight basis generally increases with greater light intensity, the amount of increase is much less than for protein and RuDP carboxylase (table 24). This result is not surprising since the content of light-harvesting pigment per se would not be

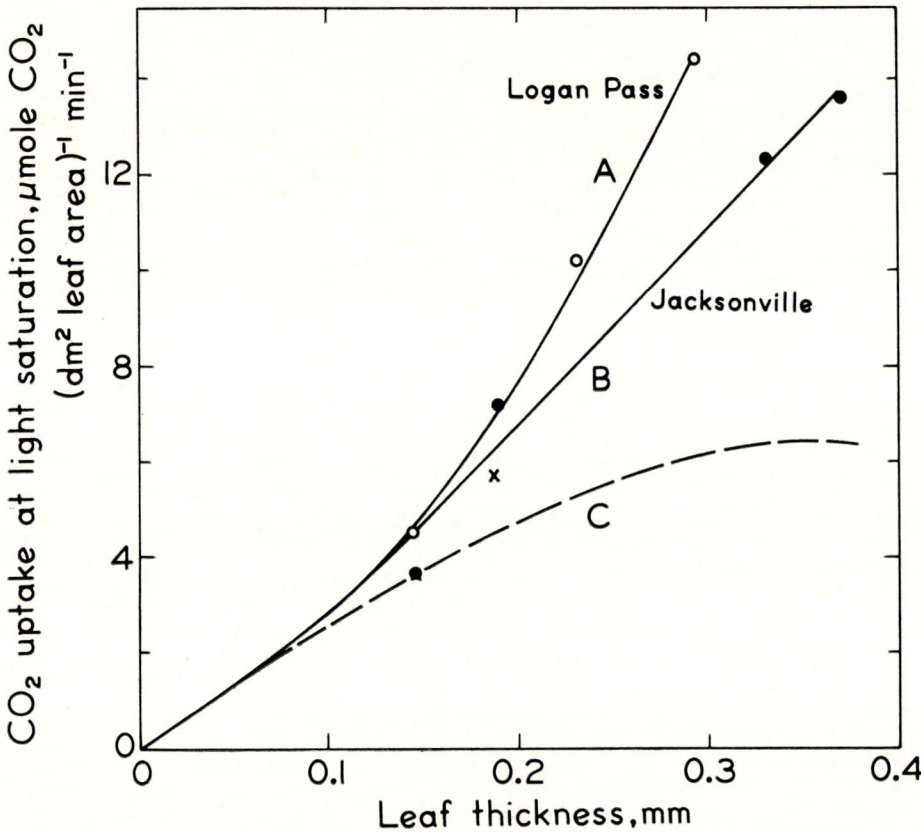

Figure 47. Rate of CO_2 uptake at light saturation as a function of leaf thickness by *Mimulus lewisii,* clone 7635-2 Logan, and *M. cardinalis,* clone 7211-4 Jacksonville. See text.

expected to have much effect on the light-saturated photosynthetic rate (cf. Björkman, 1968).

The data presented above demonstrate (1) that *Mimulus* clones have the ability to adjust to increased light intensity during growth by increasing their capacity for light-saturated photosynthesis; and (2) that this is achieved both through an increased ratio of leaf volume to leaf area and through an increased level of photosynthetic enzymes, as determined on the basis of leaf volume.

TABLE 23

Effect of Light Intensity during Growth on the Activity of RuDP Carboxylase
in Leaf Extracts of *Mimulus* Clones

Light Intensity during Growth, erg cm^{-2} sec^{-1}	RuDP Carboxylase Activity,* μ mol CO$_2$ $\times$ min^{-1} $\times$ (g fresh wt)$^{-1}$	
	Logan Pass (7635-2)	Jacksonville (7211-4)
18,000	4.7	4.4
53,000	10.0	7.9
106,000	11.3	13.5

* Enzyme assay: 0.05 M NaHCO$_3$, 4 $\times$ 10^{-4} M RuDP, pH 8.0, 30° C.

EFFECT OF LIGHT INTENSITY ON THE PRODUCTION OF DRY MATTER. From the data just presented, one would expect that up to the limit of light-saturating intensities, higher light intensities should result in a faster rate of growth, i.e., in greater production of dry matter per unit of time. Experimental evidence confirms this conclusion.

Figure 48 shows the growth of propagules of the *M. lewisii* clone 7635-2 from Logan Pass in comparison with comparable propagules of the *M. cardinalis* clone 7211-4 from Jacksonville under the three light intensities mentioned previously. With the exception of light intensity, all the propagules were grown under exactly comparable conditions over a period of 17 days (cf. footnote, figure 48). It is evident from the illustration that both the Logan and Jacksonville clones made more growth under the highest light intensity than under the lowest.

Table 25 shows the average net dry weight increase of the two clones in this same experiment. The dry weight increase in both the Logan and Jacksonville clones was linearly proportional to light intensity under the conditions of this experiment, as shown by the graph in figure 49. The slope or rate of increase in growth with light intensity for the Logan Pass clone was greater than for

TABLE 24

Effect of Light Intensity during Growth on Chlorophyll
and Soluble Protein Content in Leaves of *Mimulus* Clones *

Light Intensity during Growth, erg cm^{-2} sec^{-1}	Chlorophyll (a + b), mg (g fresh wt)$^{-1}$		Soluble Protein, mg (g fresh wt)$^{-1}$	
	Logan Pass (7635-2)	Jacksonville (7211-4)	Logan Pass (7635-2)	Jacksonville (7211-4)
18,000	1.33	1.44	9.3	8.2
53,000	1.53	1.25	20.6	15.9
106,000	1.70	1.87	20.7	25.1

* Chlorophyll determined by method of Arnon (1951), protein by the Folin-Lowry method.

Jacksonville, a fact that may be related to the inherently greater leaf thickness of the Logan clone, as shown in figure 44.

A highly significant difference illustrated in figure 48 is the more rapid development of flowering stems and flower buds in the *M. lewisii* clone than in

Figure 48. Growth of clone 7635-2, *Mimulus lewisii* Logan, in comparison with clone 7211-4, *M. cardinalis* Jacksonville, under light intensities of 18,000, 53,000 and 106,000 ergs cm^{-2} sec^{-1}. Plants grown for a 17-day period under a 16-hour photoperiod at 20°; CO_2 concentration, 300 ppm; O_2, 21.0%. See also figure 49.

M. cardinalis. This marked acceleration in rate of flowering development in the alpine plant is clearly of ecological significance, since in its native habitat the growing season is very short compared with that of the foothil *M. cardinalis* from Jacksonville.

TABLE 25

Dry Weight Increase in *Mimulus* Clones during Growth under Different Light Intensities

Light Intensity during Growth, erg cm^{-2} sec^{-1}	Net Dry Weight Increase per Propagule, g *	
	M. lewisii Logan Pass (7635-2)	*M. cardinalis* Jacksonville (7211-4)
18,000	0.165 ± 0.016	0.233 ± 0.035
53,000	0.650 ± 0.034	0.615 ± 0.233
106,000	1.350 ± 0.171	1.150 ± 0.261

* Values are means of 8 propagules for each treatment during the 17-day experimental period; cf. figures 48 and 49.

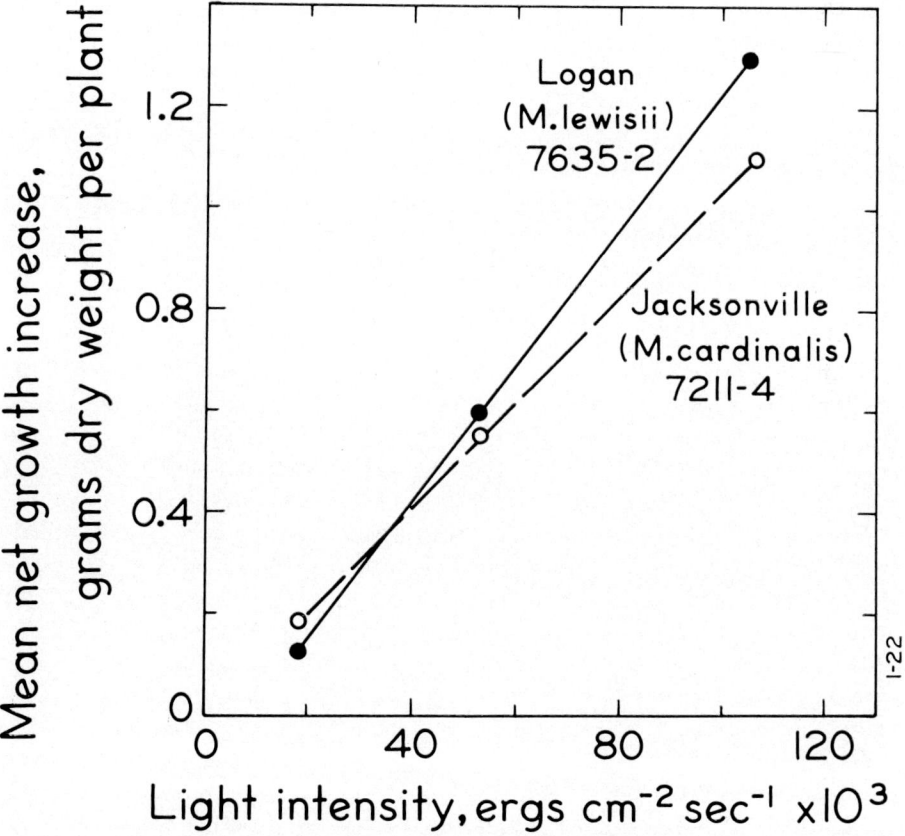

Figure 49. Dry weight increase in the clone 7635-2, *Mimulus lewisii* Logan, and 7211-4, *M. cardinalis* Jacksonville, as a function of light intensity. See figure 48.

In figure 48 it can also be seen that more flower buds are produced by the Logan Pass clone at the higher light intensities than at the lower intensities. In controlled cabinet experiments, more flowers have been observed under high than under low light intensities in clones of both *M. lewisii* and *M. cardinalis*. Light intensity, in conjunction with other external variables, notably day length and temperature, is therefore an important factor influencing flowering response in these species of *Mimulus*.

Typical long-term responses of the Jacksonville (7211-4) and San Antonio Peak (7120-8) clones of *Mimulus cardinalis* to differences in light intensity are shown in figure 50. In this experiment the light intensity was approximately 125,000 erg cm^{-2} sec^{-1} for the propagules shown at the left, and 25,000 erg cm^{-2} sec^{-1} for those shown at right. The plants illustrated were started as small rooted cuttings of matched size and grown for 32 days at a temperature of 22° C during the day and 15° C at night under a 16-hour photoperiod. Detailed data on the photosynthetic performance and leaf structure of the same two clones under the two light intensities were presented earlier on pages 98–100.

Modifications in leaf thickness, size, and texture at the two light intensities are parallel in the two clones, as is evident in figure 50. A typical feature is the shorter internodes with more leafy shoots emerging from the axils of the leaves on the propagules grown under the high light intensity. Very evident also is the greater overall growth, and the greater number of flower buds formed at the high intensity than at the low intensity.

EFFECTS OF O_2 AND CO_2 CONCENTRATION ON PHOTOSYNTHESIS AND GROWTH

During the past several years it has become well established that higher plant photosynthesis is strongly inhibited by the oxygen content of normal air (Björkman, 1966; Fock and Egle, 1966; Tregunna et al., 1966). Both photosynthetic O_2 evolution and CO_2 uptake are affected, with the notable exception that CO_2 exchange is unaffected by O_2 in higher plant species that possess the β-carboxylation (C-4 dicarboxylic acid) pathway of photosynthetic CO_2 fixation (Forrester et al., 1966; Hesketh, 1967; Björkman, 1967; Downes and Hesketh, 1968).

In species lacking the β-carboxylation pathway of photosynthesis, including *Mimulus*, a reduction in O_2 concentration from the usual 21% of air to a few percent typically results in an enhancement of CO_2 uptake in the order of 40 to 50% when the CO_2 concentration is kept at the level of normal air, i.e., approx. 300 ppm. As shown in figure 51, the inhibition is rapid, and it is also rapidly and fully reversible. The speed of the response strongly suggests that the phenomenon is not caused by an increase of stomatal aperture under low O_2 concentration. Conclusive evidence that stomatal regulation is not involved has been provided by Gauhl and Björkman (1969). Changes in O_2 concentration in

Figure 50. Effect of differences in light intensity on the growth of *Mimulus cardinalis* clones originally from San Antonio Peak (clone 7120-8, above) and Jacksonville (clone 7211-4, below). Propagules at the left were grown under a light intensity of 125,000 erg cm^{-2} sec^{-1}, those at the right, at 25,000 erg cm^{-2} sec^{-1}, both on a 16-hour photoperiod. Day temperature, 20°, night temperature, 15°; CO_2 concentration, 300 ppm; O_2, 21.0%; duration of experiment, 32 days.

the range 1% to 21% had no effect on transpiration rate in the several species investigated in spite of the fact that the rate of photosynthesis was strongly affected. Very recent experiments with *Mimulus cardinalis* Jacksonville yielded the same negative results. Transpiration in the clone was unaffected when the O_2 concentration was decreased from 21% to 1.5% O_2 even though CO_2 uptake increased by about 50%.

The O_2 inhibition affects both the light-limited and the light-saturated rate of photosynthesis. As shown in table 26 this is true of *Mimulus* as well as other

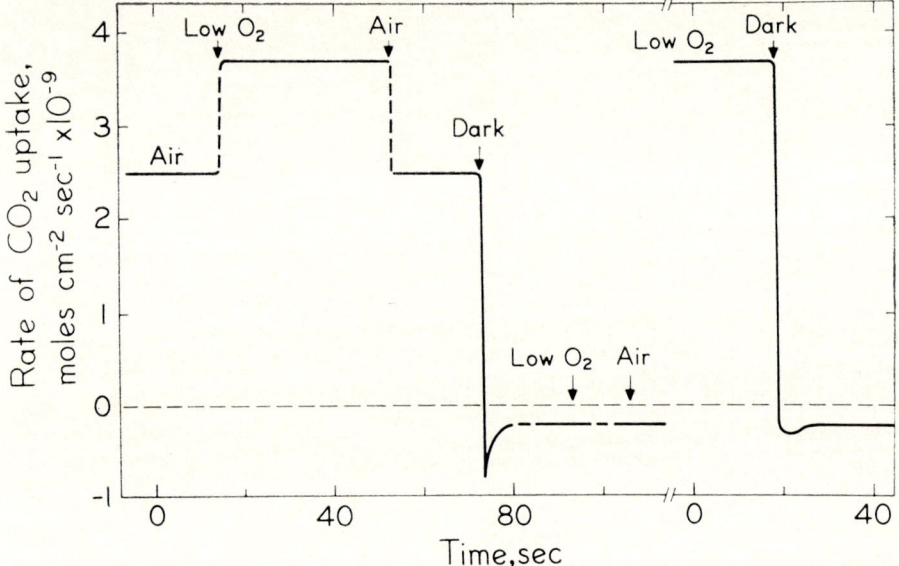

Figure 51. Time course of the rate of CO_2 exchange in response to changes in oxygen concentration in *Mimulus cardinalis* Jacksonville, clone 7211-4. Red light ($\lambda_{max}=665$ nm, half-bandwidth, 35 nm) providing 100 nanoeinstein cm^{-2} sec^{-1}. Leaf temperature, 22°.

species. Moreover, the effect is the same at different wavelengths throughout the visible spectrum (table 27).

At a given temperature the inhibiting effect of O_2 on the light-saturated rate of photosynthesis increases as the CO_2 concentration is decreased (figure 52). Expressed in different terms, for any given photosynthetic rate, a higher CO_2 concentration is required in 21% O_2 than when the O_2 concentration is kept low. Similarly, the CO_2 concentration required for CO_2 saturation of photosynthesis increases with increasing O_2 concentration. It is likely, therefore, that the CO_2 dependence curve of photosynthesis determined in low O_2 concentration relates more closely to the intrinsic CO_2 dependence of the carboxylation (plus the diffusion) process than does the CO_2 dependence curve determined in air of normal O_2 content.

TABLE 26

Inhibition of CO_2 Uptake in 21% O_2 at Different Light Intensities *

Light Absorbed, einsteins $cm^{-2} sec^{-1} \times 10^{-9}$	Photosynthetic Inhibition, Percent		
	Solidago virgaurea	*Plantago lanceolata*	*Mimulus cardinalis*
1–2	29	31	30
3–5	30	31	30
7–10	30	31	30
15–20	26	31	...
23–29	26	32	...
100	...	33	31

* Measurements made at 22° C, 0.03% CO_2; incident light, 654 nm; half bandwidth 10 nm for absorbed values up to 30×10^{-9} einsteins $cm^{-2} sec^{-1}$; for highest value, 665 nm, half bandwidth 35 nm.

At a given CO_2 concentration of the gas surrounding the leaf, the inhibition by O_2 increases with increasing leaf temperature. As shown in figure 53 the light-saturated photosynthetic rate of 300 μl CO_2 per liter of air increases strongly with temperature above 15° C. The point at which a further increase in temperature leads to a marked decline in the rate of CO_2 uptake is, however, essentially unaffected by CO_2 concentration.

It is likely that the effect of temperature on the O_2 inhibition is, at least in part, closely related to the effect of CO_2 concentration. The amount of dissolved CO_2 in a water solution in equilibrium with air of a constant CO_2 concentration decreases markedly as temperature is increased. For example, at 30° the concentration of dissolved CO_2 (e.g. in mg/l) is only about 52% of that at 10°. An increase in temperature would therefore be expected to decrease the effective CO_2 concentration in the mesophyll. The marked influence of

TABLE 27

Photosynthetic CO_2 Uptake under 2.0% O_2 and under Air (21.0% O_2) at Different Wavelengths in *Mimulus cardinalis* (Clone 7120-7)

Wavelength, nm	Half Bandwidth, nm	CO_2 Uptake, μM $cm^{-2} sec^{-1}$ *		Inhibition, Percent
		Low O_2	Air	
440	37	1.39	0.93	33
540	48	1.33	0.89	33
590	30	1.38	0.94	32
650	49	1.38	0.93	32
700	55	1.40	0.91	35

* Measurements made at 23° C and 300 ppm CO_2; light intensity, 10^4 erg $cm^{-2} sec^{-1}$ at 650 nm. At other wavelengths the intensity was adjusted so that rates of CO_2 uptake were approximately the same as at 650 nm. The rates in part were light-saturated.

temperature on the inhibition by O_2 may thus largely be accounted for by its effect on CO_2 concentration.

It is well known that under low light intensities photosynthesis is much less influenced by temperature and CO_2 concentration than it is under high light intensities. This was also found to be true of the inhibiting effect of O_2; the O_2

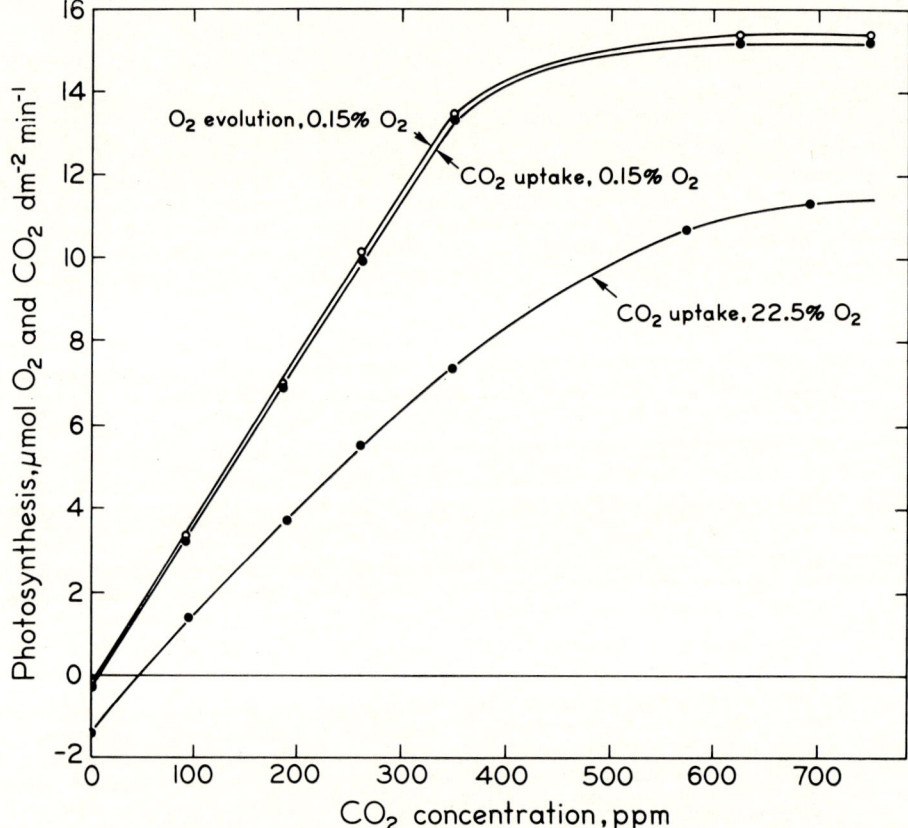

Figure 52. Carbon dioxide dependence of light-saturated photosynthesis under 0.15% and 22.5% O_2 in *Mimulus cardinalis* Jacksonville, clone 7211-4. Light intensity held constant at 340,000 erg cm^{-2} sec^{-1} (400–700 nm). Leaf temperature, 27°.

inhibition of the light-limited photosynthetic rate was nearly constant over a CO_2 concentration range of 200 to 300 ppm and a temperature range of 15° to 32° C.

With the notable exception of species utilizing the β-carboxylation pathway of photosynthesis (these lack an effect of O_2 on CO_2 uptake), different species of higher plants appear to be remarkably similar with regard to their photosynthetic response to O_2 concentration. Our studies of the effect of O_2 on photosynthesis also did not reveal any marked differences in this respect among the different species and races of *Mimulus*.

In spite of much recent work in several laboratories aimed at resolving the mechanism for the inhibitory effect of oxygen, the process that underlies the

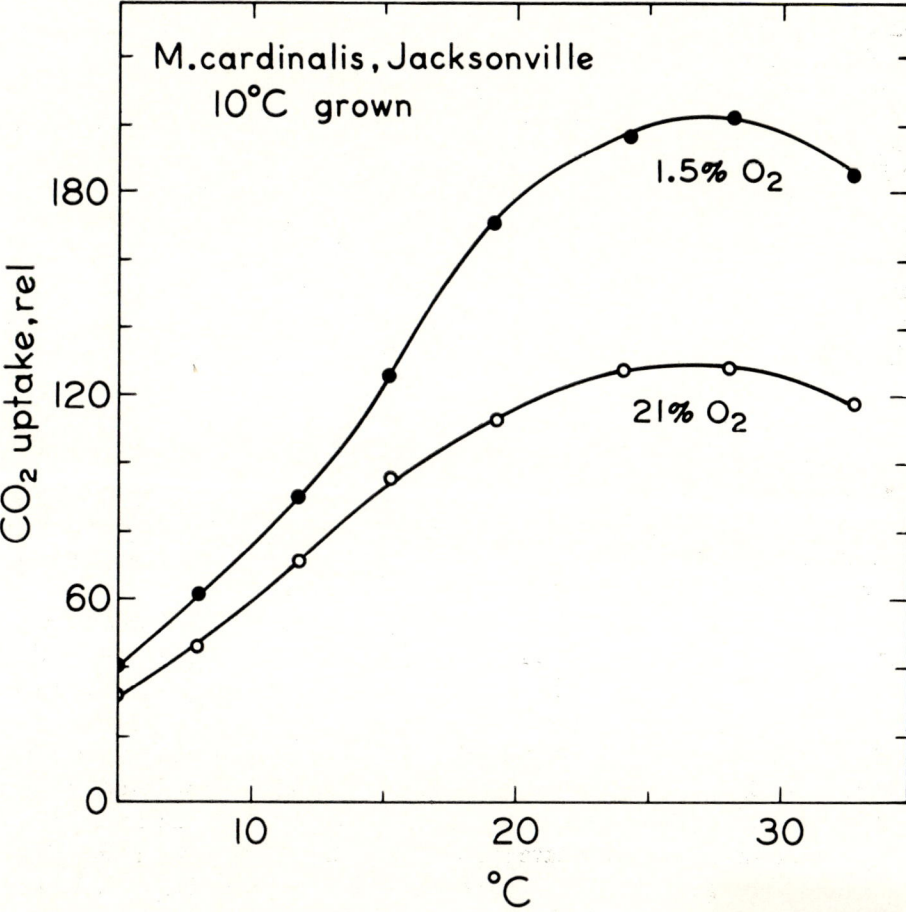

Figure 53. Temperature dependence of light-saturated photosynthesis under 1.5% and 21.0% O_2 in *Mimulus cardinalis* Jacksonville, clone 7211-4. Light intensity held constant at 340,000 erg cm^{-2} sec^{-1} (400-700 nm); CO_2 concentration, 320-340 ppm.

effect is as yet largely unknown. Several workers have used the term "photorespiration" to designate this process. There is evidence that the inhibitory effect is caused primarily by an oxidation of immediate or intermediate products of photosynthesis, and that glycolate production and metabolism are involved. The rate of glycolate production is known to be stimulated by high oxygen concentration and by low CO_2 concentration. As yet the origin of glycolate is obscure, but there is some evidence that it is produced by the oxidation of a Calvin cycle intermediate such as a sugar phosphate (RuDP?). The oxidant could be an early product of the photoacts or might perhaps be formed by the reoxidation of a highly reduced photosynthetic intermediate by oxygen in a Mehler type reaction. The hypothesis that RuDP is the source of glycolate is attractive in that it would be consistent with the observation that the O_2 effect on CO_2 uptake is present under rate-limiting light intensities, and that under conditions of saturating light the inhibition increases with decreasing CO_2 concentration. At the present time there is no indication what function the unknown process underlying the inhibiting effect of O_2 on photosynthesis ("photorespiration") might serve.

If "photorespiration" does serve a critical biosynthetic function, it would be expected that growing plants under low O_2 concentration would inhibit growth, since "photorespiration" would then be strongly suppressed. An enhancement of growth under lower O_2 concentration than that of normal air would be expected only if photorespiration does not serve an essential biosynthetic function under the conditions used (this is not to exclude the possibility that it has a useful function in normal air) and if the enhancement of apparent photosynthesis under low O_2 concentration is not caused by a diversion of reducing power to CO_2 fixation at the expense of other vital biosynthetic processes. For an enhancement of growth to be observed, it would also be necessary that secondary growth processes are not adversely affected by low O_2 concentration, and that the growth experiments are made under conditions where growth rate is substantially limited by photosynthetic rate.

Comparative growth experiments were therefore made with *Mimulus* and other species under different O_2 concentrations, in order to elucidate the relationship between the effects of O_2 concentration on photosynthesis and on productivity.

Although many studies have been made on the effects of different partial pressures of O_2 and CO_2 in the root media of higher plants, few investigations have been concerned with the effect of O_2 concentration in the atmosphere. Siegel and co-workers (1963) have shown that such plant processes as germination, root development, and coleoptile elongation are essentially unaffected, and sometimes even enhanced, by subatmospheric O_2 levels, whereas senescence is suppressed. In some cases seedling growth was found to be somewhat greater at 10% than at 20% O_2, and young seedlings were able to grow at concentrations as low as 5%.

So far as we are aware, with the exception of our own studies (Björkman et al., 1967, 1968) and very recent work by Fock and Egle,[1] there have been no experiments under precise control of temperature, light intensity, and CO_2 and O_2 concentration to determine whether or not the enhancement of net CO_2

---

[1] Egle, personal communication.

uptake by leaves in low ambient O_2 concentration is related to increases in dry matter production.

METHOD OF GAS CONTROL IN GROWTH CABINETS. In order to conduct satisfactory comparative growth experiments upon the effects of varying CO_2 and O_2 concentrations on *Mimulus* and other species, several technical problems must be resolved: precise control must be maintained over temperature, CO_2 concentration, O_2 concentration, and the quality and intensity of light. The achievement of such control requires considerable development, and merits some detailed description.

In order to avoid as far as possible any effects (positive or negative) on root metabolism that may result when the O_2 concentration is lowered, it is necessary to isolate the roots from the tops of the experimental plants with gas-tight seals.

The experimenal plants were grown in the pair of cabinets shown in figure 34. The air circulation system inside the cabinets is closed to the external atmosphere, and each cabinet is connected to a large collapsible plastic bag of approximately 500 l capacity to equalize internal and external pressures. The bag prevents leakage from the external air into the cabinets that would otherwise take place when the external atmospheric pressure increases, or when the internal pressure varies due to slight changes in temperature during cycling of the controls.

A schematic diagram of the control system is shown in figure 35. This diagram should be considered in relation to figure 34. Thermistor-operated controllers provide precise temperature control ($\pm 0.1°$). Gas from the cabinet chambers is continuously pumped through a paramagnetic O_2 analyzer (Beckman, Model F3) and an infrared CO_2 analyzer (Beckman, Model L/B 15A, or Lira Model 300, Mine Safety Appliances). Both the O_2 analyzer and the CO_2 analyzer are equipped with electronic controllers specifically designed for this purpose. Each controller consists of a solid-state operational amplifier used in a voltage comparator circuit that compares the output of the gas analyzer with an internal reference. When the gas concentration deviates from the preset reference level, a transistor switch activates a solenoid in the controlling gas line to correct this condition.

To avoid undesirable differences in CO_2 or O_2 concentration between the two cabinets, the same analyzers are used for both. An electronic timer switches the gas sampling and controlling circuits alternately between the two cabinets at preset intervals (usually 60 sec). When a cabinet is being operated at or above atmospheric O_2 concentrations, CO_2-free air is slowly fed into the cabinet to prevent the CO_2 concentration from increasing beyond the preset value. At subatmospheric O_2 concentrations, the CO_2-free air is replaced with CO_2-free N_2. The absolute accuracy of CO_2 control when monitored by the Beckman Model L/B 15A infrared analyzer is about ± 5 ppm in the range 200 to 400 ppm. The maximum difference between the cabinets (if both are set to the same value) is only about ±2 ppm. With the Lira Model 300 infrared analyzer the latter difference is about ±10 ppm. The accuracy of the O_2 control is about ±0.5% in the range between 0 and 25%.

Light is provided by 96-inch Sylvania cool-white VHO fluorescent tubes (2.4 m long) supplemented with incandescent lamps. Since a single light bank is used for the illumination of both cabinets, differences in light intensity and quality between the two cabinets can be kept very small.

The liquid nutrient medium for the roots can be aerated with gas whose composition is independent of that of the cabinet atmosphere. Gas-tight seals between the root and the shoot are obtained from foam neoprene gaskets 4 mm thick. Prior to an experiment, circular gaskets ca. 4 cm diameter are cut from a sheet of foam neoprene. Holes ca. 1 mm in diameter are punched in the center. Cuttings of Mimulus made from tips of stems or side shoots about 6–8 cm long are carefully inserted through the holes in the gaskets. The cuttings, with the gaskets surrounding them, are then rooted in Hoagland's nutrient solution. As the cuttings become rooted and the stems expand in diameter, air-tight seals are formed around the stems by the foam neoprene gaskets that do not cause injury or undesirable effects on the subsequent growth of the propagules. This same technique has been used successfully both with cuttings and with very young seedlings of other species.

After rooting, the cuttings are transferred to aquarium-like reservoirs 12 × 14 cm high × 66 cm long. The cuttings are supported by cementing the top surfaces of the neoprene gaskets to which they are attached to the underside of the black plastic cover (made of heavy plexiglass) of the reservoirs. Holes large enough to accommodate the plants are spaced at intervals through the covers. The covers are then sealed to the nutrient reservoirs by means of foam neoprene gaskets that are cemented along the sides and ends of both the reservoirs and their covers. Air from one of the cabinets or from the outside can be pumped continuously through the liquid nutrient solution in the reservoirs and then returned to the cabinet from which it was taken, or simply exhausted outside the cabinets.

In the growth chambers transpiration water released by the plants is condensed on the cooling coils of the refrigerator system and drained through a trap below.

GROWTH RESPONSES OF MIMULUS UNDER DIFFERENT O_2 AND CO_2 CONCENTRATIONS. Figure 54 illustrates results from two experiments on the Jacksonville clone 7211-4 of *M. cardinalis* in which O_2 and CO_2 concentrations were variables. The top row shows propagules grown for 12 days in an atmosphere containing 4% O_2, as compared with the 21% O_2 concentration of normal air. In this experiment the CO_2 concentration under both treatments was maintained at 0.0110% or 110 ppm. This concentration is about one-third that of normal air, and close to the CO_2 compensation point for whole plants of this clone of *Mimulus* at the 25° temperature at which they were grown.

The rooted cuttings shown at the right were placed in the cabinet having normal air concentration of O_2 at 21%, in contrast with those at the left, with only 4% O_2. Light of an intensity of 71,500 erg cm^{-2} sec^{-1} was supplied con-

Figure 54. Growth of *Mimulus cardinalis* Jacksonville, clone 7211-4, under 4% and 21% oxygen at two levels of CO_2 concentration.

tinuously over the 24-hour photoperiod. The roots were aerated with normal air.

As shown at the upper left of figure 54, growth took place in the cuttings maintained at 4% O_2, whereas those under 21% O_2 (upper right) barely maintained their original size at the end of the 12-day experimental period. These results are also made evident by comparing their mean dry weights, shown in the left-hand columns of table 28. At the low CO_2 concentration at 110 ppm the photosynthetic rate of the plants grown in air was close to the CO_2 compensation point with no net gain per propagule. Under the same CO_2 concentration, the propagules in 4% O_2 were able to maintain a high enough photosynthetic rate to allow considerable new growth and accumulation of dry matter, a mean of 0.189 g per propagule. When these same experimental conditions were repeated, except that the CO_2 level was maintained at a normal air concentration of approximately 0.032%, or 320 ppm, good growth was obtained under both

TABLE 28

Effect of Reduced O_2 Concentration on Growth of *Mimulus cardinalis* (Clone 7411-4) at Two CO_2 Concentrations *

	CO_2 Concentration 110 ppm †		CO_2 Concentration 640 ppm †	
	21% O_2	4.0% O_2	21% O_2	4.0% O_2
Mean final dry weight per propagule, g	0.117 ± 0.25	0.306 ± 0.75	0.493 ± 0.119	0.605 ± 0.185
Minus mean initial dry weight, g	0.117	0.117	0.126	0.126
Mean net dry weight increase, g	**0.000**	**0.189**	**0.367**	**0.479**

All propagules were grown at 24° under continuous white light at 71,500 ergs cm^{-2} sec^{-1} intensity; cf. figure 53.

* Values are means of 15 matched propagules for a 12-day experimental period.

† Values are means of 10 matched propagules over an 8-day experimental period.

O_2 levels, but the dry weight increase was 90% greater under 4% than under 21% O_2 (cf. table 29).

At the bottom of figure 54 the results of another experiment are shown in which the same differential with respect to O_2 concentration was maintained but the CO_2 concentration was increased to 0.064%, or 640 ppm, about twice that of the normal concentration of air. Under these conditions the propagules under both 21% and 4% O_2 showed very rapid growth, but even with these high growth rates the propagules under 4% O_2 made a 30% greater increase than the propagules under 21% O_2, as shown by the net increases in dry weight in the right-hand columns of table 28.

Table 29 summarizes data from the three experiments with the Jacksonville clone in which the O_2 level was kept constant at 4%, while CO_2 was maintained at three concentrations, 100, 320, and 640 ppm. It is clear that there is a significantly greater growth of the propagules under 4% as compared with 21% O_2 at all three CO_2 concentrations, but the relative increase becomes smaller as CO_2 concentration is increased. These data suggest that further increases in CO_2 concentration would further diminish the growth differential between

TABLE 29

EFFECT OF O_2 CONCENTRATION ON GROWTH OF *Mimulus cardinalis* [*]
AT DIFFERENT CO_2 CONCENTRATIONS

CO_2 Concentration of Surrounding Air, ppm	Increase in Dry Weight per Propagule, mg		Ratio, Increase in 4% O_2
	Grown in 4% O_2	Grown in 21% O_2	Increase in 21% O_2
110	150	10	>10.00
320	1076	565	1.90
640	1144	804	1.42

[*] Data are from the clone 7211-4 from Jacksonville; the values are means of 10 propagules in each treatment over 10-day experimental periods. Temperature was held constant at 25° C, and light was continuous at 71,500 ergs cm^{-2} sec^{-1} intensity (cf. fig. 53).

low and high O_2 levels, a prediction that follows logically from the data presented in figure 52.

A question that naturally arises from these experiments is whether further reduction of the O_2 concentration below the 4% level would enhance growth even more in comparison with propagules in 21% O_2. The results of two experiments designed to answer this question are presented in table 30. In experiment 03 comparison was made of the growth of propagules of the same clone of *M. cardinalis* under an O_2 concentration of 4% and under 21% O_2. In experiment 04 immediately following, the same conditions were repeated with the same clone, except that the low O_2 level was reduced to 2.5%. It is evident that the degree of enhancement in growth was less under 2.5% O_2 than under 4% O_2. The ratio of dry weight increase at low:high O_2 concentration in the 10-day experiments was found to be 1.58 under 2.5% O_2 as compared with 1.90

TABLE 30

EFFECT OF DIFFERENT LEVELS OF O_2 CONCENTRATION ON GROWTH
OF *Mimulus cardinalis* [*]

	O_2 in Control	Low O_2 Concentration	Ratio, Low O_2 Control (21%)
Experiment No. 03...................	21%	4.0%	
Mean final dry weight per propagule, g	0.675 ± 0.029	1.186 ± 0.043	
Mean initial dry weight per propagule, g	**0.110**	**0.110**	
Net dry weight increase, g	0.565	1.076	**1.90**
Experiment No. 04...................	21%	2.5%	
Mean final dry weight per propagule, g	0.589 ± 0.017	0.887 ± 0.036	
Mean initial dry weight per propagule, g	**0.70**	**0.70**	
Net dry weight increase, g	0.519	0.817	**1.58**

[*] Data are from clone 7211-4, Jacksonville; values are means of 10 propagules over 10-day experiments. Temperature was held constant at 25° C, light continuous 71,500 ergs cm^{-2} sec^{-1} intensity.

under 4% O_2. Both from the appearance of the plants at the end of the experimental periods, and from the data on dry weights, it appears that an O_2 level of 2.5% may be too low for maximum enhancement of growth of this clone, although it is not too low for enhancement of the light-saturated photosynthetic rate, as mentioned earlier.

The above experiments were facilitated by the fact that the *Mimulus cardinalis* clone used is not adversely affected in growth by continuous illumination over a 24-hour period. In experiments designed to investigate whether the enhancement of photosynthetic rate by low O_2 is accompanied by corresponding increases in net dry weight, it is important to eliminate possible harmful secondary effects such as might be caused by a low O_2 level on respiration during a dark period. Moreover, it is technically rather difficult to control O_2 and CO_2 concentrations precisely with alternate illuminated and dark periods during an experiment. Some species are adversely affected by continuous light, as for example, *Phaseolus vulgaris,* which became chlorotic under continuous light under 21% O_2, but not under 4% O_2 (cf. Björkman et al., 1966).

Enhancement of growth in O_2 concentration lower than that of normal air has been demonstrated also in the liverwort *Marchantia polymorpha* Betal, (Björkman and Gauhl, 1968). On the basis of data obtained from measurements of photosynthetic response to O_2 concentration, and of the CO_2 compensation point, one would expect that the enhancement of growth by low O_2 is widespread among higher plants, with the exception of certain tropical species of grasses and also of dicotyledonous plants that possess the β-carboxylation pathway of CO_2 fixation (see pp. 124–131 for further discussion and references to literature). An example of a species in this category is *Zea mays* which, when grown under the same oxygen concentrations of 4% and 21% as used in the *Mimulus* experiments, failed to show significant differences in net dry weight, although growth was markedly enhanced by an increase in CO_2 concentration from 110 to 320 ppm, as shown in table 31.

The data thus far obtained in our comparative growth experiments with different oxygen concentrations indicate that the strong depression of "photorespiration" that results when the O_2 concentration is reduced does not lead to a reduction in the rate of growth, but instead, to an enhancement analogous to the effect of O_2 concentration on the photosynthetic rate, the effect on growth increasing with decreasing CO_2 concentration. The results therefore strongly suggest that "photorespiration" does not serve a critical biosynthetic function, and that its suppression by low O_2 concentration causes a true increase in photosynthetic productivity.

This, however, does not imply that during the course of evolution plants have acquired a process that is useless, or even detrimental, to plant growth; attempts to increase photosynthesis and yield in air of normal O_2 and CO_2 content by inhibiting "photorespiration" by chemicals or other means are probably not likely to be successful. Species with β-carboxylation provide examples of plants which have overcome the inhibiting effect of O_2 on photosynthetic CO_2 uptake (although photosynthetic O_2 evolution is markedly inhibited). This has probably not been accomplished by elimination of a biochemical system, but rather by acquisition of an additional system that serves to overcome the disadvantages of high O_2 and low CO_2 concentration. In order to gain this increased effectiveness of carbon dioxide fixation in normal air, these plants may have to pay an intrinsically greater energy cost in terms of the number of moles of ATP required for each mole of CO_2 fixed.

MODIFICATIONS INDUCED ON MIMULUS BY VARYING O_2 CONCENTRATION. Although our observations on the growth of *Mimulus* under different O_2 concentrations are limited to the single clone 7211-4 *M. cardinalis* Jacksonville, modifications in propagules grown under 4% O_2 rather than 21% O_2 merit

TABLE 31

Growth of *Zea mays* at Different CO_2 and O_2 Concentrations

	CO_2 Concentration 110 ppm			CO_2 Concentration 320 ppm		
	O_2 Concentration		Difference	O_2 Concentration		Difference
	4.0%	21.0%		4.0%	21.0%	
Mean dry weight increase per seedling, g *	0.196	0.218	insignificant, $p => 0.5$	1.473	1.269	scarcely significant, $0.3 < P < 0.4$

* Values are means of 5 seedlings over 10-day experimental periods. Temperature was held constant at 25° C, light intensity at 71,500 erg^{-2} sec^{-1} with a 24-hour photoperiod.

description. Under low O_2 the growth habit is more compact and the stems are thicker and leaves are somewhat larger and thicker than on those grown under 21% O_2. Root development is notably greater in propagules whose tops are subjected to 4% O_2 than in those grown in 21% O_2, when the plants are grown in nutrient solution and aerated with normal air. The larger root systems indicate that much of the added photosynthate produced under low O_2 is translocated in large part to them.

Light-saturated photosynthetic rates on a leaf area basis appear to be significantly greater on leaves of the same clone grown under 4% O_2 than on those grown under 21% O_2. Table 32 lists light-saturated photosynthetic rates measured on leaves of the Jacksonville clone developed under 4% and 21% O_2 when the CO_2 concentration was that of normal air at approximately 320 ppm. The photosynthetic rates were measured both in normal air and under low O_2 (1.5%), and are listed in the table. From these data it is evident that the apparent light-saturated photosynthetic rates as measured in air are approximately 29% greater in leaves of propagules previously grown under 4% O_2 than in those grown under 21% O_2. The same relative difference is found also when the rates are measured in an atmosphere containing only 1.5% O_2. In the latter measurements the light-saturated photosynthetic rates on both low- and high-O_2-grown propagules show the usual enhancement of approximately 40% under low O_2 mentioned in previous pages of this chapter.

TABLE 32

Effect of O_2 Concentration during Growth on Subsequent Light-Saturated Photosynthetic Rates of *Mimulus cardinalis*

	Light-Saturated Photosynthetic Rates *					
	Measured in 21% O_2			Measured in 1.5% O_2		
	A. Grown in 4.0% O_2	B. Grown in 21.0% O_2	Percentage Increase of A over B	C. Grown in 4.0% O_2	D. Grown in 21.0% O_2	Percentage Increase of C over D
Apparent photosynthetic rates, clone 7211-4, μ mole CO_2 dm^{-2} min^{-1}	9.80	7.31	**34.2**	15.20	10.90	**39.5**

* Means of measurements on two propagules under each experimental treatment. Measurements with 21% and 1.5% O_2 were made on the same leaves after a 10-day experimental period. Grown at a constant temperature of 25° C; light intensity, 71,500 erg cm^{-2} sec^{-1} over a 24-hour photoperiod; CO_2 concentration, 320 ppm.

Growth experiments with varied CO_2 concentrations. The effect of varying the CO_2 content of the surrounding air on the growth of *Mimulus* plants has been studied in experiments in growth cabinets. In these comparisons, clones were propagated as cuttings rooted in a mixture of sand and vermiculite and were potted in soil in 4-inch pots before being subjected to the experimental treatments. The plants were watered frequently with nutrient solution throughout the experimental periods. The O_2 concentration was held constant at normal atmospheric composition. The CO_2 concentration was varied at predetermined levels ranging in different experiments from approximately 0.015% (150 ppm) to 0.150% (1500 ppm) by means of apparatus previously described.[1] Cool-white fluorescent lamps (Sylvania VHO) were used as light sources. Examples of experimental results, and the principal conclusions derived from them, follow.

Figure 55 illustrates the growth of two clones of *Mimulus cardinalis* grown for a 25-day period under 300 ppm CO_2 (right) as compared with 1250 ppm (left). The responses of the coastal clone 6546-5 from Los Trancos are shown below, and those of the Sierran foothill form from Priests Grade, 7210-1, above. At the start of this experiment all the propagules of both clones were comparable rooted cuttings 5–7 cm high. Both day and night temperatures were

[1] See French, Clair, and Hiesey (1962) and later improvements by Björkman et al. (1967).

kept constant at 25°, and light intensity was maintained at approximately 71,500 erg cm^{-2} sec^{-1} over a 12-hour photoperiod.

The marked enhancement in growth that took place in both clones at the higher CO_2 concentration is clearly evident in figure 55. At 1250 ppm CO_2 the leaves became somewhat modified, being narrower and thicker than those of propagules grown at 300 ppm, a difference that is not readily apparent in the illustration.

The somewhat greater degree of enhancement in growth of the coastal Los Trancos clone 6546-5 at the higher CO_2 concentration than of the Sierran foothill clone 7210-1 from Priests Grade is also evident in figure 55. Table 33 lists the dry weight increases per propagule for the two clones, and also their mean stem heights under the two CO_2 treatments at the end of the experimental period. From this table it is seen that the mean dry weight per propagule of the Los Trancos clone is 113% greater under the higher CO_2 concentration than under the lower, as compared with 74.3% for the Priests Grade clone. A similar differential between the two clones applies to stem heights.

In another experiment the growth of the same two clones was compared under a subatmospheric CO_2 concentration of 175 ppm and at the 300 ppm of normal air. Thus the low-CO_2 propagules were supplied with approximately half the CO_2 concentration present in the normal air with which the others were supplied. After a 39-day experimental treatment the dry weight increase of the Los Trancos clone was 268% greater in the propagules grown under 300 ppm CO_2 than in those grown under 175 ppm, whereas the corresponding gain was only 53% in the Priests Grade clone.

The difference in degree of enhancement of growth at high CO_2 concentration shown by the Los Trancos and Priests Grade clones of *M. cardinalis* suggests that a clone of the same species native to a higher elevation might show a still greater difference. Figure 56 shows the results of a comparison of the growth at 300 ppm and 1250 ppm CO_2 of two clones: clone 7210-1 from Priests Grade, at 300 m elevation (the same clone used in the previous experiments) and clone 7120-8 from San Antonio Peak, originally from an altitude of 2500 m. In this 31-day experiment the day temperature was again maintained at 25° and the light intensity held at approximately 71,500 erg cm^{-2} sec^{-1}. The greater growth of the Priests Grade clone under 1250 ppm CO_2 (shown at the lower left of the figure) than at 300 ppm (lower right) is clearly evident. The responses of the San Antonio Peak clone 7120-8 shown in the upper part of the figure may on first sight appear to be slight reversal of those observed in the Priests Grade clone. However, the difference in mean net dry weight increase between high and low CO_2 treatments of propagules of the San Antonio Peak clone is insignificant, as shown in table 34. This is in marked contrast with the Priests clone, whose net dry weight increases 100% at the higher CO_2 concentration.

There are also marked differences in the kinds of modifications in the leaves

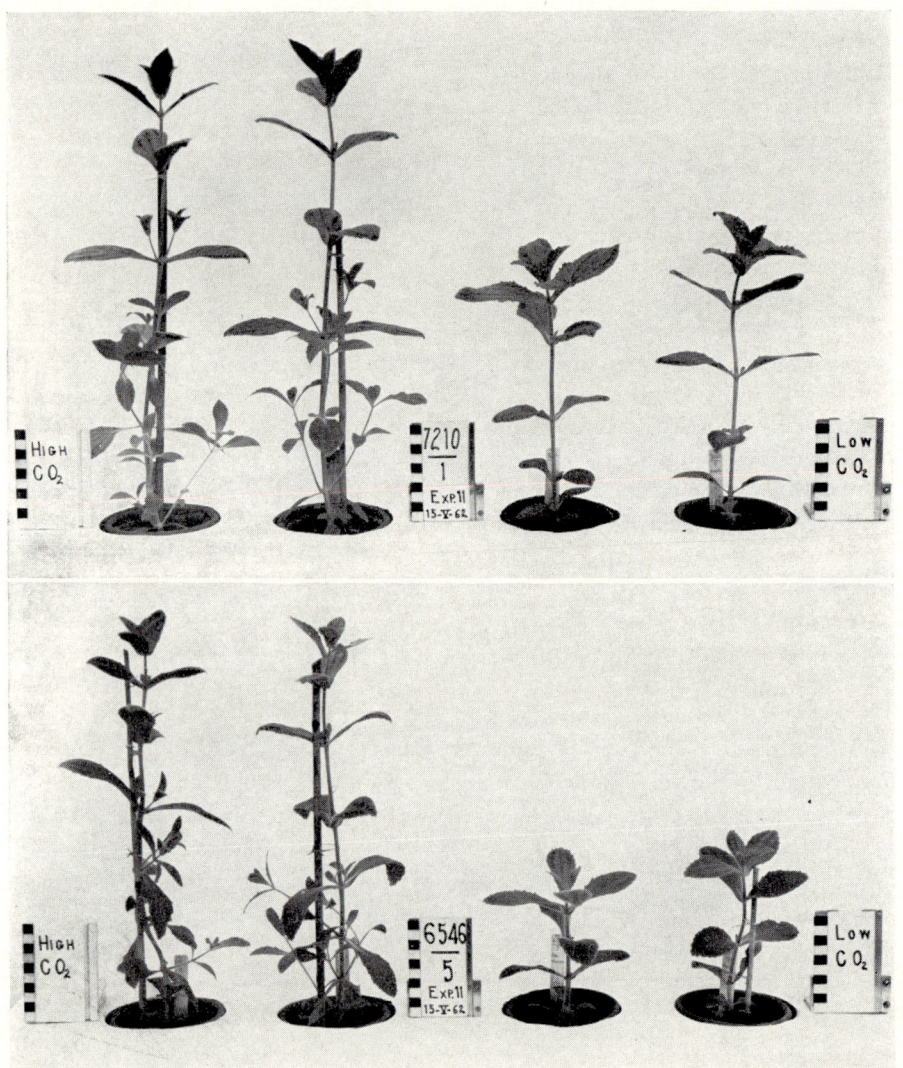

Figure 55. Growth of two clones of *Mimulus cardinalis* under high CO_2 concentration (*left*, 1250 ppm) and under low CO_2 concentration (*right*, 300 ppm).
Above: Clone 7210-1 originally from Priests Grade at 400 m elevation in the foothills of the Sierra Nevada of California.
Below: Clone 6546-5 from Los Trancos Creek from near sea-level along the coast of central California.
Temperature held constant at 25°; light intensity, approximately 71,500 erg cm^{-2} sec^{-1}; photoperiod, 12 hours; O_2 concentration, 21.0%; duration of experiment, 25 days.

TABLE 33

Effect of CO_2 Concentration on Growth of *Mimulus cardinalis* *

	6546-5 Los Trancos			7210-1 Priests Grade		
	CO_2 Concentration		Percentage Increase at 1250 ppm	CO_2 Concentration		Percentage Increase at 1250 ppm
	300 ppm	1250 ppm		300 ppm	1250 ppm	
Mean increase in dry weight per propagule, g	0.53 ± 0.09	1.13 ± 0.12	**113.0**	0.74 ± 0.12	1.29 ± 0.16	**74.3**
Mean increase in stem height, cm	17.7 ± 3.7	33.4 ± 3.5	**88.5**	25.8 ± 2.6	39.8 ± 4.3	**54.5**

* Values are means of 8 propagules for each treatment for a 25-day experiment. Temperature held constant at 25° C; light intensity, 71,500 ergs cm^{-2} sec^{-1} for a 12-hour photoperiod; O_2 concentration 21%; cf. figure 54.

Figure 56. Growth responses of contrasting altitudinal races of *Mimulus cardinalis* under high (*left*, 1250 ppm) and under low (*right*, 300 ppm) CO_2 concentrations.
Above: Clone 7120-8 from San Antonio Peak at 2200 m elevation.
Below: Clone 7210-1 from Priests Grade at 400 m elevation.

Day temperature, 25°, night temperature, 15°; light intensity, 71,500 erg cm^{-2} sec^{-1}; photoperiod, 12 hours; O_2 concentration, 21.0%; duration of experiment, 31 days. See also table 31.

TABLE 34

Effect of CO_2 Concentration on Growth of Low-Altitude and High-Altitude Clones of *Mimulus cardinalis*

	7210-1 Priests (400 m)			7120-8 San Antonio Peak (2200 m)		
	CO_2 concentration		Percentage Increase at 1250 ppm	CO_2 concentration		Percentage Increase at 1250 ppm
	300 ppm	1250 ppm		300 ppm	1250 ppm	
Mean increase in dry weight per propagule, grams*	0.42 ± 0.13	0.86 ± 0.25	100.4	1.10 ± 0.30	1.23 ± 0.28	insignificant

*Values are means of 10 propagules for each treatment over a 31-day experimental period. Temperature 25° during days with 15° nights; 12-hour photoperiod; light held at 71,500 ergs cm^{-2} sec^{-1} intensity, and O_2 at 21.0%; cf. figure 55.

and stems of the two clones under the high and low CO_2 treatments. The leaves of the San Antonio Peak clone become much thicker under high CO_2 concentration than under the lower concentration, and they have an additional one or two layers of palisade cells. The thickening of the leaves and stems of this clone at the high CO_2 concentration is accompanied by a reduction in leaf area, so that the overall appearance of this plant changes rather markedly, as shown in figure 56. Conversely, the leaves of the Priests Grade clone show only a small increase in leaf thickness, and no increase in the number of palisade layers. On the other hand, stems of the Priests clone are larger in diameter at the higher CO_2 concentration as a result of the overall enhanced growth.

Figure 57 compares the growth of a clone of the subalpine form of *M. lewisii* from near the Timberline station and that of the clone 7210-2 of *M. cardinalis* from Priests Grade, under high CO_2 concentration, with growth under low CO_2 concentration. In this 24-day experiment the propagules were grown at a day temperature of $25°$ and a night temperature of $15°$, conditions that are suitable for growth of both clones of these contrasting altitudinal races. Light intensity was maintained at 71,500 erg cm^{-2} sec^{-1}. The greater growth of the Priests Grade clone at the higher CO_2 concentration is obvious from the illustration, and is consistent with the previous experiments. As shown in table 35, the average dry weight increase per propagule of this clone was 65% higher when grown under the higher CO_2 concentration. The clone of subalpine *M. lewisii* likewise increased its mean dry weight at the higher CO_2 concentration, but only by 20%.

Under the conditions of this experiment the modifications induced by the higher CO_2 concentration in the leaves of the *M. lewisii* clone are marked, as can be seen in figure 57. The leaves are much narrower, shorter, and thicker under the higher CO_2 concentration, and the internodes on the stems are much shorter. Anatomical sections of leaves reveal one or two more layers of palisade parenchyma cells in propagules grown under 1250 ppm CO_2 than in those grown under 300 ppm, as well as more layers of spongy parenchyma. The light absorption of the high-CO_2 leaves is also measurably increased, especially in the 500–550-nm wavelength range. The modifications on the Priests Grade clone, on the other hand, are much less marked under the same two CO_2 concentrations.

McMahon and Bogorad (1966) compared the RuDP-carboxylase activity in leaf extracts of four clones of *M. cardinalis*, including the races represented in figure 56, and found marked differences in their Michaelis constants for $CO_{2\ total}$, which is equal to the sum of $CO_2 + HCO_3^- + H_2CO_3$. All four clones were grown at normal atmospheric concentration of CO_2. For 7210-1, a clone from Priests Grade, these Km values were in the range 18 to 20 mM as compared with 5 to 10 mM for San Antonio Peak clone 7120-15, a sister plant of 7120-8, illustrated in figure 56. From the data on the four clones studied (table 36) these authors concluded that the Michaelis constants for $CO_{2\ total}$

Figure 57. *Above:* Propagules of *Mimulus lewisii* (clone 7424-4) originally from near Timberline in the Harvey Monroe Hall Natural Area at 3200 m elevation, grown under 1250 ppm CO_2 (*left*) and 300 ppm (*right*).
Below: Propagules of *M. cardinalis* (clone 7210-2, originally from Priests Grade at 400 m elevation) grown under the same treatments.
Day temperature, 25°; night temperature, 15°; photoperiod, 12 hours; light intensity, 71,500 erg cm^{-2} sec^{-1}; O_2 concentration, 21.0%; duration of experiment, 24 days. See also table 32.

TABLE 35

Effect of CO_2 Concentration on Growth of *Mimulus cardinalis* and *M. lewisii*

	M. cardinalis Clone 7210-2, Priests			*M. lewisii* Clone 7424-4, Timberline		
	CO_2 concentration, ppm		Percentage Increase at 1250 ppm	CO_2 concentration, ppm		Percentage Increase at 1250 ppm
	300 ppm	1250 ppm		300 ppm	1250 ppm	
Mean increase in dry weight per propagule, g*	0.46 ± 0.08	0.76 ± 0.14	65.3	0.77 ± 0.13	0.93 ± 0.14	20.8

*Values are means of 10 propagules for each treatment over a 24-day experimental period. Temperature, 25° C during days and 15° C nights; light intensity, 71,500 ergs cm^{-2} sec^{-1} with a 12-hour photoperiod; O_2 concentration 21.0%; cf. figure 56.

appear to be inversely related to the native altitude of the *Mimulus* races. Since low Michaelis constants reflect a high affinity of the enzyme for CO_2 total, and vice versa, these *in vitro* biochemical data appear to be consistent with the conclusion, based on growth experiments, that races of *M. cardinalis* from higher altitudes have a greater capacity to absorb CO_2 from the surrounding atmosphere, when it is present in low concentrations, than races from lower altitudes. The Michaelis constants given above are 500 to 2,000 times higher than the CO_2 concentrations occurring in water in equilibrium with air, and would therefore seem to be of little relevance to CO_2 fixation *in vivo*. A very recent report by Cooper et al. (1969) provides evidence that of these molecular species of CO_2 total, only CO_2 itself can serve as an active substrate for the enzyme. Since the concentration of CO_2 at the pH used for the enzyme assay is

TABLE 36

Michaelis Constants for RuDP Carboxylase in Leaf Extracts of Different Races of *Mimulus cardinalis*

Clone	Native Altitude, m	Michaelis Constants,* K_m, mM Na H CO_3
7113-8 Los Trancos	45	19–22
7119-16 Baja California	550	12–15
7210-1 Priests Grade	400	18–23
7120-15 San Antonio Peak	2200	5–10

* For bicarbonate with crude preparations of RuDP carboxylase; mean values of five determinations (data from McMahon and Bogorad, 1966).

less than 1% of CO_2 total, the Michaelis constants, if recalculated for CO_2, would become more reasonable, but still about 5 to 20 times higher than the CO_2 concentration in water in equilibrium with air.

Evidence relating light-saturated photosynthetic rates with RuDP carboxylase activity in sun and shade plants has been presented by Björkman (1968). It is possible that the different growth responses of diverse species and races to CO_2 concentration are not related to differences in affinity of the carboxylation enzyme to CO_2, but rather to the inhibiting effect of O_2 on CO_2 uptake (see pages 124–131 of this chapter). If different species and races of plants differ in their sensitivity to high O_2 concentration, then different degrees of CO_2 dependence in the presence of normal air may be related to the O_2 effect.

It is well known that, in general, the degree of stomatal opening decreases with increasing CO_2 concentration. This suggests that the different degrees of enhancement of growth by increased CO_2 concentration could be related to differences among races and species in the degree of sensitivity to CO_2 of their stomatal control systems. At present, we have no direct evidence either to support or to negate such a hypothesis. Recent results obtained in this laboratory from simultaneous measurements of CO_2 uptake and transpiration rate under varying O_2 concentrations on leaves of *Atriplex patula* and *Mimulus cardinalis* indicate, however, that stomatal resistance may not be a critical factor in limiting CO_2 uptake under conditions of ample water supply and normal air.

Measurements by Billings, Clebsch, and Mooney (1961) on photosynthetic rates of high-altitude vs. low-altitude races of *Oxyria digyna* (a race from Logan Pass, at 2000 m elevation, and one from near sea-level, at the mouth of the Pitmegea River in Alaska) indicated higher photosynthetic rates for the high-altitude race than for the lowland race at CO_2 concentrations in the range 400 to 100 ppm. These authors suggest that the high-altitude ecotype may have a greater inherent capacity than the lowland form to absorb CO_2 under the reduced partial pressure of this gas at high altitudes.

Whether or not species and races of plants from high altitudes, where the partial pressure of CO_2 is relatively low, have evolved forms that are in general more efficient than lowland forms in absorbing CO_2 at low CO_2 concentrations is a question that merits further investigation. The various pieces of evidence reviewed above suggest that this may be the case.

EFFECTS OF TEMPERATURE

As may be expected, temperature has a profound influence on the growth of all those races of *M. cardinalis* and *M. lewisii* that have been studied. The magnitude and sometimes even the direction of the growth responses to varying temperatures could not, however, have been accurately predicted from the responses at the altitudinal field stations described in Chapter II. Photosynthetic rate and the activity of photosynthetic enzymes are directly and markedly influenced by temperature. Moreover, as indicated by the examples given below, photosynthetic responses as well as biochemical characteristics, including chlorophyll and protein content and levels of carboxylation enzymes in the leaves, are influenced by the temperature under which the plants have previously been grown.

EFFECTS OF TEMPERATURE ON GROWTH. During 1962–1966 a number of experiments in controlled growth chambers were conducted to compare the growth of clones of *M. cardinalis* and *M. lewisii* under different temperature treatments. Some examples will be presented to indicate the kinds of responses that have been observed.

Figure 58 shows the growth responses of three contrasting clones of *M. cardinalis* when grown at constant day and night temperatures of 10° and 20° C, respectively, with a 12-hour photoperiod. The three clones are 6546-5, Los Trancos, from near sea-level along the central California coast; 6694-105, Yosemite, from the central Sierra Nevada at 1200 m elevation; and 7120-15, San Antonio Peak, from 2200 m elevation in the San Gabriel range of southern California. At 10° C all three grow slowly, with no evidence of flowering during the experimental period. At this cool temperature, however, the coastal,

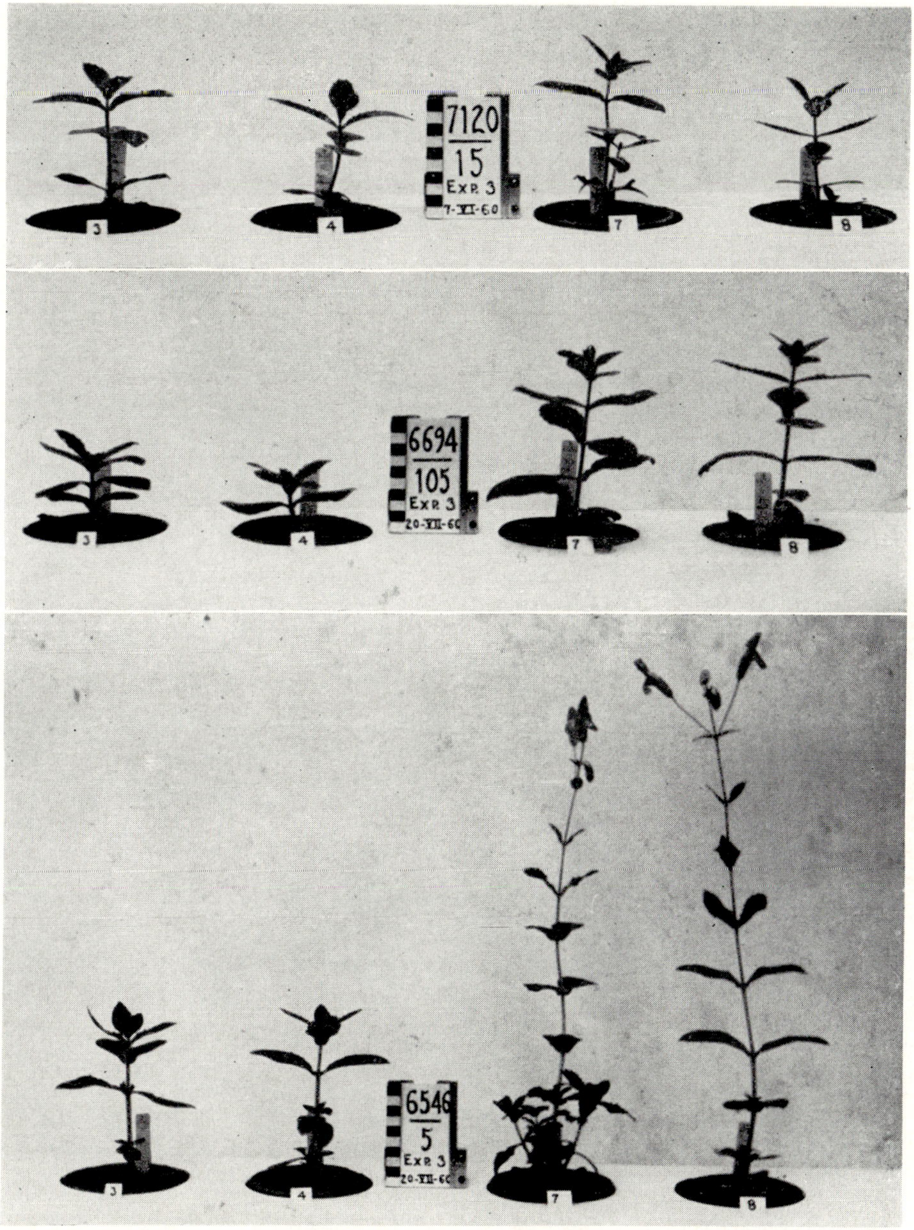

Figure 58. Growth responses of *Mimulus cardinalis* clones at 10° (*left*) and 20° (*right*).
Above: Clone 7120-15, originally from San Antonio Peak at 2200 m elevation.
Center: Clone 6694-105, originally from Yosemite Valley at an altitude of 1200 m elevation.
Below: Clone 6546-5, originally from Los Trancos Creek near sea-level.
Temperatures held constant during days and nights; light intensity, 71,500 erg cm^{-2} sec^{-1}; photoperiod, 10 hours; CO_2 concentration, 300 ppm; O_2, 21.0%; duration of experiment, 41 days.

normally winter-active Los Trancos clone shows somewhat more growth activity than either of the two other clones originating from montane habitats with colder winter climates.

At 20° C growth in all three clones is greater than at 10° C. This is especially visible in the coastal Los Trancos clone which attained full flowering during the 41-day experimental period. Its propagules attained a net dry weight increase of 72 percent over the propagule grown at 10° C (table 37). At 20° C the Yosemite clone increased by a comparable amount in relation to its growth at 10° C, but did not flower. The San Antonio Peak clone weighed only 32 percent more at 20° than at 10°, and, like Yosemite, produced no visible flower buds under these conditions. At the beginning of the experiment all three clones were started as comparable small rooted cuttings approximately 4 cm in height.

TABLE 37

Dry Weight Increase in *Mimulus cardinalis* Clones at Two Temperatures

Clone	mg per Propagule *		Increase at 20° over 10° C	
	10° C	20° C	mg dry wt	percent
6546-5 Los Trancos, coastal	0.656 ± 0.041	1.179 ± 0.085	0.523	79.5
6694-105 Yosemite, 1200 m	0.402 ± 0.018	0.796 ± 0.049	0.393	98.0
7120-15 San Antonio Peak, 2200 m	0.391 ± 0.022	0.586 ± 0.059	0.195	49.8

* Mean values of 4 propagules of each clone for a 41-day experimental period. Temperature held constant; light intensity, 71,500 erg cm^{-2} sec^{-1} for a 10-hour photoperiod; CO_2 concentration, 300 ppm; O_2, 21.0%; cf. figure 57.

The temperature responses of the three clones, illustrated in figure 58, thus appear to be consistent with the climatic differences in their native habitats. Los Trancos is from a coastal climate having winter rains during which the plants are in active growth. Summer temperatures are likewise mild, and seldom as high as the summer temperatures in montane areas such as Yosemite and San Antonio Peak. Both Yosemite and San Antonio Peak are winter dormant in the mild Stanford garden, as in their native habitats.

At the mid-altitude Mather transplant station the winter-active Los Trancos clone typically sends out new shoots during occasional warm, snow-free, periods of winter and in early spring, after the snow melts, only to be frozen shortly thereafter by frosts. This usually results in fatal injury, as the food reserves become exhausted. The winter-dormant, slower-moving Yosemite and San Antonio Peak clones are less vulnerable to these early-season freezes and are able to survive at this mid-altitude station.

Other experiments in the controlled cabinets with these and other clones of *M. cardinalis* show that, in general, most forms of this species grow slowly at

15° or below, appreciably more rapidly at 20°, and even more rapidly at 25° C or higher. As shown earlier by Went (1957), many other species of higher plants may show substantial increases in dry weight yield when cool night temperatures are alternated with warm day temperatures, compared with growth under constant temperature. This has also been found to be true of *Mimulus*. Figure 59 shows propagules of two clones of *Mimulus cardinalis* started as small rooted cuttings, after a 35-day period in which one group was maintained at a constant day and night temperature of 20° C; another was maintained at a constant 30° C; and a third was maintained at 30° C during the day and 15° during the night. In these experiments the plants were provided with a 12-hour photoperiod. The large enhancement in growth of both clones at the alternating day and night temperatures, as compared with the growth at either of the constant temperatures, is clearly evident. The differences are even more impressive when compared on the basis of dry weight yields, shown at the left in table 38.

A point of special interest is the differential responses between the Los Trancos and Priests Grade clones, illustrated in figure 59. Under the relatively low light intensity in which these plants were grown (35,000 erg cm^{-2} sec^{-1}, 12-hour day), the coastal clone 6546-5 from Los Trancos produced at 30° C only one-fifth the dry weight increase made at 20° C. Clone 7210-1 from the warm Sierran foothills at Priests Grade yielded at 30° two-thirds of the dry weight increase recorded at 20° C (left half of table 38). That both clones produced less dry matter at 30° than at 20° C can probably be attributed to a greater respiratory loss at 30° C, especially during the dark period. When the same clones are grown under the lower night temperature of 15° C, marked enhancement in dry weight increase occurs in both.

Parallel experiments with the same two clones grown at the same temperatures but under more than twice the light intensity (100,000 erg cm^{-2} sec^{-1}), resulted in higher overall dry weight growth increases. The relative degree of differential response between the two clones was altered, however. In Los Trancos the dry weight increment of growth was approximately the same at 20° as at 30° C, whereas in Priests the increment was 50 percent higher at 30° C than at 20° C (right half of table 38). Thus the Priests clone again was relatively more efficient in growth at 30° C than Los Trancos. To the eye of the observer, the growth of both clones would appear vigorous at 20° C at both the low and the high light intensities. Alternating a day temperature of 30° with 15° at night increased the growth of both clones under the high light intensity, but the degree of enhancement was less evident than under the lower light (table 38).

These results are consistent with our knowledge of the importance of light intensity for growth in *Mimulus*, as described on pages 94–96. The light intensity required for saturation of photosynthesis in both the Los Trancos and Priests clones is in the order of about 250,000 erg cm^{-2} sec^{-1}. For the plants

TABLE 38

Effect of Alternating Day and Night Temperatures on Growth of *Mimulus cardinalis* Clones *

	Growth under Low Light, 35,000 erg cm^{-2} sec^{-1}			Growth under High Light, 100,000 erg cm^{-2} sec^{-1}		
	Constant Temperatures		Alternating Temperatures	Constant Temperatures		Alternating Temperatures
	20° C	30° C	30° D, 15° N	20° C	30° C	30° D, 15° N
6546-5 Los Trancos, dry weight increase, g	1.24 ± 0.14	0.22 ± 0.06	2.21 ± 0.12	1.43 ± 0.19	1.15 ± 0.21	2.39 ± 0.08
7210-1 Priests, dry weight increase, g	1.62 ± 0.14	1.13 ± 0.14	2.42 ± 0.17	1.39 ± 0.13	1.88 ± 0.26	2.66 ± 0.27

* Values are means of 8 replicated propagules over an experimental period of 35 days with 12-hour photoperiod; O$_2$ and CO$_2$ at normal air concentration.

grown under low light illustrated in figure 59 the intensity was approximately one-seventh that of saturation; under the high light intensity, less than one-half.

When alternating day and night temperatures are maintained at the ex-

Figure 59. Growth of *Mimulus cardinalis* clones at constant temperatures as compared with alternating day and night temperatures.
Above: Propagules of clone 7210-1, originally from Priests Grade in the foothills of the Sierra Nevada of California, grown at a constant temperature of 20° (*left*), 30° (*center*), and alternating day and night temperatures of 30° and 15° (*right*).
Below: Propagules of clone 6546-5, originally from Los Trancos along the central California coast, grown under the same conditions.
Light intensity, 35,000 erg cm^{-2} sec^{-1}; photoperiod, 12 hours; CO_2 concentration, 300 ppm; O_2, 21.0%; duration of experiment, 35 days.

tremes of 35°–25° C as compared with 15°–5° C, marked differences in rate of growth and in flowering development are evident in *M. cardinalis*. A temperature of 15° C during the day and 5° C during the night results in slow growth in all races of *M. cardinalis*, irrespective of their altitudinal origin. An extremely high day temperature of 35° combined with a 25° C night temperature results in a greatly increased growth and flowering. Table 39 summarizes data from an experiment in which the growth of clone 7210-2 from Priests Grade was compared with clone 7120-15 from San Antonio Peak at the 35°–25° and 15°–5° combinations. The capacity of such distinct altitudinal forms of *Mimulus cardinalis* to grow at such contrasting temperatures reflects the wide overall tolerance of this species whose forms nevertheless show such differential responses as are illustrated in figures 58 and 59.

A study reported by Vickery (1967) on the growth of a botanical garden form of *M. cardinalis* in the Earhart Laboratory of the California Institute of Technology at Pasadena also points to a wide tolerance for the growth of this species at different temperatures. In another investigation conducted in the

TABLE 39

Growth of *Mimulus cardinalis* Clones at Contrasting Alternating Day and Night Temperatures

	7210-2 Priests Grade		7120-15 San Antonio Peak	
	35° D, 25° N	15° D, 5° N	35° D, 25° N	15° D, 15° N
Dry weight increase, g	1.85 ± 0.27	0.75 ± 0.23	1.19 ± 0.30	0.36 ± 0.09
Increase in stem height, cm	45.2 ± 0.3	8.6 ± 0.02	34.7 ± 0.3	5.65 ± 0.01
Mean number of flowers per stem	6.1 ± 0.5	none	4.5 ± 0.6	none

* Values are means of 10 propagules of each clone for a 37-day experimental period. Light intensity, 71,500 erg cm^{-2} sec^{-1}; 12-hour photoperiod; normal air concentration of CO_2 and O_2.

Earhart Laboratory, Dr. Morris Cline (1970)[1] compared the growth of seedlings of the Priests Grade race of *M. cardinalis* with that of seedlings of *M. lewisii* from near Timberline at constant day and night temperatures of 3°, 7°, 11°, 15°, 19°, 23°, and 27° C over an 8-month period during 1967. One set of seedlings of each species was grown under a 16-hour day and another under an 8-hour day. Light was supplied by fluorescent lamps supplemented by incandescent light and was of an intensity much below saturation for both species. Under the 16-hour day both *M. cardinalis* and *M. lewisii* seedlings (7 replicates in each experiment) attained maximum stem growth and dry weight yield at 19° C. At 27° *M. lewisii* succumbed to the high temperature, whereas *M. cardinalis* maintained active growth. At 3° C both *M. lewisii* and *M. cardinalis* made very little growth, but the increment of increase in *M. lewisii* was approximately twice that in *M. cardinalis*. Under the short 8-hour day the mortality of *M. lewisii* seedlings was very high, with measurable growth only at 7°, 11°, 15°, and 19°, with maximum dry weight yield at 19°. The *M. cardinalis*

[1] We are indebted to Dr. Cline, now at the Ohio State University, for data relating to his experiments, and for permission to summarize some of the results of his study.

seedlings under the same 8-hour day survived over the entire range from 3° to 27°, with maximum dry weight yield again at 19°C. Under the 8-hour day flowering stem development was markedly retarded as compared with the 16-hour day, but *M. cardinalis* at 23° and 27° C developed elongated flowering stems. The results from Dr. Cline's experiments reflect the interaction between temperature and the supply of light energy for growth of these ecologically contrasting species of *Mimulus*.

Although the field measurements on leaf temperatures in contrasting natural habitats of *M. cardinalis* and *M. lewisii* described on pages 93–94 show a less pronounced difference than might be expected, experiments in the controlled growth cabinets reveal that *M. lewisii* is less tolerant of warm temperatures than *M. cardinalis*. Consistently successful results for vegetative propagation by cuttings and for growing cloned propagules of *M. lewisii* for photosynthetic measurements were realized only when day temperatures were maintained within the range of 20° to 23° C, and night temperatures between 15° and 17° C. In contrast, cuttings of *M. cardinalis* of different races can easily be rooted and established not only under these conditions, but also under a wide range of temperatures (both in controlled cabinets and in uncontrolled greenhouse conditions) including extremes at which all forms of *M. lewisii* invariably fail.

Studies on responses to temperature of growth and photosynthetic and biochemical characteristics were made during 1968 and 1969 with the clone 7211-4, *M. cardinalis* Jacksonville, from the warm Sierran foothills of California at 200 m elevation, and with clone 7635-2, *M. lewisii* Logan Pass, originally from an alpine habitat in Glacier National Park at 2,000 m elevation. The upper half of figure 60 illustrates the growth response of the two clones at 10° and 30° C after 17 days, and the lower half of the same figure depicts the same clones after a 30-day experiment at the same temperatures. In these experiments both clones were started from comparable rooted cuttings established under identical conditions in a growth cabinet. The light intensity was maintained at 53,000 erg cm^{-2} sec^{-1} for a 16-hour photoperiod, the day and night temperature remaining constant. The CO_2 concentration was held at 0.032% (320 ppm) and the O_2 concentration at 21.0%.

As is evident from the upper photographs in figure 60, the Jacksonville clone at 30° C developed normal, healthy leaves and stems, whereas the Logan clone produced weak, slender stems with abnormally reduced leaves and precocious flower buds after the 17-day experimental period. During this 17-day period the increase in growth of the Jacksonville clone was 2.4 times greater at 30° than at 10°, whereas in Logan the increment of growth at these contrasting temperatures was approximately the same (a ratio of 0.9) as shown in table 40. The differential growth responses of the two clones at the two temperatures reveal a breakdown of the Logan clone at 30° C in contrast with the Jacksonville clone which grows successfully both at 30° and at 10° C.

Figure 60. Growth of *Mimulus lewisii* Logan (clone 7635-2) in comparison with *M. cardinalis* Jacksonville (clone 7211-4) at 10° and 30°, after 17 days (above) and after 31 days (below).

Day and night temperatures held constant; light intensity, 53,000 erg cm^{-2} sec^{-1}; photoperiod, 16 hours; CO_2 concentration, 0.032%; O_2, 21.0%. See also table 37.

This is clearly illustrated in the lower half of figure 60; whereas after 31 days at these temperatures Logan dies at 30°, Jacksonville continues to thrive.

In view of the marked hybrid vigor observed at the altitudinal transplant stations in the F_1 progeny of *M. lewisii* and *M. cardinalis*, as described in Chapter II, the growth of the F_1 seedling progeny of the *M. lewisii* clone 7635-2 and the *M. cardinalis* clone 7211-4 was compared with the growth of rooted cuttings of the parents at 10° and 30° C. The conditions of illumination and CO_2 and O_2 concentration were the same as in the preceding temperature experiment. Although the 14 seedling replicates grown at each temperature were fairly variable, their growth response at 30° was intermediate between the parents, as shown by the mean dry weight increases of the F_1 progeny listed

TABLE 40

Growth of *Mimulus lewisii* Logan, *M. cardinalis* Jacksonville, and Their F_1 Hybrids at 10° and 30° C

	Dry Weight Increase, g		Ratio
			Growth at 30° C
	10° C	30° C	Growth at 10° C
Mimulus lewisii (clone 7635-2) *	0.139 ± 0.023	0.126 ± 0.064	**0.9**
Mimulus cardinalis (clone 7211-4) *	0.149 ± 0.038	0.337 ± 0.077	**2.4**
F_1 hybrids (culture 7718) †	0.232 ± 0.015	0.277 ± 0.025	**1.1**

* Values are means of 7 replicated propagules. Experimental period, 17 days; day and night temperatures held constant; light intensity, 53,000 erg cm^{-2} sec^{-1} with a 16-hour photoperiod. Concentration of CO_2, 0.032%; O_2, 21.0%.

† Values are means of 14 replicated seedlings grown under same conditions as the parents.

at the bottom of table 40. Evidence of hybrid vigor under the high temperature is therefore lacking, but at 10° C the growth of the hybrid is apparently greater than that of either parent, indicating heterosis at this temperature.

Effect of temperature on photosynthetic and biochemical characteristics. Light-saturated photosynthetic rates in *Mimulus* and in many other plants are often characterized by a comparatively small dependence on temperature in the range 15° to 30° C. This relatively small effect of temperature on light-saturated photosynthesis has generally been interpreted to mean that photosynthesis is limited primarily by physical barriers to CO_2 diffusion, since any process that is limited by enzyme activity may be expected to exhibit a marked temperature dependence.

Recent evidence indicates that the weak influence of temperature on photosynthetic rate as measured in air is largely attributable to the inhibiting effect of O_2 in photosynthetic uptake. As shown in figure 61, the temperature dependence in both the Jacksonville and Logan clones is much greater when measured in 1.5% O_2, where the inhibiting effect of oxygen is greatly reduced, than in the presence of 21.0% O_2. These results are in agreement with those obtained by Joliffe and Tregunna (1968) for wheat leaves and by Björkman and Gauhl (1968) for *Marchantia*.

In 1.5% O_2 and 0.03% CO_2 the Arrhenius equation was found to be approximately valid for both the Logan and Jacksonville clones of *Mimulus* in the lower temperature range 5° to 15° C. It is likely that the deviation from the Arrhenius equation at higher temperatures under 1.5% O_2 and 0.03% CO_2 is largely attributable to the circumstance that the solubility of CO_2 in the liquid

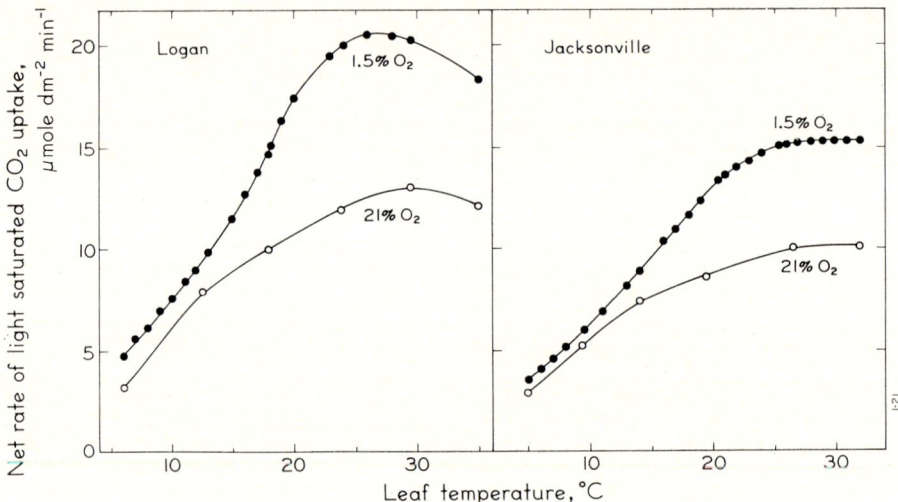

Figure 61. Light-saturated photosynthetic rates of *Mimulus lewisii* Logan (clone 7635-2) and *M. cardinalis* Jacksonville (clone 7211-4) as a function of temperature when measured in 1.5% and 21.0% O_2.

Plants previously grown at a constant temperature of 20°; light intensity, 53,000 erg cm^{-2} sec^{-1}; CO_2 concentration, 320 ppm; O_2, 21.0%.

phase decreases with increasing temperature. Similarly, the increased inhibition by 21% O_2 with increased temperature may be related to the effect of temperature on the solubility of CO_2 (see page 127). At the higher CO_2 concentration of 0.07% the linear relationship between the logarithm of the photosynthetic rate and the increase of absolute temperature is obtained up to at least 27° C. An example of such an Arrhenius plot is shown in figure 62. The energies of activation calculated from the Arrhenius plots yielded values of approximately 16–19 Kcal mol^{-1}, equivalent to a Q_{10} value between 2.5 and 3.3. These values are comparatively high for biological reactions.

We have obtained very similar high values for CO_2 fixation *in vitro* with partially purified preparations of RuDP carboxylase from *Mimulus* and *Marchantia*. The close agreement between the activation energies for photosynthesis

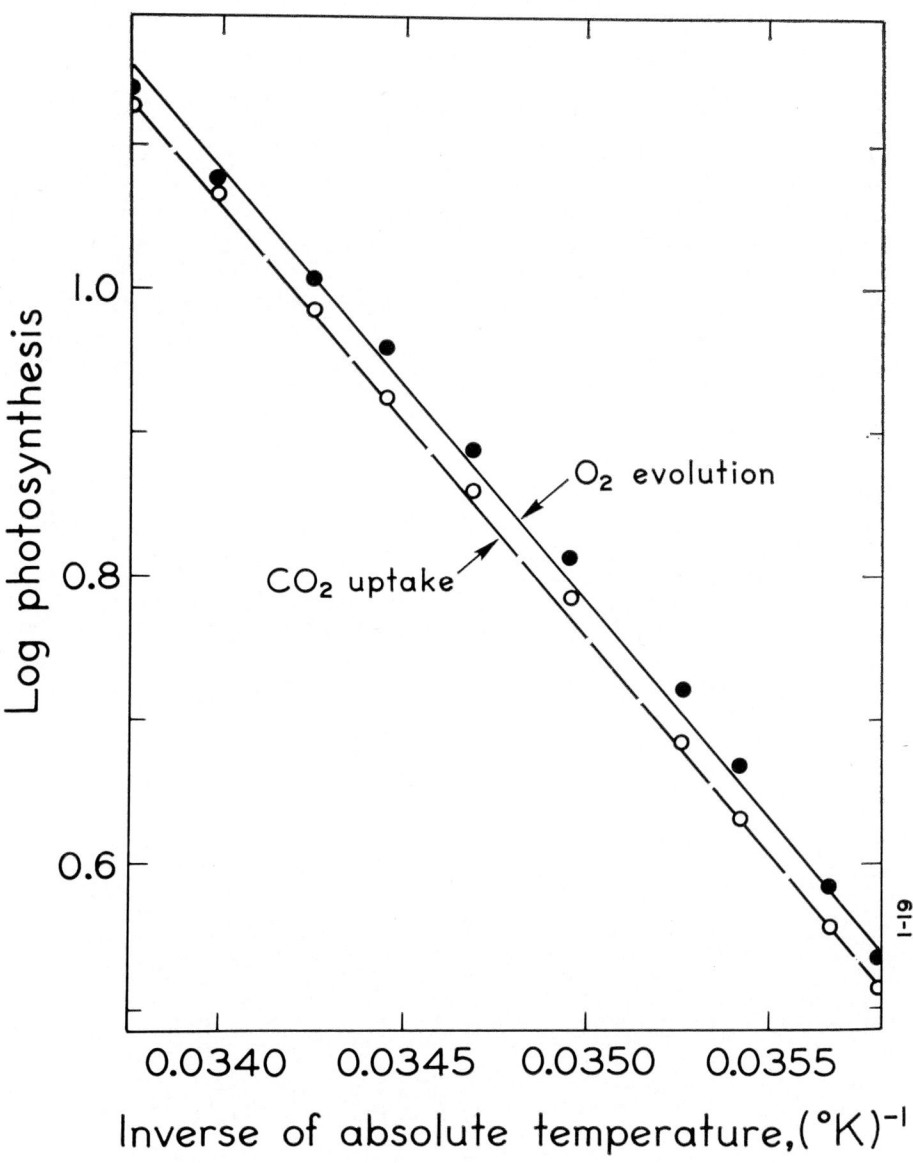

Figure 62. Arrhenius plots of the effect of temperature on the rates of photosynthetic O_2 evolution and CO_2 uptake in a leaf of *Mimulus verbenaceus* (clone 7637-2).
The CO_2 concentration was held at 700 ppm and O_2 at 0.160% (1600 ppm). Saturating white light of 2.5×10^5 erg cm^{-2} sec^{-1} intensity (400–700 nm) was used.

and the carboxylation reaction *in vitro* might, of course, be coincidental. On the other hand, it could reflect a causal relationship. A close agreement between the two processes would be expected if the activation energies for the RuDP carboxylase-catalyzed reaction *in vitro* is approximately the same as *in vivo*, and if the carboxylation reaction is a major limiting step in light-saturated photosynthesis at low temperatures.

No marked differences in activation energy for light-saturated photosynthesis were found between the Logan and the Jacksonville clones when both were previously grown at 20° C and at a light intensity of 53,000 erg cm^{-2} sec^{-1} (400–700 nm). The main difference between the two clones is that Logan exhibits a higher rate of photosynthesis than Jacksonville at all temperatures in the range 5° to 30° C, as shown in figure 61. Another difference is that in Logan the photosynthetic rate declines at temperatures above 25°, whereas in Jacksonville such a decline is not apparent until the temperature considerably exceeds 30° C.

A question of great importance is the extent to which the photosynthetic characteristics of a given genotype are affected by the temperature under which the plant is grown. This question has been investigated by Mooney and West (1964) and Mooney and Shropshire (1967) with several higher plant species including *Encelia californica* and *Polygonium bistortoides,* and in our laboratory with the liverwort *Marchantia polymorpha* (Björkman and Gauhl, 1968).

Mooney and co-workers found that both short-term (less than 24 hours) and long-term (three weeks or more) acclimation to cold and warm temperatures markedly affected both the rate and the optimum temperature of photosynthesis in normal air. Plants acclimated to cold were more efficient, in terms of percentage of maximum photosynthesis, at low temperatures, whereas plants acclimated to warm temperatures were more efficient at higher temperatures.

In *Marchantia* the rate of photosynthesis in normal air expressed on the basis of dry weight of the thallus tissue was higher at all temperatures when the plant had been grown at 30° or 20° than when grown at 10°. Slightly higher temperatures were required to reach maximum rates of photosynthesis when the clone was grown at 30° than when it was grown at 10° or 20° C. The dependence of photosynthesis on temperature was much greater when rates were measured under 2% O_2 than under 21.0% O_2, but the differences in rate and temperature dependence among clones grown at different temperatures during growth were essentially the same at 2% and 21%. The Arrhenius energy of activation in the range 5° to 15° C was unaffected by the temperatures under which a given clone was grown. The main effect of temperature during growth on subsequent photosynthetic performance was that higher temperatures were required for maximum photosynthetic rate when the temperature during growth was high. Expressed on the basis of protein, the photosynthetic rate at all temperatures was highest when the clone was grown at 30° and lowest when grown at 10°. Apparently, the *Marchantia* clone used in this study lacks the ability to increase its photosynthetic rate at higher temperatures when it has been subjected to low temperatures during growth.

Similar experiments were conducted on the Jacksonville clone of *Mimulus cardinalis*, the results of which are shown in figure 63. The dependence of the light-saturated rate of CO_2 uptake on temperature was determined on intact, single, attached leaves of the clone 7211-4 at 10°, 20°, and 30° C. The rate of photosynthesis at 15° as measured under 1.5% O_2 was little affected by the temperatures under which the clone member was grown. To facilitate direct comparisons of the temperature curves shown in figure 63, the light-saturated photosynthetic rate for each leaf at 15° C and under 1.5% O_2 is plotted as equal to unity.

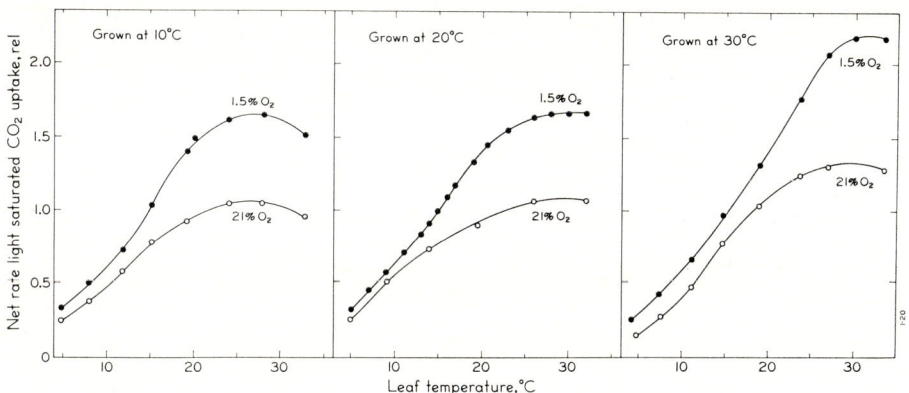

Figure 63. Effect of temperature during growth on subsequent temperature dependence of light-saturated photosynthetic rates under 1.5% and 21.0% O_2 in *Mimulus cardinalis* Jacksonville, clone 7211-4.

Measurements were made with a CO_2 concentration of 300 ppm. Saturating light of 3.4×10^5 erg cm^{-2} sec^{-1} intensity (400–700 nm) was used.

The temperature dependence of photosynthesis under 1.5% and 21% O_2 is very similar for leaves that were grown at 10° and 20° C, even though there is a slight shift of the optimum toward lower temperatures when the plant was grown at 10° as compared with 20°. When the temperature during growth is increased to 30°, a more pronounced change in the shape of the temperature curve takes place, with considerably higher rates of photosynthesis at the higher temperatures than when grown at 10° or 20° C. This effect is present when measured under 1.5% and under 21.0% O_2, but it is more evident at the lower O_2 concentration. This indicates strongly that the modification in temperature dependence is not caused primarily by changes in the rate of the processes underlying the inhibiting effect of O_2 on photosynthesis (i.e., "photorespiration"). The activation energy for photosynthesis in the range 5°–10° C is nevertheless not significantly affected by the temperature under which the clone was grown.

Determinations of RuDP carboxylase activity and of the content of soluble protein and chlorophyll in the leaves were made on the Logan and Jacksonville clones grown at 10°, 20°, and 30° C. All analyses were made during the period in which both clones were in active growth at the three temperatures. The results of this study are summarized in table 41.

In both clones the soluble protein content of the leaves was higher at 10° than at 20° or 30° C. This accumulation of soluble protein in *Mimulus* is particularly great in the Jacksonville clone. Steemann-Nielsen and Jørgensen (1968) found that the soluble protein content in the diatom *Skeletonema costatum*, a species occurring in cool Danish waters, was far greater when cultured at 7° than at 20° C, and that the photosynthetic rate was essentially

TABLE 41

EFFECT OF TEMPERATURE DURING GROWTH ON LEVELS OF RuDP CARBOXYLASE CHLOROPHYLL AND SOLUBLE PROTEIN ON *Mimulus* CLONES

	Mimulus lewisii Logan, 7635-2			*M. cardinalis* Jacksonville, 7211-4		
	10° C	20° C	30° C	10° C	20° C	30° C
RuDP carboxylase activity,* μmol CO_2 (g fresh wt.)$^{-1}$ min^{-1}	10.6	10.0	3.62	5.2	7.9	6.5
Chlorophyll content, a + b mg (g fresh wt.)$^{-1}$	1.62	1.53	0.78	1.21	1.25	1.00
Soluble protein,† mg (g fresh wt.)$^{-1}$	26.2	20.0	13.9	39.9	15.9	16.3

* Assay conditions: 0.05 M Na H CO_3; 10^{-4} M ribulose 1,5-diphosphate; pH 8.0, 30° C.
† Protein was determined by the Folin-Lowry method.

the same at all light intensities when measured at these two temperatures. These results suggested to them the attractive hypothesis that at lower temperatures the diatom produces more photosynthetic enzymes, which compensate for the reduction in light-saturated photosynthetic rate that would otherwise be expected at the lower temperature. In *Mimulus,* however, the RuDP carboxylase content of the leaves was found not to increase at the lower temperatures as did the soluble protein content, as shown in table 41. There appears, therefore, to be no satisfactory explanation for the observed increase in total soluble protein content at low temperatures.

In the Logan clone growth at 30° results in a very much reduced RuDP carboxylase activity. Similarly, the chlorophyll content of its leaves was much lower at 30° than at 10° or 20°, whereas in the Jacksonville clone the corresponding values were essentially the same at the three different temperatures. These results provide evidence of a breakdown of the photosynthetic apparatus in the Logan clone at 30°, but there is no evidence of any detrimental effects of high temperature on the Jacksonville clone. These data therefore suggest that *Mimulus* races from warm environments are capable of high rates of photosynthesis and growth at temperatures that cause a breakdown of the photosynthetic apparatus in races from cold habitats. We do not know whether the detrimental effects of high temperature on the Logan clone are primarily due to an intrinsically low degree of temperature stability of its photosynthetic apparatus, or whether processes responsible for the continuous synthesis of its components, such as photosynthetic pigments and enzymes, are adversely affected by high temperature, so that the rate of their synthesis does not keep up with the rate of their breakdown.

PHOTOSYNTHETIC PERFORMANCE OF PARENTAL AND HYBRID COMBINATIONS

Of particular interest are comparisons between the photosynthetic performance of hybrids of contrasting species and ecological races of *Mimulus* and that of their parents. Through such comparisons information may be gained regarding the inheritance of differences in performance between races. It is furthermore of interest to determine whether or not hybrid vigor between contrasting races, as expressed in different environments, can be related to photosynthetic capacity.

Hybrids between M. lewisii and M. cardinalis. Figure 64 shows curves of light-saturated apparent photosynthetic rates of clone 7405-4, *M. lewisii* from Timberline (above), and 6546-5, *M. cardinalis* from Los Trancos (below), for propagules of each clone grown under strong and weak light. The measurements were made at 20.0° C, using light of wavelengths between 600 and 700 nm. The most striking feature of the curves is the higher light-saturated rate for *M. cardinalis* as compared with *M. lewisii*. Another is the difference in the degree to which the photosynthetic rates of the two clones are influenced by their previous growth under the two light intensities. When grown under weak light, the light-saturated photosynthetic rate of the Los Trancos clone was reduced to approximately 50% of that of the propagule grown under strong light, whereas in the Timberline clone the corresponding reduction was only about 21%.

In these measurements the propagules of both clones were grown under identical conditions in controlled growth cabinets. The day temperature was maintained at 22° and the night temperature at 15° C, with a 12-hour photoperiod. Both clones have the capacity to grow under a wide range of light intensities when subjected to the relatively cool temperatures (20–22° C days and 15–17° nights) that are compatible with comparably vigorous growth for both of these altitudinally contrasting plants (see also the discussion on pages 102–105).

The light-saturated photosynthetic rates of both reciprocal F_1 hybrids of these clones, grown under the same conditions, were intermediate between those of the parents. Moreover, three F_2 individuals having diverse morphological characters inherited as recombinations from the contrasting parents were

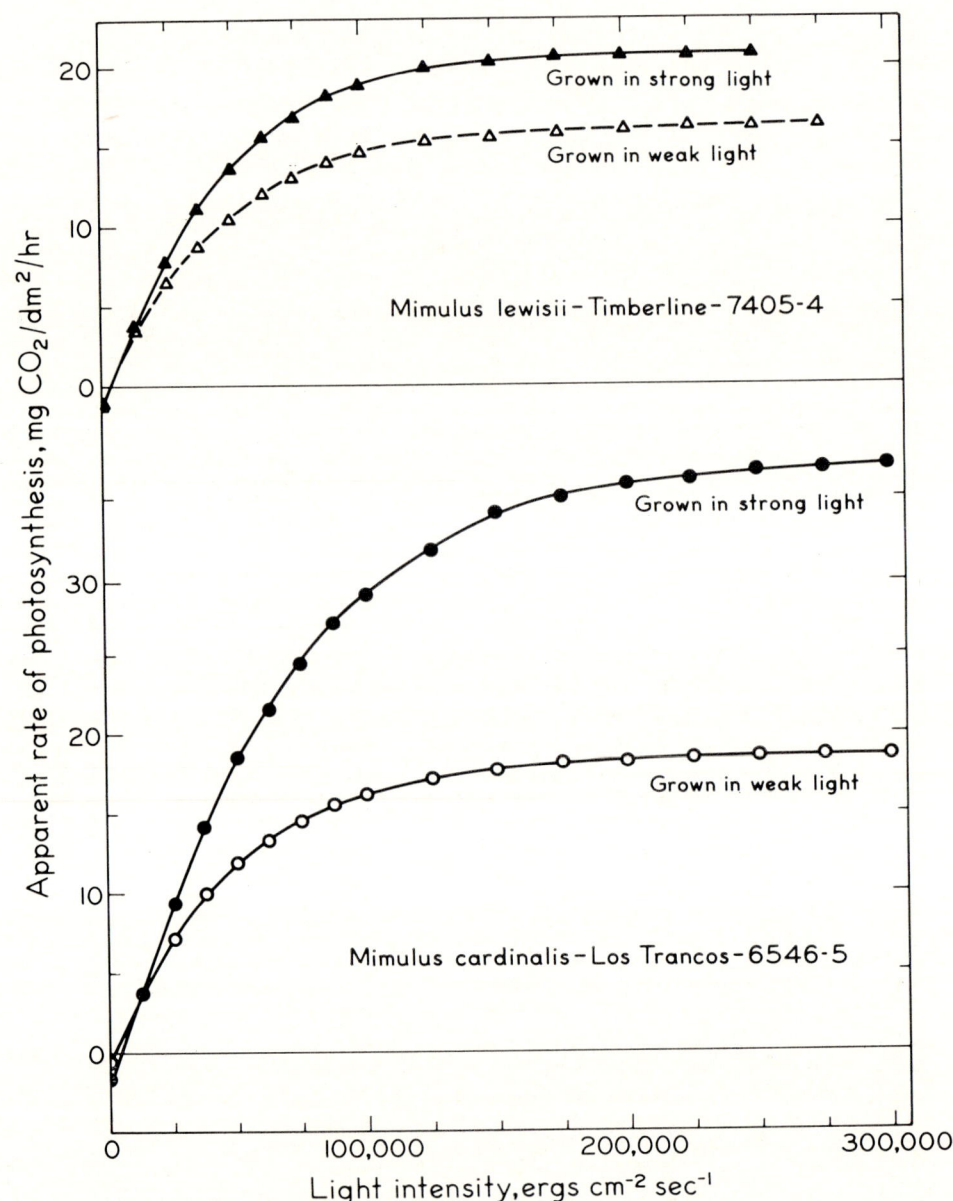

Figure 64. *Above:* Photosynthetic rates of *Mimulus lewisii* Timberline, clone 7405-4, as a function of light intensity when previously grown under strong light (100,000 erg cm^{-2} sec^{-1}) and under weak light (25,000 erg cm^{-2} sec^{-1}).
Below: Photosynthetic rates of *M. cardinalis* Los Trancos, clone 6546-5, previously grown under the same conditions as above.
All measurements made at 20° with light of 600–700 nm wavelength; CO_2 concentration, 300 ppm; O_2, 21.0%.

also intermediate in their light-saturated photosynthetic rates. Figure 65 shows light saturation curves of the parents, F_1 hybrids, and the two most contrasting F_2 plants, all previously grown under the same high light intensity. The light-saturated photosynthetic rates for the F_2 plants are shown in figure 65 only

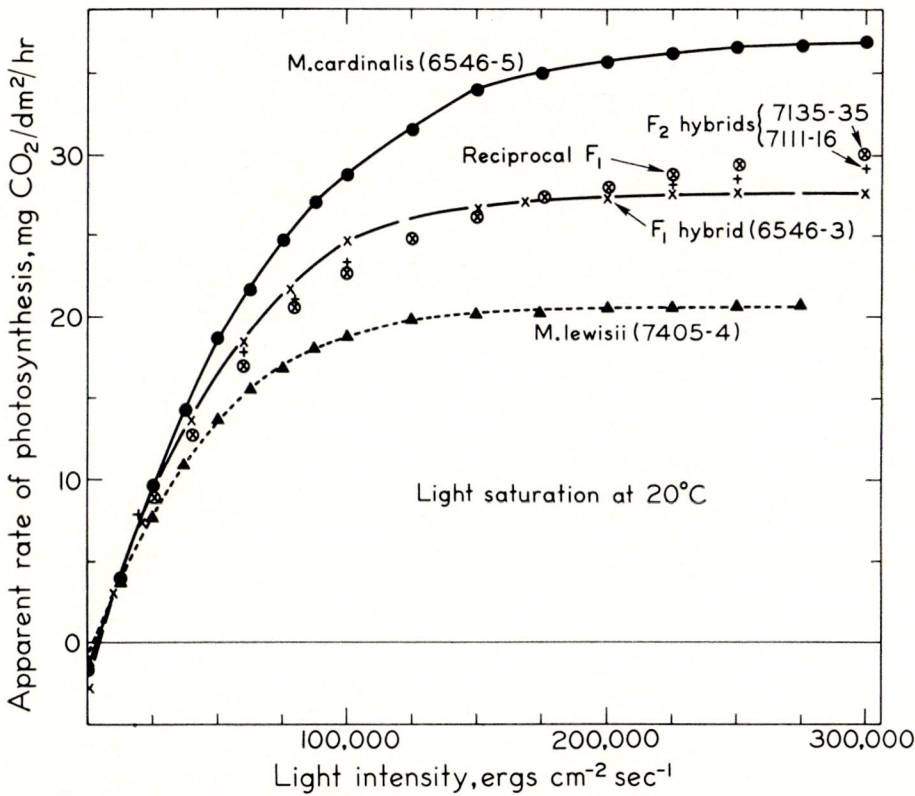

Figure 65. Photosynthetic rates as a function of light intensity for *Mimulus cardinalis* Los Trancos, clone 6546-5, *M. lewisii* Timberline, clone 7405-5, and their reciprocal F_1 hybrids.

Prior to measurement all plants were grown under identical controlled conditions with temperatures of 20°–22° during days and 15°–17° during nights with a 12-hour photoperiod under a light intensity of 100,000 erg cm^{-2} sec^{-1}. All measurements made with light of 600–700 nm wavelength; CO_2 concentration, 300 ppm; O_2, 21.0%.

as points and include clone 7135-35, having a preponderance of *cardinalis*-like characters, and clone 7111-16, having mostly *lewisii*-like characters. These two F_2 individuals are among the most highly contrasting with respect to morphological characters. The light-saturation curves of these divergent F_2 plants are remarkably similar to the light-saturation curves of the reciprocal F_1's. The curves are clearly intermediate between the widely differing parental races—

a correspondence which suggests that the differences in photosynthetic characteristics between the parental clones are governed by complex multiple-gene systems.

The relative efficiency with which the *M. cardinalis* and *M. lewisii* parents

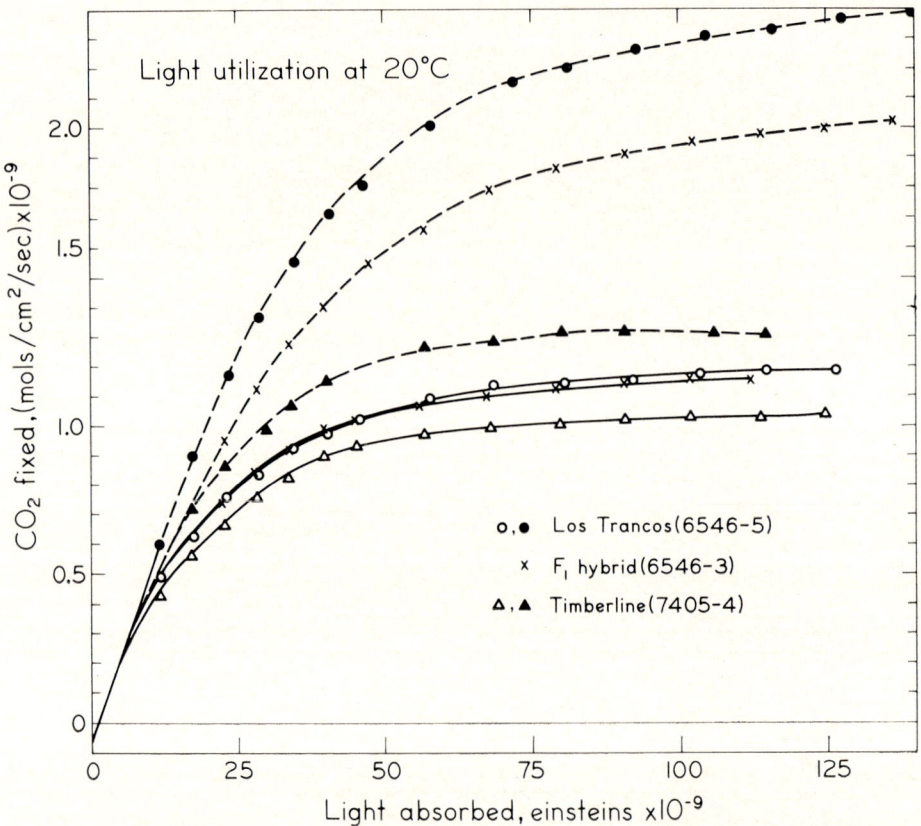

Figure 66. Efficiency of light utilization in photosynthesis of *Mimulus cardinalis* Los Trancos, clone 6546-5, *M. lewisii* Timberline, clone 7405-4, and their F_1 hybrid, clone 6546-3, previously grown under strong and under weak light.

Einsteins of light absorbed per mole of CO_2 absorbed are plotted as a function of incident light intensity. These values were computed from photosynthetic percentage of incident light absorbed by the same leaves with an Ulbricht sphere. Black symbols indicate clones grown under high light intensity; open symbols, clones grown under low light.

and their F_1 hybrids utilize incident light of wavelengths between 600 and 700 nm for fixing CO_2 at intensities ranging from darkness to 250,000 erg cm^{-2} sec^{-1} is shown in figure 66. The number of nano-moles of CO_2 fixed per square centimeter of leaf surface per second is plotted as a function of the number of nano-einsteins of light energy absorbed per square centimeter per second.

Values for propagules previously grown both under strong light and under weak light are shown. From the curves in figure 65 it is evident that clone 6546-5, *M. cardinalis* Los Trancos, when previously grown under strong light, is much more efficient in utilizing the available incident light energy for photosynthesis under conditions of strong illumination than is the clone of *M. lewisii* 7405-4, from Timberline, previously grown under identical conditions. The F_1 hybrid, although intermediate between the parents, is closer to *M. cardinalis* than to *M. lewisii* in light-utilizing efficiency.

When the two parental races and the F_1 are all grown under weak light prior to measurement, their differences in efficiency of light utilization are greatly diminished although their relative order of efficiency remains the same. At very low intensities of incident light, i.e., the range within which the photosynthetic rates are linearly proportional to light intensity, the differences in light-utilizing efficiency between all of the clones grown either under strong or under weak light disappear entirely.

Anatomical studies of cross-sections of leaves of the parental *M. cardinalis* and *M. lewisii* clones and their F_1 hybrids grown under the same conditions under which the photosynthetic rates were measured reveal characteristic differences, as shown in figure 67. In both the parental and F_1 hybrid clones, leaf thickness is less under weak light than under strong light. The chloroplasts tend to be larger and more densely distributed in the palisade and spongy parenchyma cells in leaves grown under weak light. In either strong or weak light, *M. lewisii* and *M. cardinalis* leaves are of approximately the same thickness, in contrast with the F_1 hybrid, which is thinner-leaved than either parent.

The chloroplasts of *Mimulus cardinalis* Los Trancos leaves are considerably smaller in diameter and fewer in number in the palisade cells of leaves grown in strong light than those of leaves developed under weak light, as illustrated in figure 67. *Mimulus lewisii* shows a somewhat parallel but much less pronounced modification in chloroplast size, and the F_1 hybrid is clearly intermediate in this respect. The chlorophyll content of the leaves from the Los Trancos clone is considerably higher than in the *M. lewisii* parent whether expressed on the basis of leaf area or of fresh weight, while corresponding values of the reciprocal F_1 hybrids are intermediate, as shown in table 42. The *cardinalis*-like F_2 plant 7135-35 matches the *M. cardinalis* parent in chlorophyll content, whereas the *lewisii*-like F_2 plant 7111-16 was intermediate, like the F_1's.

A comparison of the photosynthetic rates of the parental and F_1 hybrid clones as a function of temperature over the range $5°$–$38°$ C is shown in figure 68. These measurements were made with light in the wavelength region between 600 and 700 nm with a constant intensity of 175,000 erg cm^{-2} sec^{-1}, which is essentially saturating for these clones (cf. figure 65).

As is evident by the shapes of the curves in figure 68, the apparent photosynthetic rate of the *M. cardinalis* parent is influenced by differences in temperature to a greater degree than is that of the *M. lewisii* parent. In this respect the F_1 hybrid again is intermediate between the parents. The remarkable flatness of the curve for the Timberline parent is, on first consideration, surprising, in view of the highly distinctive subalpine environment to which it is native. However, since photosynthetic rates show much greater temperature dependence when measured under low O_2 concentrations of 1%–2% than

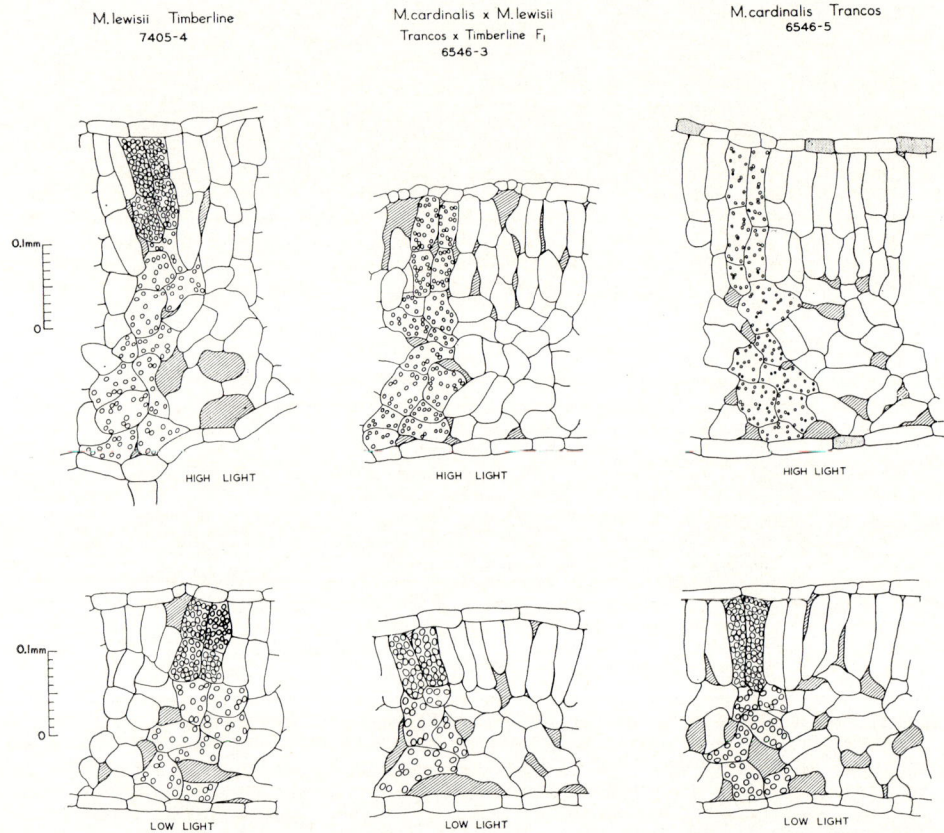

Figure 67. Cross sections of leaves of clones of *Mimulus lewisii* Timberline, *M. cardinalis* Los Trancos, and their F_1 hybrid grown under low light intensity (25,000 erg cm^{-2} sec^{-1}) as compared with high light intensity (100,000 erg cm^{-2} sec^{-1}). Cross-hatched areas indicate intercellular spaces. See also figures 64, 65, and 66 for photosynthetic data from the same clones grown under the same conditions.

under 21.0% O_2 (as described on pages 155–157 for *M. lewisii* Logan and *M. cardinalis* Jacksonville), the curves shown in figure 68 obviously reveal only one aspect of the photosynthetic picture. It seems evident that the clone 7405-4, *M. lewisii* Timberline, possesses compensating mechanisms for minimizing the effects of varying ambient temperatures on the rate of photosynthetic uptake of CO_2. What these mechanisms are is unknown.

The observed photosynthetic characteristics of *M. cardinalis* Los Trancos, *M. lewisii* Timberline, and their F_1 and F_2 hybrids could not have been predicted. Some findings are contrary to our earlier speculations, formulated on the basis of growth responses at the altitudinal transplant stations. For example, on the basis of the marked vigor and extended seasonal activity of the F_1 hybrid at the transplant stations (cf. figure 22), one might anticipate that the F_1 hybrid might have a higher light-saturated photosynthetic rate than either parent, and perhaps a greater range of temperature tolerance. Neither of these expectations is supported by the measurements.

The light-saturated photosynthetic rates of *Mimulus lewisii* Logan (clone 7635-2), *M. cardinalis* Jacksonville (clone 7211-4), and their F_1 hybrid (clone 7718-4) when measured as a function of temperature under normal air and

TABLE 42

Photosynthetic Rate and Chlorophyll Content of *Mimulus* Parents and Hybrids

Clone	Light-Saturated Photosynthetic Rate, μmol CO_2 dm^{-2} min^{-1}	Ratio, p Rate of Leaves Grown under High/Low Light Intensity	Chlorophyll Content of Leaves	
			mg/dm^2 of Surface	mg/g Fresh Weight
M. cardinalis Los Trancos, 6546-5	14.71	1.8	5.07	1.60
M. lewisii Timberline, 7405-4	9.95	1.4	3.40	0.90
M. cardinalis × *lewisii*, F_1, 6546-3	10.00	1.5	4.35	1.41
M. lewisii × *cardinalis*, F_1, 6547-1	11.42	1.5	4.00	1.42
M. cardinalis × *lewisii*, F_2, 7135-35, (*cardinalis*-like)	12.53	1.9	4.94	1.62
M. cardinalis × *lewisii*, F_2, 7116-16, (*lewisii*-like)	11.88	1.8	3.93	1.05

* All plants previously grown under a light intensity of 100,000 erg cm^{-2} sec^{-1} on a 12-hour photoperiod. Photosynthetic measurements made under a CO_2 concentration of 300 ppm, O_2 at 21.0%.

under an oxygen concentration of 1.5% are shown in figure 69. From these measurements it is evident that the maximum light-saturated rate of the F_1 hybrid is greater than that of either parent, when measured in 1.5% O_2, but not when measured under 21.0% O_2. Moreover, above 25° C, the temperature at which maximum photosynthesis occurs in the Logan clone of *M. lewisii*, the rate for this plant drops, as contrasted with the Jacksonville clone of *M. cardinalis* whose maximum rate levels off in the same temperature range. In the F_1 hybrid the maximum rate is attained at approximately 30° C. It is evident that measurements of rates of CO_2 uptake made only under air with an oxygen concentration of 21.0% reveal only part of the story regarding the intrinsic photosynthetic capacities of parents and hybrids.

That clones of *M. lewisii* originating from different habitats differ in their light-saturated photosynthetic rate when grown and measured under identical conditions in air has been demonstrated on races from Logan Pass (clone

7635-2), Tamarack Flat (clone 7399-3), and Timberline (clones 7405-4, 7423-3). In these comparisons the rates for both Timberline clones were found to be approximately 33% lower than for Logan, Tamarack being intermediate.

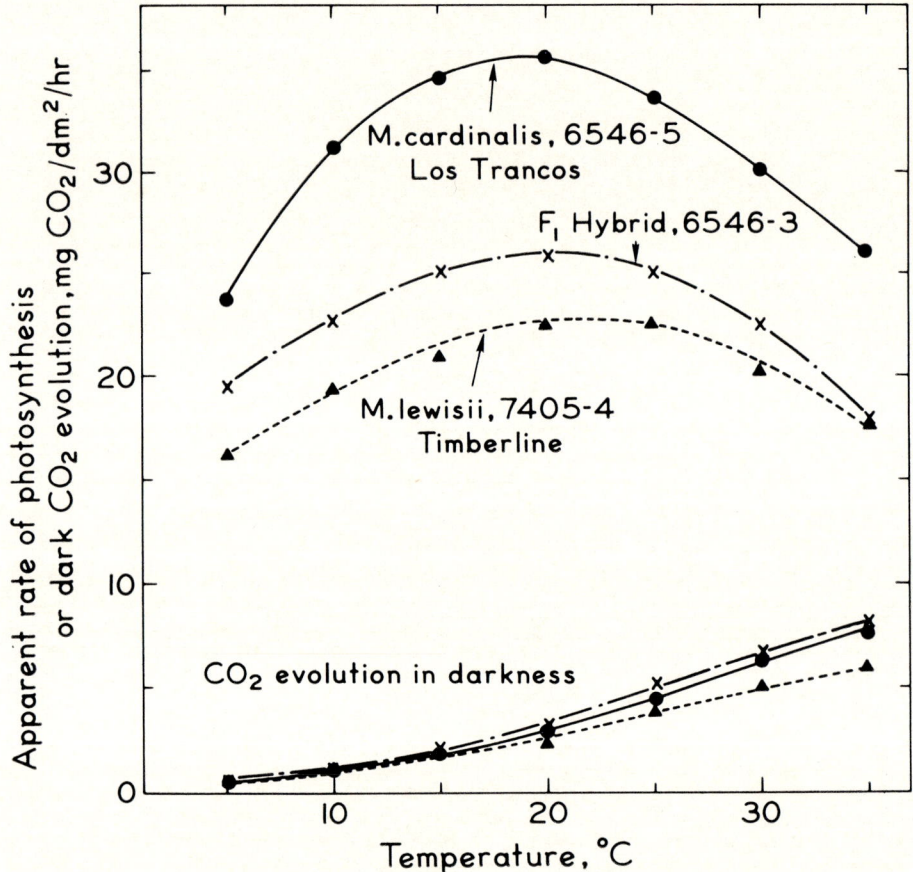

Figure 68. Apparent photosynthetic CO_2 uptake and dark CO_2 evolution rates of *Mimulus lewisii* Timberline, clone 7405-4, *M. cardinalis* Los Trancos, clone 6546-5, and their F_1 hybrid as a function of temperature.

All measurements were made on propagules previously grown under a high light intensity (100,000 erg cm^{-2} sec^{-1}) with a 12-hour photoperiod. Rates of photosynthesis shown above were measured under a constant incident light intensity of 175,000 erg cm^{-2} sec^{-1} (600–700 nm).

AMPHIPLOID BETWEEN M. NELSONII AND M. LEWISII. The derivation of a stable, fertile amphiploid from a tetraploid sector of a sterile F_1 hybrid between the clone 7422-12, *M. nelsonii,* originally from Mexico, and 7405-4, *M. lewisii* from Timberline, as described on pages 23–24, provided an opportunity to compare the photosynthetic characteristics of the parents, the sterile diploid F_1 hybrid, the fertile autotetraploid derived from it, and the fertile, nonsegregating F_2 tetraploid progeny. In this instance we are dealing with the interaction of the same sets of two distinct genomes combined on both the diploid and tetraploid levels.

Light saturation curves for both parental clones and the amphiploid, all previously grown under the high light intensity of 100,000 ergs cm^{-2} sec^{-1}, are shown in the lower part of figure 70. The comparable light-saturated values of the F_1 hybrid on both the diploid and tetraploid levels are also indicated as points in this same figure. Similar data for the same clones previously grown

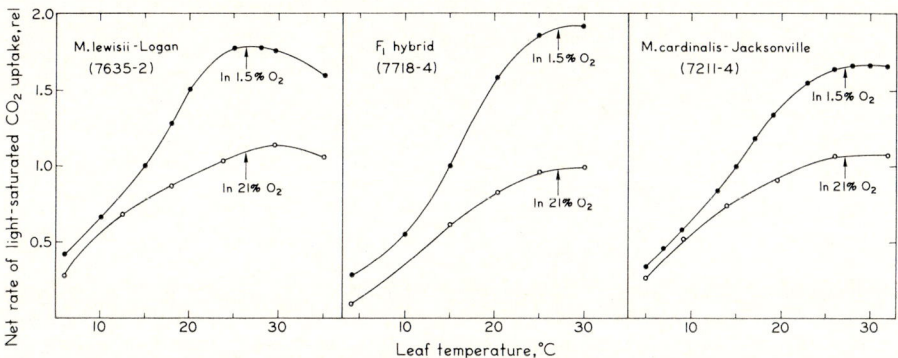

Figure 69. Temperature dependence of light-saturated photosynthetic rate of *Mimulus lewisii* Logan, *M. cardinalis* Jacksonville, and their F_1 hybrid when measured under an O_2 concentration of 1.5% and 21.0%. Light intensity held constant at 340,000 erg cm^{-2} sec^{-1} (400–700 nm); CO_2 concentration, 280–320 ppm.

The plants were previously grown at 20° under a light intensity of 53,000 erg cm^{-2} sec^{-1} on a 16-hour photoperiod with normal air concentration of O_2 and CO_2. In the above graphs the photosynthetic rate under 1.5% O_2 at 15° for each leaf has been set as equal to unity to facilitate comparison. See also figure 65.

under the low intensity of 15,000 ergs cm^{-2} sec^{-1} are plotted in the upper part of the same figure.

At very low incident light intensities ranging from almost darkness to approximately 25,000 erg cm^{-2} sec^{-1} all the clones under the two contrasting light intensities have essentially identical curves for photosynthetic rates. As light-saturating intensities are approached, the curves of the clones grown under the high and the low light intensities diverge and show differences both in the light intensity required for saturation and in the maximum light-saturated photosynthetic rates attained. The *M. lewisii* clone 7405-4 saturates at a lower light intensity than either *M. nelsonii* or the F_2 amphiploid derivative. The amphiploid has a significantly higher light-saturated rate than either parent irrespective of whether it was previously grown under high or low light. The

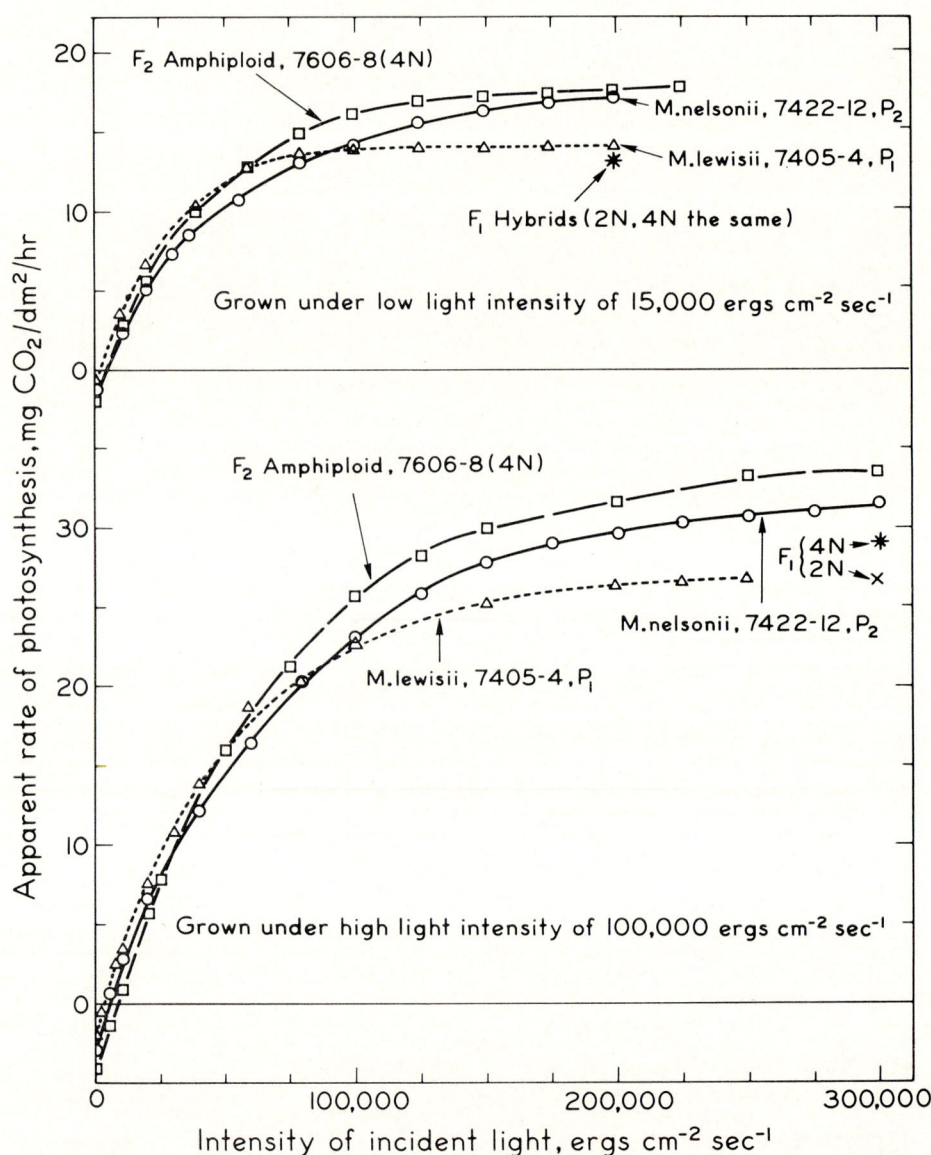

Figure 70. Apparent photosynthetic rates as a function of light intensity for *Mimulus lewisii* Timberline, clone 7405-4, *M. nelsonii* El Salto, clone 7422-12, and their tetraploid F_2 amphiploid derivative, clone 7606-8, previously grown under high (*below*) and under low (*above*) light intensities on a 16-hour photoperiod. The corresponding light-saturated photosynthetic rates of the F_1 hybrid on both the diploid and tetraploid levels are shown as points.

All measurements made at 20° with light of wavelengths between 600 and 700 nm; CO_2 concentration was 300 ppm, and O_2 was 21.0%.

F_1 progenitor, whether on the diploid or tetraploid level, is intermediate between the parents.

Of greater interest than the light-saturated photosynthetic rates when measured at a given temperature are comparisons between rates of CO_2 assimilation at different temperatures. The curves in figure 71 show the photosynthetic rates of the parental clones, the F_1 on both the diploid and tetraploid levels,

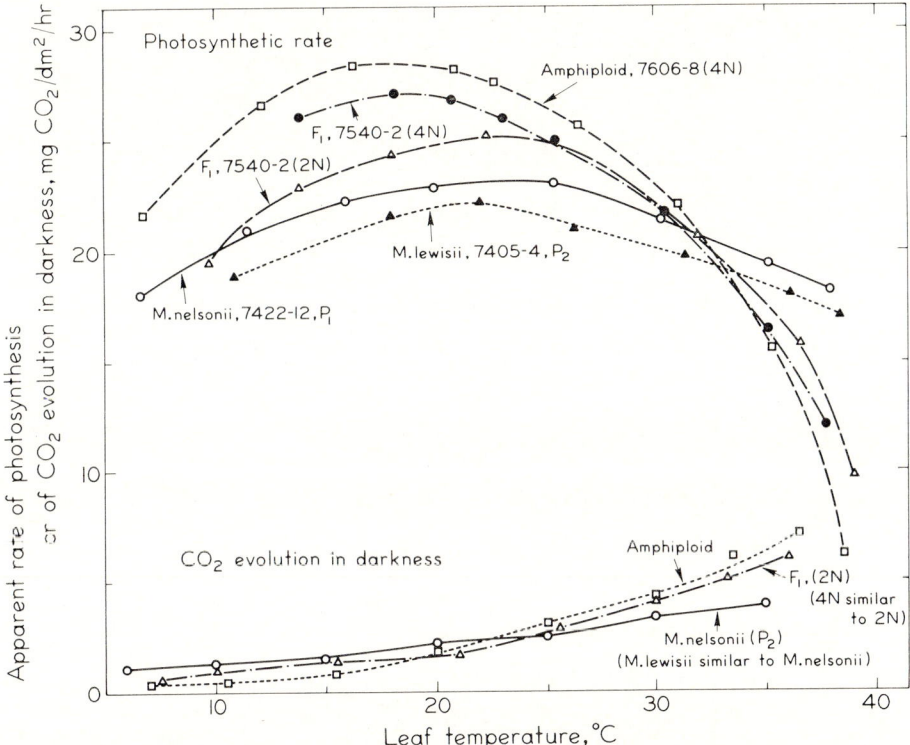

Figure 71. Temperature dependence of apparent photosynthesis and dark CO_2 evolution of *Mimulus nelsonii* El Salto (P_1), *M. lewisii* Timberline (P_2), their F_1 hybrids on the diploid ($2n$) and tetraploid ($4n$) levels, and of the F_2 amphiploid derivative ($4n$).

All plants were previously grown under a light intensity of 100,000 erg cm^{-2} sec^{-1} on a 16-hour photoperiod with day temperatures of 20–22°C and nights of 15–17°C. The photosynthetic measurements were made under a constant light intensity of 175,000 erg cm^{-2} sec^{-1} (600–700 nm); average CO_2 concentration, 300 ppm; O_2, 21.0%.

and the F_2 amphiploid 7606-8 as a function of temperature. These curves were all determined on propagules of clones previously grown under a light intensity of 100,000 ergs cm^{-2} sec^{-1} with a 16-hour photoperiod at a day temperature of 22° C and nights at 15° C. The measurements on photosynthetic rates were made at a constant and essentially light-saturating intensity of 175,000 ergs cm^{-2} sec^{-1}. The rates of CO_2 evolution in darkness shown at the bottom of the figure were made on the same leaves on which photosynthetic rates were determined.

As shown in figure 71, the remarkable flatness of the temperature curve for 7405-4, the parental *M. lewisii* from Timberline, is matched by the other parent, 7422-12, *M. nelsonii* El Salto. The photosynthetic rate of *M. nelsonii* measured under the same conditions was slightly but consistently higher than that of the Timberline *M. lewisii* parent throughout the temperature range.

In striking contrast with the parents, the F_1 hybrid on both the diploid and tetraploid levels and the amphiploid were found to be highly sensitive to temperature changes. In the range between 10° and 25° C the hybrids have a considerably higher photosynthetic rate than either parent, the tetraploid being higher than the diploid derivative of the same individual F_1 hybrid, and the amphiploid, in turn, having a rate significantly higher than the tetraploid F_1. In the 30–33° C range the apparent photosynthetic rates of all these hybrid derivatives drop sharply, and cross below the curves of the two parental species. Interestingly enough, the rates of dark CO_2 evolution of the hybrid derivatives likewise seem to be more responsive to temperature than are the parental species previously grown under identical conditions.

That *Mimulus nelsonii* from the highlands of Mexico and *M. lewisii* from the high Sierra Nevada of California have essentially the same photosynthetic response with respect to temperature indicates that the inability of *M. nelsonii* to survive at the Timberline transplant station as compared with the success of *M. lewisii* is not due to differences in their photosynthetic efficiency at different temperatures.

In the F_1 hybrid evidently a shift in genic balance results in the expression of physiological differences that are of importance in controlling light-saturated photosynthetic rates at different temperatures. Doubling the chromosome number in the F_1 hybrid appears to increase this effect, and in the stabilized F_2 amphiploid this effect is further enhanced. There also seems to be a correlation between the higher photosynthetic rates observed in the hybrid derivatives and in the rates of dark CO_2 evolution (figure 71).

The amphiploid derivatives grown as a population thrive with considerable vigor in the Stanford garden. The F_2 and F_3 generations that have been tested in this environment far exceed in vigor the nonsurviving *M. lewisii* parent. The *M. nelsonii* parent, although a successful survivor at Stanford, does not equal the amphiploid in vigor of growth in this environment. Tests on the F_1 and F_2 amphiploid progeny at the Timberline transplant station in comparison with the parents reveal that the F_1 hybrids on both the diploid and tetraploid levels are at least as successful as the *M. lewisii* parent at Timberline, and that F_2 amphiploid progeny appear to have even greater vigor. At Mather, where neither *M. nelsonii* nor *M. lewisii* succeeds, the F_1 hybrids and the amphiploid are reasonably successful survivors.

The evolutionary importance of amphiploidy for the synthesis of new species of higher plants is well established, a subject dealt with in an earlier volume of this series (Clausen, Keck, and Hiesey, 1945). The physiological basis for the marked success of some amphiploid species in occupying new environmental niches has been assumed to be due to complementation of gene-controlled physiological capacities contributed by the parental species. The data presented above appear to support this hypothesis, and suggest that through such interspecific recombination physiological traits not expressed in either parent may be realized. Doubling the chromosome complement without change in composition of the genomes appears to cause a shift in physiological balance.

PHOTOSYNTHETIC PERFORMANCE OF ECOLOGICAL RACES OF MIMULUS COMPARED WITH OTHER SPECIES

Although at the present writing relatively few comparative studies have been made on the photosynthetic performance of contrasting ecological races of the same or related species under reproducible controlled laboratory conditions, evidence already available demonstrates that different species-groups have evolved strikingly different kinds of heredity-controlled mechanisms regulating photosynthetic performance. A review of investigations bearing on this question seems to be appropriate.

Comparative studies in this laboratory of photosynthetic characteristics of ecological species and races of other genera than *Mimulus* have been made on *Solidago, Solanum,* and *Atriplex*. We will consider first the investigations on members of these three genera in relation to those in *Mimulus*.

ECOTYPIC DIFFERENTIATION IN THE SOLIDAGO VIRGAUREA COMPLEX. In his classic studies on ecotypes, Turesson (1922, 1926) featured, among other species, ecological races of the geographically widespread species *Solidago virgaurea,* which occupies many kinds of contrasting habitats throughout Eurasia. Later Björkman, Florell, and Holmgren (1960) compared the photosynthetic rates of contrasting ecological races of this species at different temperatures. Swedish alpine forms were found to have optimal photosynthetic rates at lower temperatures than lowland populations. Races from higher elevations were also found to have higher respiratory rates than those from low elevations (Björkman and Holmgren, 1961).

Later studies (Björkman and Holmgren, 1963; Björkman, 1968a; Holmgren, 1968) were concentrated on detailed investigations of races from shaded as contrasted with sunny habitats. On the basis of many controlled growth experiments, quantitative measurements of photosynthetic rates and quantum yields, anatomical studies on leaves, and biochemical investigations, a picture revealing important differences in the capacity of different photosynthetic steps between such races has been realized.

Races from sunny habitats such as an open meadow (Ronneberga, in south Sweden) and exposed alpine tundra (Beskades in northern Norway) thrive under the same high light intensities that cause severe light damage in races from deeply shaded habitats such as the floors of a dense beech forest (Norreskov in Denmark) or oak forest (Hallands Vädero, an island on the southwest coast of Sweden). Conversely, the sun races fail to grow at the same low light intensity that results in good growth in the shade races.

Growing the sun races under high light intensities results in much higher light-saturated rates of photosynthesis, and higher activities of RuDP carboxylase than when the same clones are grown under low light intensities. These responses are very similar to those found for *Mimulus* (pages 112–121). In sun races of *Solidago* growth under high light intensities also resulted in a lower resistance to gas diffusion than did growth under low light intensities. Thus sun races have the ability to adjust to the efficient use of high light intensities for photosynthesis.

Shade races of *Solidago* were found to lack this ability. Growing the shade clones under high light intensity as compared with low light intensity did not result in a higher light-saturated photosynthetic rate. Also, the activity of RuDP carboxylase and the resistance to gas diffusion did not increase with increasing light intensity during growth in the shade clones. In addition, growing the shade clones under high intensities resulted in reduced quantum yield for photosynthesis. This is probably caused by an inhibition of primary reaction centers of photosynthesis, and there is some evidence that photosystem II is more affected than photosystem I. Secondary detrimental effects of high light intensity include chlorophyll bleaching and disturbances in chloroplast structure.

Clones of coastal *Mimulus cardinalis* Los Trancos (6546-5) as well as of subalpine *M. lewisii* Timberline (7405-4) grown in controlled cabinets under the same high light intensity (120,000 erg cm^{-2} sec^{-1}) that proved to be highly detrimental to the shade forms of *Solidago* both thrive under this intensity as well as under a low light intensity (25,000 erg cm^{-2} sec^{-1}) that is highly favorable for the growth of the shade races but too low for survival of the sun races of *Solidago*. Under such contrasting light intensities, both races of *Mimulus* have lower light-saturated photosynthetic rates when grown under a low intensity than under a high intensity. In this respect the *Mimulus* races resemble the sun races of *Solidago* when grown under different light intensities of narrower range.

Mimulus and *Solidago* races therefore share a number of photosynthetic characteristics, but *Mimulus* differs in having ecological races with a wider range of tolerance to light intensity than the highly specialized shade and sun forms of *Solidago* studied by Björkman and Holmgren.

Altitudinal races of *Mimulus* differ from each other in their capacity to survive at extremes of temperature, as described on pages 148 to 150 for the alpine *M. lewisii* from Logan Pass in comparison with the Sierran foothill race of *M. cardinalis* from Jacksonville. Whether or not similar differences in tolerance to temperature extremes exist among ecologic races of the *Solidago virgaurea* complex is a question that has not yet been adequately explored.

PHOTOSYNTHETIC DIFFERENTIATION IN SOLANUM. Recent studies by Gauhl (1967, 1968, 1969) on clones of ecological races of the widely distributed species *Solanum dulcamara* L. of central Europe and Asia reveal the occurrence of sun and shade races that appear to be almost as markedly different in tolerance as the *Solidago* races just mentioned.

A race native to a densely shaded *Fragmites* marsh near Mönchbruch, Germany, grown under a high (111,000 erg cm^{-2} sec^{-1}) and a low (24,000 erg cm^{-2} sec^{-1}) light intensity showed clear symptoms of damage to the photosynthetic mechanism under the high intensity, but thrived under the low. The damage under high light was evidenced by a lower quantum yield for photosynthetic CO_2 fixation and reduced chlorophyll concentration of the leaves. Another race of *Solanum dulcamara*, originally from an open sand dune on Fehmarn Island off the Baltic coast of Germany, was capable of healthy growth and survival when grown under both the high light intensity and the low light intensity just mentioned and, in common with races of *Mimulus* and the sun forms of *Solidago,* had lower light-saturated photosynthetic rates and RuDP carboxylase activity than propagules of clones previously grown under the lower intensity.

That not all forms of *Solanum dulcamara* from shaded habitats show photodamage to the photosynthetic apparatus when grown under high light intensities is apparent from the responses of another race originating from a shaded *Alnus glutinosa* swamp near Frankfurt-Schwanheim, Germany. When grown under a high light intensity the Frankfurt ecotype proved to be capable of sustaining a high light-saturated photosynthetic rate like the Fehmarn Island clone, and did not show the photodamage characteristic of the Mönchbruch clone when grown under ample water supply. However, when grown under high light intensity and limited supply of water, the Frankfurt clone showed pronounced photodamage to the photosynthetic apparatus. Propagules of a clone of this same race grown under low light intensities thrived vigorously.

All three of the above races of *Solanum* originated from habitats of adequate moisture supply. A fourth race, originally from a sunny dry gravel mound near Rovinj, Yugoslavia, that normally grows actively during the dry summer season was also included in Gauhl's studies. Cloned propagules of this race were subjected to water stress by growing them under full sunlight at Stanford with a limited daily water supply in comparison with adequately watered controls. Propagules of the marsh Frankfurt race treated the same way were used for the comparison. The light-saturated photosynthetic rate of the propagules of the Frankfurt race grown under water stress dropped dramatically in comparison with the adequately watered propagules of the same clone. In contrast, the Rovinj race attained approximately the same light-saturated rates under both treatments. The growth rates and the light-saturated photosynthetic rates of the adequately watered propagules of the Frankfurt race were considerably higher than those of propagules of the Rovinj race grown under the same conditions, but under water stress the Rovinj far outperformed Frankfurt on both counts.

The development of genetically differentiated races in *Solanum* with respect to photosynthetic capability under water stress is a feature not found among any of the races of *Mimulus* that we have studied, since all forms of the *Erythranthe* are highly dependent on an ample water supply for active growth.

DIFFERENCES IN PATHWAYS OF PHOTOSYNTHETIC CO_2 FIXATION IN ATRIPLEX. The results obtained on *Solidago, Solanum,* and *Mimulus* reveal pronounced adaptive differentiation in photosynthetic characteristics between ecologic races of the same species. The available evidence indicates that this kind of differentiation is achieved through changes in the relative capacities of component steps of photosynthesis. There is no indication that in such races it is caused by major changes in photosynthetic pathways. It is now clear, however, that basic differences in the biochemical pathway of photosynthesis have evolved in many genera of other plants, as mentioned earlier in this chapter.

Investigations by Burr (1962); Kortschak, Hartt, and Burr (1965); Hatch and Slack (1966); Hatch, Slack, and Johnson (1967); Slack and Hatch (1967); and Johnson and Hatch (1968) have shown that many species of both mono- and dicotyledons fix CO_2 by β-carboxylation of phospho(enol)pyruvate, leading to the formation of C_4-dicarboxylic acids as the first products of CO_2 fixation rather than 3-phosphoglyceric acid, which is normally the case with other plants. The former is commonly referred to as β-carboxylation photosynthesis, or the C_4-dicarboxylic acid pathway.

Shortly after the discovery of this pathway it was thought that it represented a major evolutionary divergence within the plant kingdom. Later contributions from several laboratories have shown that even within the same genus, as, for example, in *Atriplex, Euphorbia, Panicum,* and *Cyperus,* some species possess the β-carboxylation pathway, and others do not. Moreover, very recent work (Björkman, Gauhl, and Nobs, 1969) reveals that in *Atriplex* there is sufficient genetic compatibility between species with and without β-carboxylation photosynthesis that hybrids between them can be obtained. The male parent in this cross, *A. patula* ssp. *hastata* Hall and Clem., lacks β-carboxylation photosynthesis, whereas the female parent, *A. rosea* L., possesses this pathway. Like many other species with β-carboxylation photosynthesis, *A. rosea* is mainly distributed in hot, semiarid regions of the world. *Atriplex patula,* on the other hand, occurs mainly in cooler moist areas. Occasionally the two species occur together, as in the San Francisco Bay area, where the two *Atriplex* species studied in this laboratory were collected.

Species with β-carboxylation photosynthesis have photosynthetic characteristics profoundly different from those of plants lacking this pathway. The CO_2 compensation point for CO_2 exchange in air approaches zero, and the strong inhibiting effect of 21% oxygen in CO_2 uptake is absent. Unusually high temperatures and light intensities are required for maximum photosynthetic rates even in normal air, and these rates are considerably higher than in plants lacking β-carboxylation photosynthesis. All of these and several other characteristics of species having β-carboxylation photosynthesis are present in *A. rosea* and absent in *A. patula*.

The evolutionary and ecological significance of β-carboxylation photosynthesis is a subject of active current inquiry. On the basis of the results obtained with *Atriplex patula* and *A. rosea* it appears that the main effect of β-carboxylation photosynthesis is to enable a plant to overcome the inhibiting effect of oxygen present in normal air on CO_2 uptake. This hypothesis is supported by data showing that the marked differences in photosynthetic response to temperature and CO_2 concentration that are found in the two species in the presence of 21% O_2 are greatly diminished when the O_2 concentration is reduced to a low value.

The inhibiting effect of O_2 increases strongly with decreasing CO_2 concentration and increasing temperature in *Atriplex patula, Mimulus cardinalis* (figure 52), and in the several other species not following the β-carboxylation pathway. This suggests that the absence of an inhibiting effect of O_2 on photosynthetic CO_2 uptake might be particularly advantageous under conditions of high temperature and low CO_2 concentration. This may explain why β-carboxylation photosynthesis appears to be closely associated with plants that occupy hot semiarid habitats. Frequent occurrence of water stress resulting in stomatal closure and consequently reduced internal CO_2 concentration would further accentuate the disadvantage of oxygen inhibition. In such habitats the selective advantage of β-carboxylation photosynthesis therefore appears to be obvious.

It is possible that in order to gain the advantages associated with β-carboxylation photosynthesis, plants must pay an intrinsically greater energy cost in terms of the number of moles of ATP required for each mole of CO_2 fixed. This requirement would be expected not to be of major disadvantage in environments characterized by high light intensities, but would be expected to impose an important restriction on photosynthetic efficiency under rate-limiting light intensities.

It is hoped that current attempts to produce a segregating F_2 population from crosses between *Atriplex patula* and *A. rosea* will provide material for elucidating the inheritance of β-carboxylation photosynthesis and further information on the adaptive significance of this pathway.

PHOTOSYNTHETIC DIFFERENTIATION IN ALGAE. Although our present concern is primarily with differences in photosynthetic capacity of higher plants in relation to environment, mention should be made of particularly interesting instances of photosynthetic differentiation in algae. A high-temperature strain of the green alga *Chlorella pyrenoidosa* was isolated by Sorokin and Myers (1953) from local waters in the vicinity of Austin, Texas. This strain was used extensively in laboratory investigations of photosynthesis in comparison with standard strains such as those isolated by Emerson and Van Niel. The optimal growth temperature for the high-temperature strain, known as 17-11-05, is around 39° C, as compared with 25° for the standard strains, which are unable to grow at 39° C. The range of tolerance for active growth in the 17-11-05 strain is between 15° and 42° C as compared with 5° to 28° for the "standard" strains (Sorokin and Kraus, 1958). The 17-11-05 strain also requires higher light intensities for saturation and is much more rapid in growth (Sorokin, 1958, 1959).

More recently Sorokin (1967) isolated another strain (1-90-30) having approximately the same temperature and light responses as 17-11-05 but having larger cells and approximately a 10% faster growth rate. Such strain differences in photosynthetic and growth characteristics of *Chlorella* appear to be comparable to the kinds of differences between ecological races of higher plants found in *Solidago, Mimulus,* and *Solanum*.

Studies on thermal algae occurring in hot springs in areas of volcanic activity underscore the extremely high temperatures required for the growth of these interesting blue-green forms. Investigations reported by Brock and Brock (1966) on the density of growth of such algae growing along temperature gradients in water channels originating from hot springs in Yellowstone National Park, Wyoming, and in the vicinity of Sisjothade in Iceland indicate that maximum growth occurs in the temperature range 51–56° C at Yellowstone and at about 48° C in Iceland. The maximum temperatures at which algae were found to grow at Yellowstone are in the range 72–73° C, and in Iceland, approximately 60° C.

Measurements on photosynthetic activity of such algae made in sites in Yellowstone using a $C^{14}O_2$ technique on cored samples collected along a thermal gradient indicate that the maximal photosynthetic rates of the samples occur at the same temperature at which a given sample was collected (Brock, 1967a). Thus, although the density of algal growth at the upper temperature extremes of 72–73° C was low, the algae growing there apparently photosynthesize optimally at these temperatures, in contrast with samples collected in cooler waters, whose maxima were found to be the same as the temperature of the water in which they grow. Brock's measurements were made under full sunlight on core samples immersed in the water channels along the temperature gradient. Photosynthetic rates were computed in terms of $C^{14}O_2$ absorbed per unit time per total chlorophyll content of the cored samples.

From these studies Brock concluded that (1) distinct strains of algae having different inherent temperature optima have evolved, and grow along such thermal gradients; (2) that 72–73° C represents the upper temperature limit compatible with the survival of photosynthetic organisms (in contrast with bacteria, which are found at 90° C or even higher temperatures), and (3) that the blue-green algae of hot springs are of ancient evolutionary origin from which forms tolerant to cooler temperatures seem to have evolved. Another interesting conclusion, based on studies on relative growth rates, is that although the thermophiles grow faster at their optimal temperatures than mesophiles do at theirs, the increases in growth rate are considerably less than would be predicted on the basis of the Arrhenius equation (Brock, 1967a).

An interesting review by Castenholtz (1968) described experimental studies, made in his own and in other laboratories, on thermophilic blue-green algae in response to environment. This author points to the lack of critical information regarding the extent of genetic differentiation within and between species even in such widespread groups as *Oscillatoria* and *Synechococcus*.

In marked contrast are cryophilic diatoms that occur in antarctic regions described by Bunt, Owens, and Hoch (1966). These workers found, for example, the species *Fragilaria sublinearis* to be capable of growing under very low light intensities under ice at $-2°$ C, but unable to grow at temperatures above 10° C. Other cryophilic forms include the many species of snow algae. Experimental cultures of various species from the Pacific Northwest have been made by Stein and Brooks (1964) and Garric (1965), from the Rocky Mountains by Stein and Amundsen (1967), and from the Sierra Nevada of California by Dr. William H. Thomas [1] of the Scripps Institution of Oceanography at La Jolla. Most of these studies have been concerned with studies on identification, life histories, and culture techniques. The challenging question of how such cryophilic algae differ from mesophiles and thermophiles in physiological and biochemical functioning is one inviting future investigations.

A recent report by Halldal (1969) describes the striking characteristics of the green alga *Ostreobium reineckii* Bornet collected from the brain coral *Favia* in the Great Barrier Reef off the east coast of Australia. This species grows within the living surface of the coral under extremely low light intensities, where it is heavily shaded by a dense canopy of photosynthetic epizoic dinoflagellates growing above. Most of the light energy that penetrates and is available to the endozoic *Ostreobium* lies in the wavelength region between 700 and 750 nm, although the action spectrum for photosynthesis of this species extends through the spectral range from 300 to approximately 750 nm. The actual light intensities reaching the algal surface are estimated to be in the range of 1 to 10 lux. Incident light intensities as low as 2 erg cm^{-2} sec^{-1} were found capable of inducing measurable photosynthetic activity. The action spectrum of photosynthesis for this alga differs from the spectra of other species of the green algal group primarily in being capable of absorbing and utilizing light of long wavelengths (700 to 750 nm) where other species are photo-

[1] Personal communication.

synthetically inactive. Halldal concluded that a new form of chlorophyll *a* occurs in *Ostreobium* with an absorption peak in the vicinity of 720 nm.

Light saturation for photosynthesis of *Ostreobium* measured with 440 nm light was found to be 1000 erg cm^{-2} sec^{-1} or less, in contrast with the epizoic dinoflagellates growing above that are exposed to high sunlight and require 95,000 erg cm^{-2} sec^{-1} intensity for saturation. These results reveal that major evolutionary changes in photosynthetic properties have taken place among green algae. With the exception of Sorokin's work on *Chlorella,* however, these studies have been made on organisms whose relationships are not well understood and may belong to widely diverse taxa.

GENERAL CONCLUSIONS

At this relatively early period in the comparative study of the photosynthetic characteristics of plants from contrasting environments, it is already clear that ecological races and closely related species differing in hereditary composition may differ strikingly in the functioning of basic steps of the photosynthetic process. In different plant groups such physiological differentiation may occur in various patterns. In the *Solidago virgaurea* complex genetically distinct races, highly specialized with respect to their tolerance to different intensities of light, have been demonstrated. It seems likely that further investigations in this geographically and ecologically widespread species will uncover other aspects of photosynthetic differentiation as well. To date only a few ecologic races have been studied critically under controlled laboratory conditions.

In the *Erythranthe* section of *Mimulus* there appears to be a high degree of similarity in general photosynthetic characteristics. The diverse ecological races of this group possess in common a wide range of tolerance to differences in light intensity, but they do differ in their capacity for photosynthesis at contrasting temperatures. The divergent races appear to be quite highly buffered through compensating feedback mechanisms that make possible comparably vigorous growth of even contrasting races within mutually compatible ranges of temperature, light intensity, and CO_2 and O_2 concentrations.

None of the forms of *Mimulus* that we have studied is tolerant of even mild water stresses. In the *Solanum dulcamara* complex, however, this ecological gap appears to have been bridged by the evolution of races whose photosynthetic functioning is not seriously affected by limited water supply.

That such basic differences in the pathway of photosynthetic CO_2 fixation as the C_4-dicarboxylic acid and the reductive pentose phosphate pathways have evolved in species as closely related as *Atriplex patula* and *A. rosea* is of particular significance in considering the possible limits of physiological differentiation in ecological races of the same species. Photosynthetically, *A. rosea* has features closely resembling such taxonomically unrelated plants as the panicoid grasses, *Amaranthus,* and members of the genus *Euphorbia,* all characterized by high light-saturated photosynthetic rates, a requirement of high light intensity for photosynthetic saturation, an ability to extract CO_2 from ambient air to values approaching 0 ppm, and high temperature optima for photosynthesis.

Atriplex patula, on the other hand, has photosynthetic characteristics in common with *Mimulus, Solidago, Solanum,* and most other species of cool-temperate regions, including grasses (Downes and Hesketh, 1968). The physiological divergence that has evolved in *Atriplex* therefore is a major one that is parallel, on the one hand, to genera and species of apparently mostly hot-tropical and subtropical distribution, and on the other to genera and species of cool-temperate regions. Thus the capability of biochemical changes in pathways of photosynthesis to evolve between species and within races of higher plants is clearly an important aspect in natural selection and plant evolution.

IV
GROWTH OF EXCISED TISSUES OF MIMULUS UNDER ASEPTIC CONDITIONS

During the years 1962 through 1965 exploratory studies on culturing excised tissues and seedlings of *Mimulus cardinalis, M. lewisii,* and some of the other members of the *Erythranthe* section were undertaken. The objective was to explore the feasibility and potential value of such techniques for comparative physiological and biochemical studies on ecological races and species.

This work was started in 1962 by Dr. Ruth Elliott [1] and one of the present authors (Hiesey) and continued with the help of Kathe Picken [2] and Mr. Frank Nicholson through June, 1965. This effort demonstrated both the feasibility and potential value of excised tissues for comparative physiological and biochemical studies. It also became clear that further pursuit in depth of the possibilities afforded by this approach would require more time than was available to our small staff. The studies were therefore concluded at this point. We will summarize the salient results from these studies, which provide a starting point for further investigations.

MEDIA EMPLOYED. Three basic media whose compositions are listed in table 43 were used. The three differ primarily in their concentration of inorganic salts. For convenience we will refer to them as low (L), medium (M) and high (H) salt media. Organic carbon in the form of three percent glucose was added to all cultures in routine experiments with *Mimulus*. Modifications in each of the three media through the addition of varying proportions and concentrations of the hormones indole acetic acid (IAA); naphthalene–acetic acid (NAA); 2, 4-dichlorophenoxy-acetic acid (2, 4-D); and 6-furforylaminopurine (kinetin) were tested with different kinds of excised parts of clones of *Mimulus*.

The media were used in either solid form with agar added, or in liquid form without agar. Since the growth of cultures is characteristically slower in solid media, these were used mostly for the maintenance of stock cultures. Liquid media when kept in gentle motion on slowly rotating drums were found to promote faster growth, and were used in comparative growth experiments. Most of the cultures were grown in test tubes, but for larger amounts of material small Erlenmeyer flasks (300 cc) were used. The cultures were usually maintained at 22–26° C and illuminated by diffuse laboratory daylight supplemented with 8 hours of low-intensity (*ca.* 250–300 erg cm^{-2} sec^{-1}) light from standard cool-white fluorescent lamps.

PLANT MATERIALS AND ESTABLISHMENT OF CULTURES. Nine races of *M. cardinalis* and three of *M. lewisii* were included in these studies, in addition to one race

[1] Now with the Plant Diseases Division, Department of Scientific and Industrial Research, Auckland, New Zealand.
[2] Now Mrs. K. Standeven, Bakersfield, California.

each of *M. verbenaceus* and *M. eastwoodiae*. Some success was attained in growing excised parts of all these species, but most of the work was concentrated on several clones of *M. cardinalis* originally from different altitudes (Jacksonville, Priests Grade, and San Antonio Peak) and a single race of *M. lewisii* (Timberline). Different combinations of media were tried with different comparisons in various experiments.

Initial cultures were established from (1) peeled internodes of young, actively growing plants, following a modification of the technique described by Blakely and Steward (1964); (2) stem apexes of greenhouse or cabinet-grown plants; and (3) excised pieces of seedlings, i.e., mostly leaves or terminal apexes that

TABLE 43

Compositions of Basic Media

Elements and Supplements	L, Low Salt * mg/l	M, Intermediate Salt † mg/l	H, High Salt ‡ mg/l
Nitrogen	12.4	46.7	840.8
Potassium	16.9	65.0	783.5
Calcium	12.7	50.9	119.9
Magnesium	2.5	74.0	36.5
Sulfur	3.3	142.6	48.1
Phosphorus	5.7	4.2	38.7
Glycine	...	3.0	2.0
Nicotinic acid	...	0.5	0.5
Thiamine	...	0.1	0.1
Pyridoxine	...	0.1	0.5
Myo-inositol	...	...	100.0
Coconut milk	15% by volume	..	...

* Laetsch and Briggs (1962)
† P. R. White (1963)
‡ T. Murashige and F. O. Skoog (1962)

were first germinated aseptically on solid media in test tubes, and subsequently transferred to subcultures. Some attempts were also made to establish cultures from pith cells of *M. cardinalis* with partial success.

Mimulus lewisii in general proved to be more difficult to culture than *M. cardinalis*, and after establishment, the growth of explants from *M. lewisii* was usually much slower than that of *M. cardinalis*. A few reversals of this trend were observed, however, in certain types of media. Within *M. cardinalis*, not only different altitudinal races, but different individuals within the same race, were found to vary considerably in the rate of growth of corresponding excised parts. In the altitudinal series Jacksonville, Priests Grade, and San Antonio Peak, for example, certain clones of each race were consistently easier to establish than others. *Mimulus lewisii* cultures in general were found to be favored in growth by high salt media (H), whereas *M. cardinalis* was equally successful in both low (L) and high (H). Although in nearly all tests the growth of *M. cardinalis* explants was faster than parts of *M. lewisii*, this differential tended to disappear in media of medium (M) salt concentration.

The rate of growth of excised tissues of both species was markedly influenced by variations in the media, either in shifts among the three basic L, M, or H media, listed in table 43, or in various combinations with different concentrations of hormones. Uniformity of growth in replicated cultures of a given clone was not often obtained. Considerable improvement is needed in attaining reproducibility among replicates of a single experiment, and between successive experiments, for critical comparative growth studies.

Inasmuch as small differences among the many variables of media and such external physical factors as temperature and light have considerable effect on the resultant growth of excised tissues, the use of excised cultures may prove to be a highly sensitive means of pinpointing genetically controlled differences in metabolic characteristics. Reducing the variability in replicated cultures from a given clone to a consistently controllable level remains, however, a major technical problem.

The use of peeled internodes, following a modification of the method described by Blakely and Stewart (1964) for tobacco, proved to be a reliable means of establishing *M. cardinalis* cultures. Pieces of internodes 4 or 5 mm in length are cut with a razor from young actively growing plants of clones started as cuttings and dropped in 95 percent ethyl alcohol for a few seconds to wet the surfaces. The pieces are then treated with 1 percent hypochlorite solution for 10 minutes, and washed twice in sterile distilled water. The outer tissues are then stripped in a sterile inoculating chamber: a longitudinal slit is made the length of the internodal section down to the depth of the cambial zone, and the outer portions peeled away, leaving a central core of pith surrounded by a narrow band of xylem and some remaining pieces of cambial tissue. The stripped cores were then transferred to sterile agar or liquid media in test tubes.

Peeled internode cultures of nine different races of *M. cardinalis* were thus established. Most frequently, callus tissues are formed at the outer surfaces and at the ends of the peeled internodes, but root and leafy tissues may also be initiated, the direction of development being shifted by different compositions of hormones added to the media. Subcultures of callus tissue of the foothill races of *M. cardinalis* (Priests Grade clone 7210-2 and Jacksonville 7211-5) were made through as many as 21 successive transfers over a two-year period in the L medium, and apparently could have been continued indefinitely. Similar callus from the mid-Sierran Yosemite clone 6694-105 died after eight transfers in the same medium, while another from San Antonio Peak (clone 7120-8) grew slowly and survived through only six transfers. Subcultures of root tissues originating from peeled internodes of *M. cardinalis* have also been maintained through as many as a dozen transfers.

Early attempts to establish *M. lewisii* peeled internodal cultures failed. Later efforts (using White's agar medium with 1 mg/l 2, 4-D added) were more successful, but growth was much slower than in *M. cardinalis*. Stem apexes of *M. lewisii* were relatively easy to establish when provided with the high salt medium (H), but comparable apexes of *M. cardinalis* in either the L or H media grew considerably faster than corresponding explants of *M. lewisii*.

Success in establishing comparable explants of both *M. cardinalis* and *M. lewisii* under identical conditions was finally attained by first establishing seedling cultures of the two species in the intermediate salt medium (M). Seeds were sterilized in hypochlorite solution, washed in sterile distilled water, and transferred to sterile test tubes containing this medium. Under these conditions the seedlings of both species developed rather slender succulent stems with numerous small leaves crowded together by the shortened internodes (cf. figure 72, center). Side branchlets are frequently developed from the stems, and also roots at the base. Subcultures made from excised leaves of both species transferred to either solid or liquid media are capable of developing callus tissues which may proliferate and develop roots, shoots, or both.

EXAMPLES OF EXPERIMENTS. Some examples of experiments will serve to illustrate responses observed with excised *Mimulus* tissues. In figure 72 (center) the growth responses at 15° and 25° C of seedling cultures of *Mimulus lewisii* from Yosemite are shown in comparison with similarly treated seedlings of *M. cardinalis* from Jacksonville. In this experiment (No. 39 of the culture series) sterilized seeds of both species were grown in sterile test tubes containing 1 ml of H medium and allowed to germinate and establish for 90 days while being kept in test tube racks at a room temperature of 20–22° under fluorescent light of *ca.* 250 erg cm^{-2} sec^{-1} intensity. At this stage the seedlings of the 10 replicated cultures of *M. lewisii* were quite uniform, approximately 1 cm in height, and those of *M. cardinalis* slightly more variable, averaging 1.7 cm in height. Quintuplicate sets of cultures of each species were then placed in slowly rotating drum holders to provide gentle agitation of the liquid nutrient and evenness of exposure to lighting. To each test-tube culture 1 ml fresh nutrient was added each week during the experimental period. The rotating cultures were housed in small control chambers, one set being maintained at 15°, the other at 25°. The sides and top of the chambers were made of glass to admit penetration of diffuse laboratory daylight.

The responses of the replicated cultures of each species at each temperature treatment were consistently similar, the variation within each replicated set being less than the differences in growth between temperature treatments and between species. The photographs shown at the center in figure 72 show typical growth responses at the end of a 47-day experimental period. The mean dry weights of the cultures at the termination of this experiment are shown in table 44.

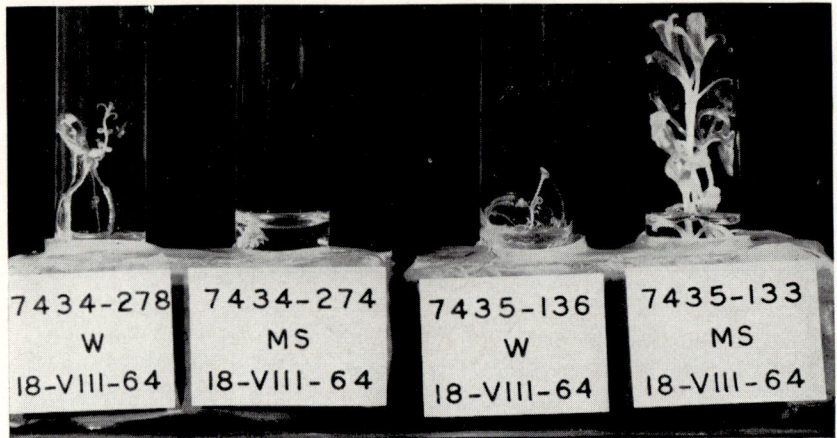

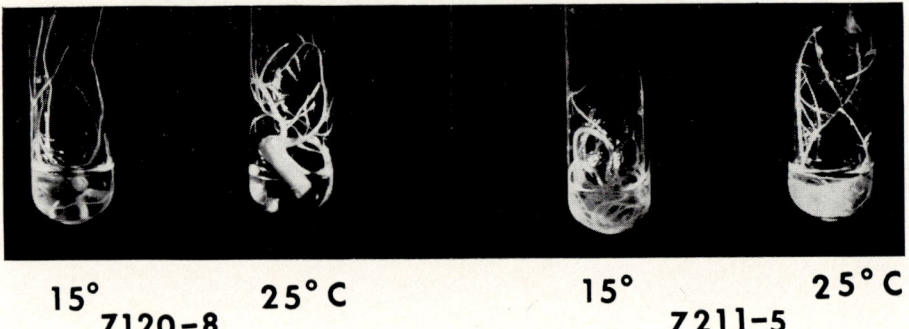

Among the interesting responses is the considerably higher growth rate observed in the seedlings of *M. lewisii* at 25° as compared with those of *M. cardinalis*, and shown in dry weight increases in table 44. The greater growth of *M. lewisii* at 25° was accompanied, however, by marked chlorosis of the numerous small leaves of the seedlings at 25° at the end of the experimental period. The seedlings of the same species maintained at 15° retained a healthy green appearance. The *M. cardinalis* seedlings at both 15° and 25° retained a healthy green color up to the end of the experimental period and did not show a significant difference in dry weight at the two temperatures, although stem elongation was greater at 25° (table 44). These results suggest that the *M. cardinalis* seedlings were more highly buffered against major shifts in metabolic balance resulting from temperature change than those of *M. lewisii*. This response seems to be consistent with the growth differences between *M.*

TABLE 44

Growth of Seedlings in Test-Tube Cultures at Different Temperatures

	M. lewisii		*M. cardinalis*	
	15° C	25° C	15° C	25° C
Mean dry weight increase, mg...	24	54	28	30
Mean height of stems, cm........	3.5 ± 0.57	6.2 ± 0.35	6.8 ± 1.08	10.9 ± 0.44

Dry weights are pooled mean values of 5 replicated cultures. Culture period was 47 days. Cf. figure 72 (center).

lewisii Logan and *M. cardinalis* Jacksonville at 10° and 30° C described on pages 155–157. It is difficult, however, on the basis of the present data to arrive at satisfactory physiological interpretations of observed growth in test-tube seedling experiments because of complicating factors. For example, the growth medium contained 3% sucrose, and we do not know the extent to which growth of the two clones was dependent on the direct absorption of organic carbon in the nutrient media in relation to what may have been contributed by photosynthesis.

An example of differential growth responses between *M. lewisii* Yosemite and *M. cardinalis* Los Trancos when grown in different liquid media is illustrated at the top of figure 72. In this experiment (No. 43a of this series) the

Figure 72. *Above:* Differential growth of *Mimulus lewisii* (Yosemite, the two cultures at the left), and *M. cardinalis* (Los Trancos, the two cultures at the right). Explants of each were established from stem apexes of aseptically grown seedlings in medium salt (M) and high salt (H) media, left and right tubes of each pair, respectively. Shown here 27 days after inoculation. See text.
Center: Seedling cultures of *M. lewisii* (Yosemite, *left*) and of *M. cardinalis* (Jacksonville, *right*) grown at 15° and 25°, 47 days after inoculation. See text.
Below: Cultures of *M. cardinalis* clones (7120-8, San Antonio Peak, and 7211-5, Jacksonville) cultured from stem internodes and grown for 48 days at 15° and 25°. See text.

growth responses of apexes of seedling cultures of both species established in agar cultures several months previously were grown in intermediate salt (M) medium containing 3% sucrose, with 0.1 mg/l IAA and 0.2 mg/l kinetin added. The excised seedling tips of each clone were placed in 1.0 ml liquid medium and incubated in roller drum holders in diffuse laboratory daylight at room temperature (20–22°). The photographs shown at the top of figure 72 were taken at the end of a 27-day experimental period.

In the intermediate salt medium (modified White's), the apical cultures of *M. lewisii* and *M. cardinalis* were quite similar in that both shoot growth and root growth took place with moderate vigor, but in the high salt medium (Murashige and Skoog) the growth of *M. cardinalis* was greatly enhanced in contrast with the very meager development of roots in cultures of *M. lewisii*. Five replicated cultures of the two species compared in these media were consistent in their differential responses, and the examples illustrated at the top of figure 72 are average. Table 45 shows the mean dry weight increase of the

TABLE 45

Growth Responses of *Mimulus lewisii* and *M. cardinalis* in Intermediate and High Salt Media

	M. lewisii		*M. cardinalis*	
	Intermediate Salt Medium	High Salt Medium	Intermediate Salt Medium	High Salt Medium
Mean net increase in dry wt., mg *	3.9	2.2	3.6	22.8

* Values are means of 5 replicates (final dry weight minus average initial dry weight of excised apexes). Cf. figure 72 (top).

cultures at the end of the experimental period. The differential responses of the same clones of both species were confirmed in subsequent experiments.

The results of another experiment in which peeled stem internodes of clones of the San Antonio Peak and Jacksonville races of *M. cardinalis* were cultured at 15° and 25° in liquid culture media are illustrated at the bottom of figure 72. The internodes were cut from stems of actively growing shoots of plants in a greenhouse and sterilized in the usual manner. The cultures were grown in 1 ml liquid modified White's medium (medium M of table 43) with 3% glucose added. The test tubes were placed in slowly rotating drums that were housed in the small temperature-controlled chambers. At weekly intervals the cultures were replenished with 1 ml nutrient medium during the experimental period. The internodes at first developed callus tissues from which active root growth took place later in both clones at both temperatures. In this experiment (No. 63 of the culture series), only slight differences were observed between the growth of the two clones of *M. cardinalis*: clone 7120-8 from San Antonio Peak, originally from 2200 m elevation (figure 72, lower left), having somewhat greater growth at 15° than at 25°, and clone 7211-5 from Jacksonville, originally from 240 m elevation in the warm Sierran foothill region (figure 72, lower right), with slightly faster growth at 25°. The photographs shown in figure 72 were taken 48 days after the inoculations were made. These responses are in contrast with a similar experiment with the clone 7246-3, *M. cardinalis* from the Santa Catalina Mountains at Bear Wallow, Arizona, at an elevation of 2280 m. In this clone the root growth in 10 replicated cultures was spectacularly greater at 15° C than at 25°, as shown at the top of figure 73 (experiment No. 52 of the culture series). In this latter experiment the same medium as used as in the one previously mentioned (White's base, with 1 mg/l IAA and 3% sucrose added).

A number of experiments on callus cultures with *Mimulus* were made. Peeled internodes of cultures of *M. cardinalis* can readily be established on agar slants in the low salt medium and carried through many successive transfers, some clones being more readily grown for longer periods, as previously mentioned. Attempts to establish similar callus cultures of *M. lewisii* with stem internodes were unsuccessful, but later efforts using pieces of excised leaves from seedlings did succeed. Figure 73 (center) shows cultures of *M. cardinalis* callus tissues grown on agar medium of high salt concentration containing three levels of IAA: (1) no IAA added, (2) 0.1 mg/l IAA, and (3) 10.0 mg/l IAA. These cultures originally were derived from peeled stem internodes of the Jacksonville clone 7211-5 grown in low salt medium in agar. The examples illustrated were derived from stock callus that had been carried through successive transfers over a two-year period. After inoculation on agar slants, they were maintained at 25° at a relative humidity of 70% and provided with 8 hours of light of 250 erg cm^{-2} sec^{-1} intensity (experiment No. 41 of the culture series). The photographs in figure 73 (center) were taken 180 days after inoculation and show representative cultures of each treatment among the 10 replicates. The inhibiting effect of IAA on the growth of callus is clearly evident.

In attempts to obtain friable callus cultures containing cells with active green chloroplasts, parts of excised leaves from previously established cultures of both *M. cardinalis* and *M. lewisii* were tried in both solid and liquid media. Figure 73 (bottom) shows such cultures of *M. lewisii* Timberline derived from single leaves of seedlings grown in test tubes (for example, from such cultures of *M. lewisii* and *M. cardinalis* as are illustrated in the center of figure 72). Pieces of bacteria-free leaves were placed with their lower surfaces in contact with agar made with intermediate salt (M) medium with NAA added. The cultures were maintained at 26° in one of the small chambers and illuminated 8 hours daily with fluorescent lamps. The pictures shown at the bottom of figure 73 show leaf callus cultures of *M. lewisii* 39 days after incubation (experiment No. 60 of the culture series). The culture at the left shows the effect of adding 0.1 mg/l NAA to the basic medium, in comparison with the one on the right

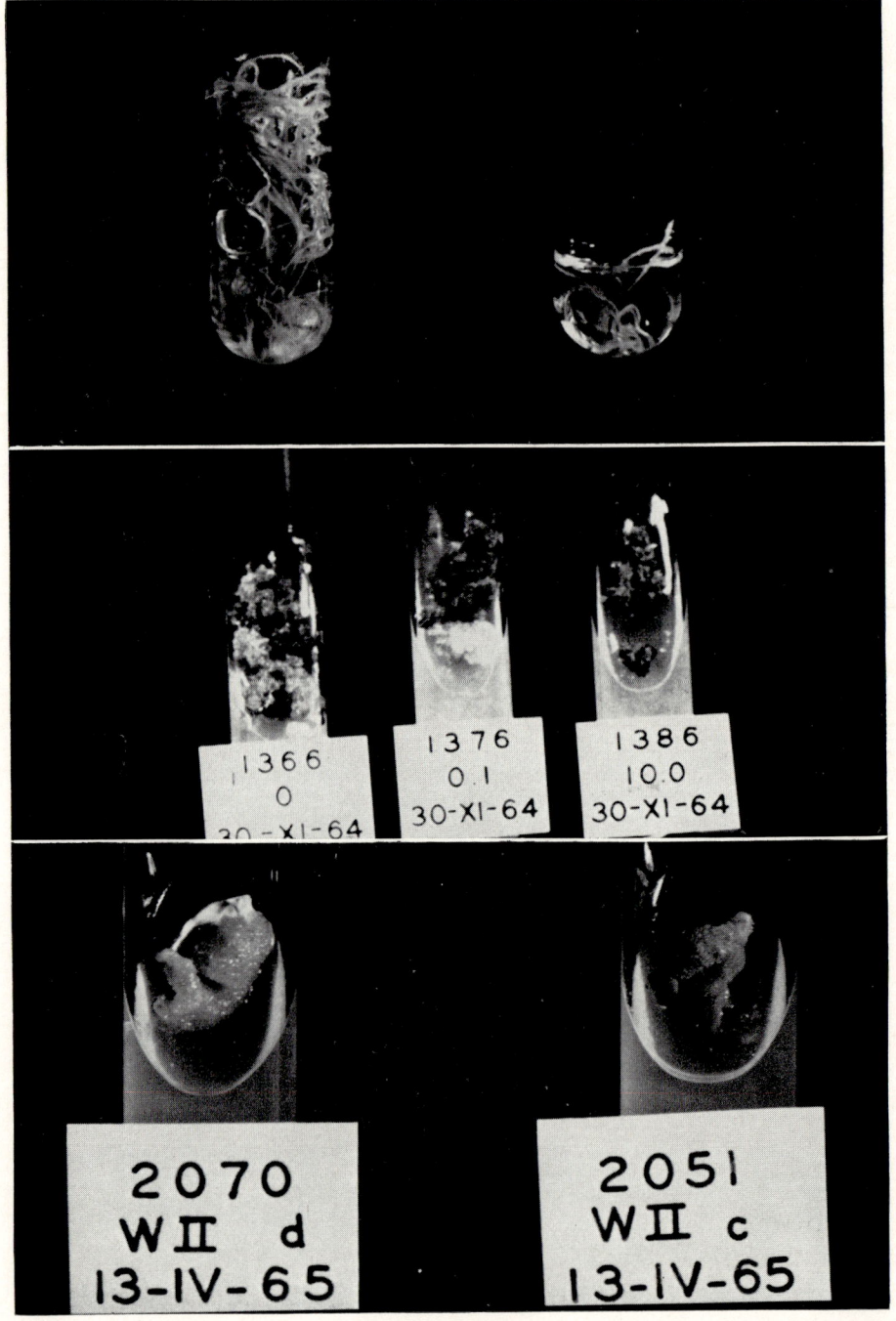

containing 10.0 mg/l. Growth was more rapid and the callus was of a more friable structure when the culture was grown in the medium containing the lower amount of NAA. Ten replicated cultures in each treatment were consistent in showing the differences illustrated.

Similar cultures of excised leaves of *M. cardinalis* produced callus tissues even more readily than *M. lewisii*. In both species the cells forming the callus were commonly aggregated in clumps, but sometimes occurred in chains, and were variously pigmented. The colors ranged from yellow to dark brown, but in neither species were callus tissues with active green chloroplasts successfully maintained over long periods of time. In some instances green callus formed which on aging became yellow to dark brown.

Limitations of space do not permit a more extended review of experiments made on excised cultures of *Mimulus*. Our primary objective was to evaluate the feasibility and potential usefulness of this approach in the comparative study of contrasting ecological races and species. The results of this exploration show that the value of this approach may be real. The number of external controllable variables available to the experimenter is far greater than in typical growth experiments on whole plants in controlled cabinets or chambers, as described in the previous chapter. A logical consequence, however, is that the problem of unscrambling the variables in critical experiments becomes greater. The potential enhancement of experimental precision due to the finer control possible in excised tissues may well compensate for the more exacting control of variables that is required. With the possibility of accurate control of substrate levels, for example, critical comparative studies on metabolic performance of ecological races should be possible.

Figure 73. *Above:* Cultures of *Mimulus cardinalis* (clone 7246-3, Santa Catalina Mountains, Arizona) started from peeled internodes and grown at 15° (*left*) and at 25° (*right*). Photograph taken 167 days after inoculation. See text.
Center: Callus cultures of *M. cardinalis* (clone 7211-5, Jacksonville) grown in the high salt (H) medium with varying amounts of indole acetic acid added (*left*, no IAA; *center*, 0.1 mg/l; *right*, 10.0 mg/l). Cultures established from previous callus after many transfers. Cultures here shown are 180 days old.
Below: Callus cultures of *M. lewisii* established from excised leaves of aseptically grown seedlings (cf. figure 72, *center*). Grown on M medium with 0.1 mg/l NAA added (*left*) and 10.0 mg/l (*right*). See text.

V
DEVELOPMENT OF APPROACHES IN EXPERIMENTAL STUDIES ON THE NATURE OF SPECIES

The overall objective of experimental studies on the nature of species is to clarify our understanding of the relative importance and interrelationships of factors that underlie plant evolution. This quest during the past half century has brought to light many previously unknown facts that profoundly influence our present thinking. The search is still continuing and recently, especially at the physiological and biochemical level, is rapidly gaining momentum. It seems appropriate to review in general terms the present status of this search in the light of such studies as have been presented in this volume.

LEVELS OF EXPERIMENTAL APPROACH. The work of the earlier taxonomists was concerned with the search and classification of species, an essential step that resulted in the orderly treatment of the great diversity of living forms into orders, families, genera, and species. As this approach became more intensively applied in detailed monographic studies of groups restricted to a few genera or even to a single section of a genus, thoughtful taxonomists became increasingly dissatisfied with their systematic treatments and sought the aid of cytologists and geneticists to help clarify relationships that proved to be too puzzling to be resolved by morphological studies alone.

This marked the beginning of experimental taxonomy, with plant materials being collected and planted in gardens where they could be hybridized and studied in the laboratory. This ushered in a period that may be termed the "grand era of cytogenetics," which evolved with such classical investigations as those of Johannsen (1909), Shull (1911), Bauer (1914), Winge (1917), Kihara (1924), Roy Clausen (1928), Jens Clausen (1929, 1931), Müntzing (1938), Goldschmidt (1938), Gregor (1939), Babcock (1947), Stebbins (1950), and Blakeslee (cf. Avery, Satina, and Reitsma, 1959), to mention only a few. The discoveries during this period uncovered the manifold devices by which species and races may become differentiated through mutations, chromosomal repatterning, aneuploidy, polyploidy, amphiploidy, apomixis, and combinations of these mechanisms. Verne Grant (1963) and Heslop-Harrison (1964) have contributed reviews covering various aspects of this productive period. Basic to all of the hereditary devices for introducing and perpetuating genetic diversity is differentiation between related forms on the diploid chromosome level such as is found in widespread groups as exemplified by the genus *Pinus* ($n=12$), *Aquilegia* ($n=7$), members of the *Potentilla glandulosa* complex ($n=7$) and in the *Erythranthe* section of *Mimulus* ($n=8$).

In the excitement of the discoveries during the "grand era of cytogenetics" the importance of environment as a selective factor in evolution was not ignored. It was the work of Turesson (1922, 1925), however, that brought the ecological viewpoint into sharp focus through his studies on ecotypes and his elaboration of the concept of "genecology." Another aspect of ecotypes, or, as we call them, ecological races, was the comparative study of responses of cloned individual plants of diverse races of the same or related species transplanted to gardens at contrasting altitudes, a subject dealt with in detail in earlier volumes of this series. These studies clarified the nature and limits of tolerance of ecological races for survival in different kinds of habitats, and, furthermore, distinguished clearly between differences due to heredity and modifications displayed by the same clone grown in different environments.

Genetic experiments involving crossing contrasting ecological races of the same species combined with tests on cloned parents and F_1 and F_2 progeny in transplant experiments were begun in 1932 (Clausen and Hiesey, 1958). These experiments demonstrated the polygenic nature of most of the hereditary differences in characters distinguishing contrasting altitudinal races, and also indicated the importance of genetic coherence, i.e., the tendency for progeny from interracial crosses to inherit assemblages of associated characters from their parents as a package rather than independently and purely at random. This finding confirmed earlier predictions by Anderson (1936) and especially by Mather (1942, 1943) relating to the genetic consequences of polygenic inheritance.

The significance of genetic coherence for storing unexpressed genetic variability that can be released in subsequent generations under stress of changed selective pressures in new environments has been emphasized by the authors cited above and has been discussed in detail by Verne Grant (1964). The genetic data from the *Erythranthe* section in *Mimulus* presented in Chapter II reveal even more clearly and in greater detail than in previous studies the significance of genetic coherence as a factor in the inheritance of characters distinguishing contrasting ecological races.

We may look forward to further advances in elucidating the mechanism of coherence, perhaps at a molecular level. This may be approached through analysis of the inheritance of enzymatic control of critical steps governing such physiological processes as the pathways of CO_2 fixation, in such species as *Atriplex patula* and *A. rosea,* discussed on pages 178–179. It is conceivable that the coherence between biochemical and physiological characteristics associated with photosynthesis in these species may be resolvable into relatively simple cause-effect relationships. The correlation between these characteristics and anatomical features that are also associated with the different pathways of CO_2 fixation is probably not a result of pleiotropism, but is more likely a result of genetic linkage.

The comparison of growth responses of cloned transplants under controlled conditions in chambers was a logical development to follow the field transplant experiments. Such studies, in turn, led directly to the next step of comparative physiological and biochemical studies of contrasting ecological races, as discussed in Chapter III. Investigations in this area have now become central in our quest for further elucidating mechanisms of natural selection.

THE PRESENT STATUS OF PHYSIOLOGICAL AND BIOCHEMICAL INQUIRIES. In addition to the general recognition of the importance of physiological and biochemical investigations for furthering our understanding of plant evolution, current interest in this relatively new field has been stimulated by the development of new technical advances that make possible precise quantitative measurements combined with excellent control of external variables with reasonable speed. Such pioneer investigations as those of Lundegård and Boysen-Jensen, for example, were limited by the necessity of using the time-consuming chemical methods available at that time for measuring photosynthetic rates. Despite these hindrances the contributions of these and other earlier investigators have established a solid basis for present and future investigations in physiological plant ecology.

Our approach to the comparative physiology of ecological races through step-by-step studies on the effects of single variables on a given process have yielded results which, together with the contributions of other laboratories, serve as starting points for future work.

There is strong evidence that ecological races of *Solidago, Solanum,* and *Mimulus* differ in the relative component steps of photosynthesis leading to different responses to external variables. The genetically controlled mechanisms that result in differences in utilization of weak and strong light for photosynthesis in sun and shade races of *Solidago,* for example, include the ratio of pigments responsible for the capture of light to the activity of enzymes responsible for the biochemical conversion of CO_2 to the level of carbohydrates. It seems likely that sun and shade plants may also differ in the size of the photosynthetic unit, i.e., that shade species have fewer photochemical reaction centers for a given number of light-harvesting chlorophyll molecules. Apparently, physical resistance to gas diffusion may also differ. There is no evidence that the differences between ecological races in *Solidago* and *Solanum* in response to light intensity, between *Mimulus cardinalis* and *M. lewisii* in temperature tolerance, or between races of *Solanum* in tolerance to water stress, involve qualitative differences in photochemical or biochemical pathways of photosynthesis.

This, of course, does not exclude the possibility that such differences do exist. The presence of the C_4-dicarboxylic acid pathway (β-carboxylation) of CO_2 fixation in some species, and its absence in other closely related species, as in *Atriplex,* suggest that qualitative differentiation in pathways of photosynthesis may be a more frequent occurrence than previously anticipated.

A striking result of studies on the kinetics of photosynthesis from studies made to date is that all plants of all ecological races, including both those that follow the C_4-dicarboxylic acid pathway of CO_2 fixation and those that do not, have been found to have the same temperature dependence for light-saturated photosynthetic rate in the temperature range of 15° C and below when measured under a low oxygen concentration in the range of 1–2%. At this low temperature range the Arrhenius equation for photosynthetic rates is valid, and a high activation energy of about 20 Kcal per mole is obtained. At higher temperatures, however, species and ecological races of the same species may differ considerably. When such photosynthetic measurements are made under higher O_2 concentrations, such as in normal air at 21.0%, such differences at higher temperatures become greatly accentuated in plants that lack β-carboxylation photosynthesis, but remain the same in plants that possess this pathway.

FUTURE INVESTIGATIONS. In view of the very large number of yet unsolved problems relating to the comparative physiology of ecological races and species, as outlined in the early part of Chapter III, future investigations may be expected to develop along a multitude of fronts. The use of excised tissues for critical studies on the as yet little understood role of respiration, for example, is an area inviting investigation. Another is the study of the physiological and biochemical basis of "heterosis," or hybrid vigor.

Fousová and Auratovščuková (1967) reported heterosis in photosynthetic rate in first-generation and backcross hybrids of *Zea mays* as compared with the inbred parental races. Their measurements, which were made manometrically on leaf disc samples, appear to be consistent with the commonly observed more rapid growth rate of hybrids as compared with their parents. Their results differ from ours on hybrids with *Mimulus* (cf. Chapter III) and those of Björkman and Holmgren (1963) in *Solidago virgaurea*, where measurements of light-saturated photosynthetic rates on hybrids were found to be intermediate between the parents. The inheritance of factors governing component steps in photosynthesis is apparently fairly complex and may, at least in many instances, be governed by polygenic hereditary factors.

Although the term "heterosis" is usually used to indicate an enhancement in vigor or in the expression of some character in hybrid derivatives as compared with the parents, one may also consider "negative heterosis" as a reduction in vigor or in expression of a given character. A striking example is the F_1 hybrid between *Atriplex rosea* and *A. patula* in which the hybrids, although clearly intermediate between the parents in morphological and anatomical characters, have a much lower photosynthetic capacity than either parent.

LITERATURE CITED

Anderson, Edgar
- 1936 Hybridization in the American *Tradescantias*. I. A method for measuring species hybrids. II. Hybridization between *T. virginicana* and *T. canaliculata*. Ann. Missouri Bot. Garden 23:511–525.
- 1939a Recombination in species crosses. Genetics 24:668–698.
- 1939b The hindrance to gene recombination imposed by linkage: an estimate of its total magnitude. Amer. Nat. 73:185–188.
- 1949 Introgressive hybridization. viii+109 pp. John Wiley & Sons, Inc. New York and London.

Auratovščuková, Naděžda
- 1968 Differences in photosynthetic rate in leaf disks in five tobacco varieties. Photosynthetica 2:149–160.

Avery, Amos G., Sophie Satina, and Jacob Rietsema
- 1959 Blakeslee: The genus *Datura*. xiii+289 pp. Ronald Press, New York.

Babcock, Ernest Brown
- 1947 The genus *Crepis*. Vol. I: The taxonomy, phylogeny, distribution, and evolution of *Crepis*. xii+198 pp. Vol. II: Systematic treatment. x+199–1030 pp. Univ. of Calif. Press, Berkeley and Los Angeles; Cambridge University Press, London.

Bauer, Erwin
- 1914 Einführung in die experimentelle Vererbungslehre. vii+401 pp. Gebrüder Borntraeger, Berlin.

Bentham, G.
- 1846 In De Candole's Prodromus Systematis Universalis Regni Vegetabilis 10:368–373.

Billings, W. D., E. E. C. Clebach, and H. A. Mooney
- 1961 Effect of low concentrations of carbon dioxide on photosynthesis rates of two races of *Oxyria*. Science 133:1834.

Björkman, Olle
- 1966a The effect of oxygen concentration on photosynthesis in higher plants. Physiol. Plantarum 19:618–633.
- 1966b Comparative studies of photosynthesis and respiration in ecological races. Brittonia 18:214–224.
- 1968a Further studies on differentiation of photosynthetic properties in sun and shade ecotypes of *Solidago virgaurea*. Physiol. Plantarum 21:84–89.
- 1968b Carboxydismutase activity in shade-adapted and sun-adapted species of higher plants. Physiol. Plantarum 21:1–10.

Björkman, Olle, Cirl Florell, and Paul Holmgren
- 1960 Studies of climatic ecotypes in higher plants. The temperature dependence of apparent photosynthesis in different populations of *Solidago virgaurea*. Annals Royal Agr. College of Sweden 26:1–10.

Björkman, Olle, and Eckard Gauhl
- 1968 Effect of temperature and oxygen concentration on photosynthesis in *Marchantia polymorpha*. Carnegie Inst. Wash. Year Book No. 67:479–482.
- 1969a Carboxydismutase activity in plants with and without β-carboxylation photosynthesis. Planta 88:197–203.
- 1969b Application of a new O_2 sensing device to measurements of higher plant photosynthesis. Carnegie Inst. Wash. Year Book No. 68:636–640.

Björkman, Olle, Eckard Gauhl, William M. Hiesey, Frank Nicholson, and Malcolm A. Nobs
- 1968 Growth of *Mimulus, Marchantia,* and *Zea* under different oxygen and carbon dioxide levels. Carnegie Inst. Wash. Year Book No. 67:477–478.

Björkman, Olle, and Paul Holmgren
- 1961 Studies of climatic ecotypes of higher plants leaf respiration in different populations of *Solidago virgaurea*. Annals Royal Agr. College of Sweden 27:297–304.
- 1963 Adaptability of the photosynthetic apparatus to light intensity in ecotypes from exposed and shaded habitats. Physiol. Plantarum 16:889–914.

LITERATURE CITED

Björkman, Olle, William M. Hiesey, Malcolm A. Nobs, Frank Nicholson, and Richard W. Hart
    1966 Effect of oxygen concentration on dry matter production in higher plants. Carnegie Inst. Wash. Year Book No. 66:228–233.

Björkman, Olle, Malcolm A. Nobs, and Eckard Gauhl
    1969 Comparative studies of *Atriplex* species with and without β-carboxylation photosynthesis, and their first-generation hybrid. Carnegie Inst. Wash. Year Book No. 68:620–633.

Blakeley, L. M., and F. C. Steward
    1964 Growth and organized development of cultured cells. V. The growth of colonies of free cells on nutrient agar. Amer. Jour. Bot. 51:780–791.

Brock, Thomas D.
    1967a Relationship between standing crop and primary productivity along a hot spring thermal gradient. Ecology 48:566–571.
    1967b Micro-organisms adapted to high temperatures. Nature 214:882–885.
    1967c Life at high temperatures. Science 158:1012–1019.

Brock, T. D., and M. Louise Brock
    1966 Temperature optima for algal development in Yellowstone and Iceland hot springs. Nature 209:733–734.

Brožek, A.
    1926 Inheritance in the monkey-flower. Jour. of Hered. 17:113–129.
    1929 Preliminary report on the genetic constitution of flower colors in the garden population of *Mimulus cardinalis* Hort. Acta Bot. Bohemica 8:80–85.
    1930 Remarks on the genetic constitution of flower-colours in *Mimulus cardinalis* Hort. Proceed. Fifth Int. Bot. Congress, Cambridge, Section G, Sect. Abstracts: 251–252.
    1931 Further investigations on the genetics of flower colors in *Mimulus cardinalis* Hort. Bull. de la Société Botanique Tchécoslovaque à Prague 10:42–46.
    1932 Mendelian analysis of the "red-orange-yellow" group of flower-colours in *Mimulus cardinalis* Hort. Preslia 11:1–10.

Bunt, J. S., Olga van H. Owens, and G. Hoch
    1966 Exploratory studies on the physiology and ecology of a psychrophilic marine diatom. Jour. Phycology 2:96–100.

Burr, G. O.
    1962 The use of radioisotopes by the Hawaiian sugar plantations. Int. Jour. Appl. Rad. 13:365–374.

Castenholz, Richard W.
    1967 Environmental requirements of blue-green algae. Proceed. Symposium, U. of Wash. and Federal Water Pollution Control Adm., Pacific Northwest Lab., Corvallis, Ore. (mimeographed).

Clausen, Jens C.
    1929 Chromosome number and relationship of some North American species of *Viola*. Annals of Bot. 43:741–764.
    1931 Cytogenetic and taxonomic investigations on Melanium violets. Hereditas 15:219–308.

Clausen, Roy E.
    1928 Interspecific hybridization in *Nicotiana*. VII. The cytology of hybrids of the synthetic species, *digluta*, with its parents, *glutinosa* and *tabacum*. Univ. of Calif. Pub. Bot. 11:177–211.

Clausen, Jens, David D. Keck, and William M. Hiesey
    1940 Experimental studies on the nature of species. I. Effect of varied environments on western North American plants. Carnegie Inst. Wash. Pub. 520, vii+452 pp.
    1945 Experimental studies on the nature of species. II. Plant evolution through amphiploidy and autoploidy, with examples from the Madiinae. Carnegie Inst. Wash. Pub. 564, vii+174 pp.
    1947 Experimental taxonomy: use of station facilities. Carnegie Inst. Wash. Year Book No. 46:103–104.
    1948 Experimental studies on the nature of species. III. Environment responses of climatic races of *Achillea*. Carnegie Inst. Wash. Pub. 581, iii+129 pp.

CLAUSEN, JENS, and WILLIAM M. HIESEY
  1958 Experimental studies on the nature of species. IV. Genetic structure of ecological races. Carnegie Inst. Wash. Pub. 615, iv+312 pp.
CLINE, M. G., and A. O. AGATEP
  1970 Temperature and photoperiodic control of developmental responses in climatic races of *Mimulus*. Plant and Cell Physiology II. In press.
COOPER, J. B.
  1968 Developmental genetics. In Report of the Welsh Plant Breeding Station for 1967. Plas Gogerddan near Aberystwyth, Wales, pp. 10–28.
COOPER, T. G., D. FILMER, MARCIA WISHNICK, and M. D. LANE
  1969 The active species of "CO_2" utilized by RuDP carboxylase. Jour. Biol. Chem. 244: 1081–1083.
DOWNES, R. W., and J. D. HESKETH
  1968 Enhanced photosynthesis at low oxygen concentrations: differential response of temperature and tropical grasses. Planta 78:79–84.
EAGLES, C. F.
  1967 The effect of temperature on vegetative growth in climatic races of *Dactylis glomerata* in controlled environments. Annals of Bot., N.S., 31:31–39.
EAGLES, C. F., and K. J. TREHARNE
  1969 Photosynthetic activity of *Dactylis glomerata* L. in different light regimes. Photosynthetica 3:29–38.
FALK, S. O.
  1966a A microwave hygrometer for measuring plant transpiration. Zeits. Pflanzenphysiol. 55: 31–37.
  1966b Quantitative determinations of the effect of excision on transpiration. Physiol. Plantarum 19:493–522.
FOCK, H., and K. EGLE
  1966 Über die "Lichtatmung" bei grünen Pflanzen. Beitr. Biol. Pfl. 42:213–239.
FOCKE, WILHELM O.
  1881 Die Pflanzen-Mischlinge. Gebrüder Bornträger, Berlin, p. 314.
FORRESTER, M. L., G. KROTOV, and C. D. NELSON
  1966 Effect of oxygen on photosynthesis, photorespiration, and respiration in detached leaves. II. Corn and other monocotyledons. Plant Physiol. 41:428–431.
FOUSOVÁ, S., and N. AURATOVŠČUKOVÁ
  1967 Hybrid vigor and photosynthetic rate of leaf disks in *Zea mays* L. Photosynthetica 1:3–12.
FRENCH, C. S., R. W. CLAIR, and W. M. HIESEY
  1962 A control system for carbon dioxide concentration in plant growth chambers. Carnegie Inst. Wash. Year Book No. 61:319–320.
GARRIC, RICHARD
  1965 The cryoflora of the Pacific Northwest. Amer. Jour. Bot. 52:1–8.
GATES, DAVID M.
  1965 Energy, plants, and ecology. Ecology 46:1–13.
  1968 Transpiration and leaf temperature. Ann. Review Plant Physiol. 19:211–238.
GATES, DAVID M., WILLIAM M. HIESEY, HAROLD W. MILNER, and MALCOLM A. NOBS
  1964 Temperatures of *Mimulus* leaves in natural environments and in a controlled chamber. Carnegie Inst. Wash. Year Book No. 63:418–430.
GAUHL, ECKARD
  1967 Comparative physiological studies on *Solanum dulcamara*. Carnegie Inst. Wash. Year Book No. 66:233–234.
  1968 Differential photosynthetic performance of *Solanum dulcamara* ecotypes from shaded and exposed habitats. Carnegie Inst. Wash. Year Book No. 67:482–491.
  1969 Leaf factors affecting the rate of light-saturated photosynthesis in ecotypes of *Solanum dulcamara*. Carnegie Inst. Wash. Year Book No. 68:633–636.
GAUHL, E., and O. BJÖRKMAN
  1969 Simultaneous measurements on the effect of oxygen concentration on water vapor and carbon dioxide exchange in leaves. Planta 88:187–191.

GOLDSCHMIDT, RICHARD B.
  1938 Physiological genetics. ix+375 pp. McGraw-Hill Book Company, New York and London.
GRANT, ADELE L.
  1924 A monograph of the genus *Mimulus*. Ann. Missouri Bot. Garden 11:99–388.
GRANT, VERNE
  1963 The origin of adaptations. x+606 pp. Columbia Univ. Press, New York and London.
  1964 The architecture of the germ plasm. John Wiley & Sons, Inc., New York. xv+236 pp.
  1966 Linkage between viability and fertility in a species cross in *Gilia*. Genetics 54:867–880.
GRAY, A.
  1876 Proceed. Ann. Acad. of Arts and Sciences 11:94–99.
  1886 Synoptical Flora of North America, second ed., 2: Supplement 442–451.
GREENE, EDWARD L.
  1885 Studies in the botany of California and parts adjacent. I. Bull. Calif. Acad. Sci. 1:66–127.
  1909 Leaflets of Botanical Observation and Criticism 2:2–3 Washington, D.C.
GREGOR, J. W.
  1939 Experimental Taxonomy. IV. Population differentiation in North American and European sea plantains allied to *Plantago maritima* L. New Phytol. 38:293–322.
HALLDAL, PER
  1968 Photosynthetic capacities and photosynthetic action spectra of endozoic algae of the massive coral *Favia*. Biol. Bulletin 134:411–424.
HATCH, M. D., and C. R. SLACK
  1966 Photosynthesis by sugar-cane leaves. Biochemical Jour. 101:103–111.
HATCH, M. D., C. R. SLACK, and H. S. JOHNSON
  1967 Further studies on a new pathway of photosynthetic carbon dioxide fixation in sugar-cane and its occurrence in other plant species. Biochemical Jour. 102:417–422.
HESKETH, J.
  1967 Enhancement of photosynthetic CO_2 assimilation in the absence of oxygen, as affected by species and temperature. Planta 76:371–374.
HESLOP-HARRISON, J.
  1964 Forty years of genecology. In Advances of Ecological Research, 2:159–247. Academic Press. London and New York. Edited by J. B. Cragg.
HIESEY, WILLIAM M., and HAROLD W. MILNER
  1962 Small cabinets for controlled environments. Bot. Gazette 124:103–118.
HIESEY, WILLIAM M., MALCOLM A. NOBS, and OLLE BJÖRKMAN
  1966 Photosynthetic rates of *M. lewisii* and *M. cardinalis* in comparison with their F_1 hybrid. Carnegie Inst. Wash. Year Book No. 65:464–468.
HOLMGREN, PAUL
  1968 Leaf factors affecting light-saturated photosynthesis in ecotypes of *Solidago virgaurea* from exposed and shaded habitats. Physiol. Plantarum 21:676–698.
JOHANNSEN, W.
  1909 Elemente der exakten Erblichkeitslehre. vi+516 pp. Gustav Fischer. Jena.
JOHNSON, H. S., and M. D. HATCH
  1968 Distribution of the C_4-dicarboxylic acid pathway of photosynthesis and its occurrence in dicotyledonous plants. Phytochem. 7:375–380.
JOLLIFFE, P. A., and E. B. TREGUNNA
  1968 Effect of temperature, CO_2 concentration, and light intensity on oxygen inhibition of photosynthesis in wheat leaves. Plant Physiol. 43:902–906.
JØRGENSEN, ERIK G.
  1968 The adaptation of plankton algae. II. Aspects of the temperature adaptation of *Skeletonema costatum*. Physiol. Plantarum 21:423–427.
KEARNEY, THOMAS H., and ROBERT H. PEEBLES
  1942 The flowering plants and ferns of Arizona. U.S. Dept. of Agriculture Miscell. Pub. 423. Government Printing Office, Washington, D.C.
KIHARA, HITOSHI
  1924 Cytologische und genetische Studien bei wichtigen Getriedarten mit besonder Rücksicht auf das Verhalten der Chromosomen und die Sterilität in den Bastarden. Mem. Coll. Sci. Kyoto Imperial Univ., ser. B, 1:1–200.

KORTSCHAK, H. P., C. E. HARTT, and G. O. BURR
   1965 Carbon dioxide fixation in sugar cane leaves. Plant Physiol. 40:209–213.
LAETSCH, W. M., and WINSLOW R. BRIGGS
   1962 Kinetin modification of sporeling ontogeny in *Marsilea vestita*. Amer. Jour. Botany 48:369–377.
LUNDEGÅRDH, HENRIK
   1924 Der Temperaturfaktor bei Kohlensaureassimilation und Atmung. Biochem. Zeitschrift 154:195–234.
   1957 Klima und Boden und ihrer Wirkung auf das Pflanzenleben. xv+584 pp. Fünfte Aufl., Gustav Fischer, Jena.
MATHER, K.
   1941 Variation and selection of polygenic characters. Jour. Genetics 41:159–193.
   1942 The polygene concept. Nature 140:731.
   1943 Polygenic inheritance in natural selection. Biol. Rev. 18:32–64.
MOONEY, H. A., and F. SHROPSHIRE
   1967 Population variability in temperature-related photosynthetic acclimation. Oeco. Planta II, 1–13.
MOONEY, H. A., and MARDA WEST
   1964 Photosynthetic acclimation of plants of diverse origin. Amer. Jour. Bot. 51:825–827.
MÜNTZING, A.
   1938 Sterility and chromosome pairing in *Galeopsis* hybrids. Hereditas 24:117–188.
MURASHIGE, T., and F. O. SKOOG
   1962 A revised medium for rapid growth and bioassays with tobacco tissue cultures. Physiol. Plantarum 15:473–497.
MUKHERJEE, B. B., and R. K. VICKERY, JR.
   1962 Chromosome counts in the section *Simiolus* of the genus *Mimulus* (Scrophularaceae). V. The chromosomal homologies of *M. guttatus* and its allied species and varieties. Madroño 16:141–155.
MCMAHON, DANIEL, and LAWRENCE BOGORAD
   1966 Some kinetic studies of ribulose-1,5-diphosphate carboxylase (carboxydismutase) from races of *Mimulus cardinalis*. Carnegie Inst. Wash. Year Book No. 65:459–461.
NUTTALL, T.
   1838 Taylor's Ann. Nat. Hist. 1:137–139.
POLLOCK, GAIL H.
   1964 The flavonoids of the section *Erythranthe* of *Mimulus*. MS. Thesis, University of Utah.
POLLOCK, GAIL, ROBERT K. VICKERY, JR., and KENNETH G. WILSON
   1967 Flavonoid pigments in *Mimulus cardinalis* and its related species. I. Anthocyanins. Amer. Jour. Bot. 54:695–701.
PROSSER, C. LADD
   1967 Molecular mechanisms of temperature adaptation. Pub. No. 84, Am. Assn. for Adv. Sci., viii+390 pp. Washington, D.C.
PURSH, FREDERICK
   1814 Flora Amer. Septentrianalis and Description of the Plants of North America 2:427. White, Cochrane and Co., London.
RYDBERG, P. A.
   1913 Bull. Torrey Bot. Club 40:483.
SCHAUB, H., W. HILGENBERG, and H. FOCK
   1968 Zeitschr. f. Pflanzenphysiol. 60:64–71.
SHULL, G. H.
   1911 Experiments with maize. Botanical Gazette 52:480–485.
SIEGEL, S. M., and L. A. ROSEN
   1962 Effects of reduced oxygen tension on germination and seedling growth. Physiol. Plantarum 15:437–444.
SIEGEL, S. M., L. A. ROSEN, and G. RENWICK
   1962 Effects of reduced oxygen tension on vascular plants. Growth and composition of red kidney bean plants in 5 per cent O_2. Physiol. Plantarum 15:304–314.
SIEGEL, S. M., L. A. ROSEN, and C. GUIMARRO
   1963 Plants at sub-atmospheric oxygen levels. Nature 198:1288–1290.

Siegel, S. M., L. Halpern, G. Davis, and C. Guimarro
    1963   The general and comparative biology of experimental atmospheres and other stress conditions. Aerospace Medicine 34:1034–1037.
Slack, C. R., and M. D. Hatch
    1967   Comparative studies on the activity of carboxylases and other enzymes in relation to the new pathway of photosynthetic carbon dioxide fixation in tropical grasses. Biochemical Jour. 103:660–665.
Sorokin, Constantine
    1958   The effect of the past history of cells of *Chlorella* on their photosynthetic capacity. Physiol. Plantarum 11:275–283.
    1967   New high-temperature *Chlorella*. Science 158:1202–1205.
Sorokin, Constantine, and Robert W. Krauss
    1958   The effects of light intensity on the growth rates of green algae. Plant Physiol. 33:109–113.
    1965   The dependence of cell division in *Chlorella* on temperature and light intensity. Amer. Jour. Bot. 52:331–339.
Sorokin, C., and J. Myers
    1953   High temperature strains of *Chlorella*. Science 117:330.
Spach, E.
    1840   Histoire Naturelle des Végétaux, 9:312–313. Boret, Paris.
Stebbins, G. Ledyard, Jr.
    1950   Variation and evolution in plants. xix+643 pp. Columbia Univ. Press, New York.
Steeman Nielsen, E., and Erik G. Jørgensen
    1968   The adaptation of plankton algae. III. With special consideration of the importance in nature. Physiol. Plantarum 21:647–654.
Stein, Janet R., and Robert C. Brooks
    1964   Red snow from Mt. Seymour, British Columbia. Canadian Jour. Bot. 42:1183–1188.
Stein, Janet R., and Clifford C. Amundsen
    1967   Studies on snow algae and fungi from the Front Range of Colorado. Canadian Jour. Bot. 45:2033–2045.
Strugger, S., and W. Baumeister
    1951   Zur Anwendung des Ultrarotabsorptionschreibers für CO_2-Assimilationsmessungen im Laboratorium. Berichte deut. Bot. Gesellschaft 64:5–22.
Tregunna, E. B., G. Krotkov, and C. D. Nelson
    1966   Effect of oxygen on the rate of photorespiration in detached tobacco leaves. Physiol. Plantarum 19:723–733.
Turesson, Göte
    1922   The genotypical response of the plant species to the habitat. Hereditas 3:211–350.
    1925   The plant species in relation to habitat and climate. Hereditas 6:147–236.
Vickery, Robert K.
    1951   Genetic differences between races and species of *Mimulus*. Carnegie Inst. Wash. Year Book No. 50:118–119.
    1952   A study of the genetic relationships in a sample of the *Mimulus guttatus* complex. PhD. dissertation, Stanford University.
    1966   Experimental hybridizations in the genus *Mimulus*. IV. Barriers to gene exchange between the main sections. Utah Academy of Sciences, Arts, and Letters. 43:115–118, pt. 1: 115–118.
    1967   Growth of *Mimulus* under controlled conditions. Proceed. Utah Acad. Sci. 44:334–338.
Vickery, Robert K., and David G. Anderson
    1967   Experimental hybridizations in the genus *Mimulus*. VI. Section *Erythranthe*. Proceed. Utah Acad. Sci. 44:321–333.
Vickery, Robert K., Barid B. Mukherjee, and Delbert Wiens
    1958   Chromosome counts in section *Erythranthe* of the genus *Mimulus* (Scrophularaceae). Madroño 14:150–153.
    1963   Chromosome counts in section *Erythranthe* of the genus *Mimulus* (Scrophularaceae) II. Madroño 17:53–56.
Vickery, Robert K., and Richard L. Olson
    1956   Flower color inheritance in the *Mimulus cardinalis* complex. Jour. of Hered. 47:195–199.

WENT, FRITS W.
    1957   The experimental control of plant growth. xvii+343 pp. Chronica Botanica Company, Waltham, Mass.

WHITE, P. R.
    1963   The cultivation of animal and plant cells. 2nd edition, vi+227 pp. Ronald Press, New York.

WILLDENOU, C. L.
    1800   Species Plantarum 3:360–362.

WINGE, ÖJVIND
    1917   The chromosomes, their number and general importance. Compt. rend. trav. lab. Carlsberg, ser. Physiol. 13:131–275.

INDEX

absorption of light by leaves
  effect of, on leaf thickness, 110, 115, 117
  factors influencing, 110–112
  importance of, in photosynthetic efficiency, 110, figs. 38, 39
  method of measurements, 110
  relation to pigment content, 110, 115–117
  wavelength dependence of, 110, figs. 40, 41, 45, 46
action spectra of CO_2 uptake
  differences in, between clones of *Mimulus* grown under low light intensities and clones grown under high light intensities, 110–112, 115–117, figs. 38, 39
  differences in, between clones of *Mimulus* of different origin, 110–112
  method of measurement, 107–110
algae
  blue-green, 180–181
  Chlorella pyrenoidosa, 179–180
  cryophyllic, 181
  evolution of strains of thermal algae with different temperature optima, 180–181
  growth of, in temperature gradients of hot springs, 180–181
  Ostreobium reineckii, 181–182
  photosynthetic differentiation in, 179–182
  snow, 181
  thermophyllic, 180–181
Alnus glutinosa, 177
amphiploidy
  between *Mimulus nelsonii* and *M. lewisii*, 23–24, 89, figs. 11, 12
  between *Mimulus tilingii* and *M. guttatus*, 24
  comparison of photosynthetic performance of, in parents and hybrid derivatives, 170–175
  evolutionary importance of, 174–175
Amundsen, Clifford C., 181
anatomy, leaf
  differences in, between clones in *Mimulus cardinalis*, 110–111, fig. 42
  modifications in, due to CO_2 concentration, 144
  modifications in, due to differences in light intensity, 107–115, fig. 44
  of an F_1 hybrid in comparison with parents, 167, fig. 67

Anderson, Edgar, 78, 81, 84, 195
anthocyanin pigments, 48–58
Aquilegia, 194
Atriplex
  geographical distribution of *A. patula* and *A. rosea*, 178
  hybrids between *A. patula* and *A. rosea*, 178, 197
  patula ssp. *hastata* Hall and Clements, 178
  photosynthetic pathways in different species, 178–179, 195
  rosea L., 178
Auratovščukova, N., 197
Avery, Amos G., 194

Babcock, E. B., 194
barriers to gene exchange
  between *Mimulus cardinalis* and *M. lewisii*, 15–23
  within the *Erythranthe* section of *Mimulus*, 12–25
  within *Mimulus lewisii* and *M. cardinalis*, 12–14
Bauer, Erwin, 194
Bell, Richie, 26
Bentham, G., 32
β-carboxylation (C-4 dicarboxylic acid) pathway
  in CO_2 fixation, 124, 136–137, 178–179
  comparison with plants lacking this pathway, 124–129, 178–179
  effect of O_2 concentration on, 179
  effects of, on temperature and light intensity, 179
  evolutionary and ecological significance, 179
Billings, W. D., 148
biochemical processes in relation to physiological functions, 92–93
biosystematic relationships within section *Erythranthe* of *Mimulus*, 24–26
Björkman, Olle, 105, 115, 120, 130, 136, 158, 175, 178, 197
Blakeley, L. M., 185
Blakeslee, A. F., 194
Bogorad, Lawrence, 144
Bombus
  balteatus Dahlbom, 20
  centralis Cresson, 20
  flavifrons Cresson, 20
Boysen-Jensen, P., 196
Breedlove, Dennis, 26

205

Brock, Thomas D., 180-181
Brooks, Robert C., 181
Brožek, A., 3, 48, 51, 58
Bunt, J. S., 181
Burr, G. O., 178

cabinets, controlled, 100-102, figs. 34, 35, p. 130-132
Calypte anna T. L., 19
carbon dioxide
   analyzers, Beckman, 131-132; Lira, Mine Safety Appliances, 131-132
   control of concentration in growth cabinets, 131-132
   differential effect of, on growth of *Mimulus* races, 138-144, 147-148
   differential responses of, in plants from low and high altitudes, 148
   effect of varied concentrations of, on growth of *Mimulus*, 138-144
   effect of varied concentrations of, on photosynthetic rates, 124-128
   equilibrium concentrations of, inside leaves, 144
   interaction with O_2, effect on photosynthetic rates, 124-126
C-4-dicarboxylic acid pathway, see β-carboxylation pathway
carotenoid pigments in *Mimulus*, 48-58
Castenholtz, Richard W., 181
Chambers, Kenton, 26
Chang, Joseph, iv
characters distinguishing species and ecological races of *Mimulus*
   classes of, 30-31
   essentially nonmodifiable vs. modifiable, 31, 58-60
   flower color, 48-50, Plate I, fig. 19
   frost-susceptibility at Timberline, 76-78
   inheritance of modifiable characters, 78
   inheritance of nonmodifiable characters, 32
   winter activity at Stanford, 76
Chlorella pyrenoidosa, high-temperature strains of, 180
chlorophyll
   breakdown in leaves of *Mimulus lewisii* at high temperature, 162
   content in leaves grown at different temperatures, 162
   content in leaves of hybrids as compared with parents, 167-170, table 42
   content in plants grown under low and high light intensity, 117-120
   content in relation to photosynthetic rate, 117-120
   long-wavelength-absorbing form in *Ostreobium*, 181-182
chloroplasts, size of, in F_1 hybrids compared with parents, 167
chromosomes
   irregularities in, pairing in crosses within *Mimulus lewisii* and *M. cardinalis*, 12-15
   number of, in species of *Mimulus* of the *Erythranthe* section, 12, fig. 8, p. 89
   pairing of, in intra- and interspecific hybrids of *Mimulus*, 12-15, fig. 9
   pairing of, in parents and amphiploid derivatives of *Mimulus lewisii* × *M. nelsonii*, 23-24, fig. 11
Clausen, Jens, iii, 1, 26, 79, 194, 195
Clausen, Roy, 194
Clebsch, E. E. C., 148
Cline, Morris, 154-155
coherence, genetic
   definition and characteristics of, 78-84, 90, 195
   between morphological characters and survival at transplant stations, 82-83, 86-87
   between morphological characters and transplant responses, 81-84
   effect of partial genetic barriers on degree of, 83, fig. 26, table 20
   effects of pleiotropy on, 79-80
   expression of, in differential survival of F_3 progenies, 84-86, fig. 28
   expression of, in F_2 progenies, 79-84, figs. 25, 26, table 19
   expression of, in floral characters in F_3 progenies, Plate II
   expression of, in "weedling" populations at transplant stations, 86-89
   historical development of concept of, 195
   in *Mimulus* as compared with *Potentilla*, 81-82
   method of determining degree of, 79-81
   role in storage of potential variability, 79
compensation point, CO_2, 179
controlled facilities, use of, in comparative physiological studies, 100-102
Cooper, T. G., 147

corolla aperture
  inheritance of, 41–43, table 6
  relation of, to survival at transplant stations, 41
conclusions, general
  regarding biosystematic relationships within the *Erythranthe* section of *Mimulus*, 24–25
  relating to genetic structure of *Mimulus* species of the *Erythranthe* section, 89–90
  relating to study of excised tissues of *Mimulus* under aseptic conditions, 193
  relative to differences in photosynthetic characteristics of ecological races and species, 182–183
  relative to future experimental studies, 197
correlation coefficients
  effect of, on partial genetic incompatibility on values, 83, fig. 26
  method of computing, 80–81
  use of, in evaluating genetic coherence, 81
crossing experiments
  between species of the *Erythranthe* section, 12–31
  interspecific combinations, 31, table 3
  intraspecific combinations, 60, table 14
  methods, 26
Cyperus, photosynthesis in, 178
cytogenetic relationships
  among species of the *Erythranthe* section, 12
  between species of the *Erythranthe* and other *Mimulus* species, 24
  summary of, within the *Erythranthe* section, 89–90

data, methods of recording and processing, 30
diatoms, cryophyllic, 181
differential pollinators
  hummingbirds *vs.* bees, 15–20
  of *Mimulus cardinalis* and *M. lewisii*, 15–20
  other pollinators of *Mimulus*, 20
Diplacus, 2
Downs, R. W., 124

Eastwood, Alice, 2
ecological races
  in *Mimulus cardinalis*, 4–7
  in *M. lewisii*, 7
  in *M. verbenaceus*, 7
  in *Solanum dulcamara*, 177–178
  in *Solidago virgaurea*, 175–177
efficiency, photosynthetic
  differences in, between ecological races, 110–112
  of hybrids in comparison with parents, 166–167, fig. 66
  of leaves grown under low and high light intensities, 107–115
  quantum yield in *Mimulus*, 110–112, figs. 38, 39
Egle, K., 130
Eldredge, Marylee, iii
Elliott, Ruth, iii, 184
Emerson, Robert, 180
Encelia californica, 160
energy of activation
  for photosynthesis of *Marchantia polymorpha*, 160
  for photosynthesis of *Mimulus cardinalis* and *M. lewisii*, 158
energy exchange between plants and natural environments, measurements on *Mimulus*, 93–99
energy utilization in plants with and without β-carboxylation photosynthesis, 178–179
enzymes, photosynthetic
  activity of, in relation to temperature, 162–163, table 41
  carboxydismutase (RuDP carboxylase), 105, 117–120, 162–163
  measurement of activity in leaves, 105
Erythranthe section of *Mimulus*
  biosystematic relationships of, 1, 4–26
  cytogenetic relationships between and within species of, 12–15, fig. 7
  geographic distribution of, 4, fig. 1
  in comparison with other species-complexes, 194
  placement within the genus, 1–4
  species of, 3–4
  summary of genetic structure of, 89–91
Eumimulus, 2
Eunamus, 2
Euphorbia, 178
excised tissues of *Mimulus*
  callus cultures, 186–187, 191–193
  conclusions regarding use of, in comparative physiological studies, 193

excised tissues of *Mimulus—continued*
  culture under aseptic conditions, 184-194
    experiments, 187-194
    media, 184
    species used, 184-187
    use of excised leaves, 191-193
    use of peeled internodes, 186-187
  experimental taxonomy studies
    historical development, 194-197
    future investigations, 197
    levels of approach, 194-196
    objectives, i–ii
    prerequisites of materials suitable for, 1
    present status of physiological and biochemical inquiries, 196-197

factors, environmental, influencing physiological functions, 91-92
Falk, S. O., 105
Favia, 181
Florell, Cirl, 175
flower color in *Mimulus*
  anthocyanins, 48-56
  carotenoids, 48-54
  factors determining, 48-58, fig. 19
  flavonoids, 48-54
flowering, dates of first anthesis
  modifications in, resulting from transplanting, 71-76
  of altitudinal races and hybrids, 71-76, figs. 23, 24
  reversal in, relative order of, at transplant stations, 74-76
  segregation in, among F_2 and F_3 progenies, 74-76, fig. 24
flowering in *Mimulus* as influenced by light intensity, day length, and temperature, 124
flower structure of *Mimulus cardinalis* and *M. lewisii* in relation to pollinators, 15-23, fig. 13
Fock, H., 130
Focke, W. O., 3
Forrester, M. L., 124
Fousova, S., 197
Fragillaris sublinearis, 181
frequency distribution in F_2 and F_3 progenies of *Mimulus* for corolla aperture, 41-43, tables 6, 7
  for date of first flowers, 74-76
  for frost susceptibility at Timberline, 76-78
  for leaf dentations, 45-48, fig. 18
  for leaf ratio, 48, table 8
  for light areas, 56-58
  for petal reflexing, 32-39, table 5
  for petal width, 39-41, fig. 14
  for pistil length, 43-45, fig. 16
  for rose, 54-56, table 12
  for star, 58, table 13
  for winter activity at Stanford, 76
  for yellow lower epidermis, 54
  for yellow upper epidermis, 50-52, table 9
frost susceptibility
  at Timberline, 76-78
  segregation in, of hybrid progenies, 77-78

Garric, Richard, 181
gas concentration, method of control of, in growth cabinets, 131-132, figs. 34, 35
Gates, David M., 93, 96
Gauhl, Eckard, 105, 124, 136, 158, 177, 178
gene systems, multiple, 78-79, 89-91
genetic composition of "weedling" populations of *Mimulus* in transplant gardens, 86-89
genetic structure of the *Erythranthe* section of *Mimulus,* 89-91
genetics of *Mimulus*
  coherence, 78-91
  early studies on, 3
  partial barriers within *Mimulus cardinalis,* 14-15
  partial barriers within *M. lewisii,* 12-14
  pollination barriers between *M. cardinalis* and *M. lewisii,* 19-23
  progeny tests of natural populations of *M. cardinalis* and *M. lewisii,* 20-23, fig. 10
  segregation of characters in F_2 and F_3 progenies of *M. lewisii-cardinalis* hybrids, 32-89; *see also* frequency distribution
  summary of genetic structure of *Erythranthe* section, 89-91
geographic distribution
  of *Mimulus* as a whole, 4-5
  of *M. cardinalis,* 4-7, 20-23
  of *M. eastwoodiae,* 12
  of *M. lewisii,* 7, 20
  of *M. nelsonii,* 10
  of *M. rupestris,* 12
  of *M. verbenaceus,* 7

of species of the *Erythranthe* section, 4, fig. 1
Gilborn, Steven, iv
Goldschmidt, Richard, 194
Grant, Adele, 2, 3, 4, 7
Grant, Verne, 79, 194, 195
Gray, Asa, 2
Greene, E. L., 3, 4
Gregor, J. W., 194
growth, comparative
  of *Marchantia polymorpha* in low and high O_2, 136
  of *Mimulus* under varied CO_2 concentrations, 138–144
  of *Mimulus* under varied light intensities, 121–124
  of *Mimulus* under varied O_2 concentrations, 130–137, fig. 54, tables 28, 29, 30
  of *Mimulus* under varied temperatures, 148–157
  of *Phaseolus vulgaris* in low and high O_2, 136
  of *Zea mays* in high and low O_2, 136–137, table 31

Halldal, Per, 181
Hart, Richard W., iii
Hartt, C. E., 178
Hatch, M. D., 178
Hesketh, J., 124, 183
Heslop-Harrison, J., 194
heterosis in hybrids
  as expressed in different environments, 61–63, table 15, p. 89, 157
  as expressed in frost resistance, 77, fig. 22
  at transplant stations, 67–70, fig. 20, table 17
  genetic instability of, 89
  negative, 197
Hiesey, William M., 1, 26, 79, 100, 195
Hoch, G., 181
Holmgren, Paul, 115, 175, 197
hummingbirds in relation to pollination, 15–19
hybrids
  anatomy of leaves in, as compared with parents, 167, fig. 67
  between *Atriplex patula* and *A. rosea*, 178–179
  photosynthetic rates of, as compared with parents, 167–170

hybrid vigor, *see* heterosis
hygrometer, microwave, 105

index values
  in relation to segregation in "weedlings" at transplant stations, 86–89
  in relation to segregation in F_3 populations, 86, fig. 28
  method of scoring, 30
infrared gas analyzers
  use of, in measurement of photosynthetic rates, 105
  use of, in monitoring CO_2 levels in cabinets, 131
inheritance of characters distinguishing species and ecological races in *Mimulus*
  corolla aperture, 41–43, table 6
  differential survival of F_3 progenies at transplant stations, 86
  essentially nonmodifiable characters, 32–58
  flower color, 48–58, Plate I, fig. 19
  frost resistance at Timberline, 76–78
  leaf dentations, 45–48, figs. 17, 18
  leaf ratio, 48, table 8
  light areas, 56–58
  modifiable characters, 78
  petal reflexing, 32–39, table 5
  petal width, 39–41, fig. 14
  phenological characters, 71–76
  rose, 54–56, table 12
  shifts in segregation ratios of "yellow upper" at transplant stations, 50–52, table 10
  star, 58, table 13
  yellow lower epidermis, 54, table 11
  yellow upper epidermis, 52–54, table 9, p. 89
integrating sphere, use of, in measuring light absorption by leaves, 105, 108–110
intraspecific hybrids
  combinations of, 60–63, table 14
  vigor of, at transplant stations, 67–70, fig. 20, table 17
interspecific hybrids
  combinations of, 31–32, table 3
  vigor of, at transplant stations, 70–71, fig. 21, table 17

Johannsen, W., 194
Johnson, H. S., 178
Joliffe, P. A., 158
Jørgensen, Erik G., 162

Kapphahn, Arline K., iv
Kearney, Thomas H., 24
Keck, David D., 1, 26
Kihara, H., 194
Kortschak, H. P., 178
Krauss, Robert W., 171

Lawrence, Mark, iv
leaf dentations, inheritance of, 45–48, fig. 17
leaf ratio, inheritance of, 48, table 8
Lenz, Andrew M., iv
Lewis, Meriweather, 2
light intensity
  differential tolerance to, in ecotypes of *Solanum dulcamara*, 177–178
  differential tolerance to, in ecotypes of *Solidago virgaurea*, 175–177
  effect of, during growth on leaf anatomy of *Mimulus*, 110–112, fig. 42, p. 167, fig. 67
  effect of, during growth on subsequent photosynthetic rates, 107–121, 163–166
  effect of, on dry matter production in *Mimulus*, 121–124, figs. 48, 49, table 25
  effect of, on number of flowers produced, 124
  effect of, on photosynthesis, 106–107, fig. 37
  effect of, on relative photosynthetic rates of parents and hybrids, 163–175
  in natural habitats of *Mimulus*, 95–96, fig. 30, p. 107
  in natural habitats of *Ostreobium reineckii*, 181–182
linkage between genetic and physiological characters, 4, 195–196, *see also* coherence
Linnaeus, C., 2
Lundegård, Henrik, 196

Marchantia polymorpha, 157–161
Mather, Kenneth, 78–79, 195
McMahon, D., 144
Mendelian ratios
  in inheritance of light areas, 56–58
  in inheritance of yellow upper epidermis, 50–52, table 9
Michaelis constants, differences in, between races of *Mimulus cardinalis*, 144–147
microwave hygrometer, 105
Milner, Harold W., iii, 100

Mimulus
  cardinalis, 1, 2, 3, 4, 7, fig. 1, fig. 2, p. 4–26, 31–91, 93–102, 107–131, 132–177, 182–198
  dentatus, 24
  eastwoodiae, 2–4, fig. 5, p. 7–12, 13–25, 41–43, 58, 67, 77, 89, 185
  Erythranthe section, 1–25
  genetics of, *see* genetics of *Mimulus*
  guttatus, 24
  guttatus–glabratus complex, 3
  history of taxonomy of, 2–3
  lewisii, 1–7, fig. 3, p. 4–25, 32–90, 94–100, 115–131, 144–177, 184–193
  luteus, 24
  moschatus, 24
  nelsonii, 3–4, 7, 10–12, fig. 6, p.11, 13, 23–24, 32, 39, 41, 58, 67, 89, 170–175
  Paradanthus section, 63
  parishii, 2
  primuloides, 24
  quinqueovulaneous, 3
  ringens, 2, 24
  rupestris, 3, 3–4, 12, 89
  Simiolus section, 3
  tigrinis, 3
  tilingii, 24
  triginoides, 3
  verbenaceus, 2–4, 7, fig. 4, p. 10, 12, 23, 24, 39, 41, 45, 58, 67, 77, 78, 89, 185
modifiable characters
  differences in, between *M. cardinalis* and *M. lewisii*, 60–63, 78
modifications
  due to growth under different O_2 concentrations, 137–144
  in characters under different light intensities, 124
  in flowering response due to transplanting, 71–76
  in leaves and stems of *Mimulus* under different CO_2 concentrations, 144, figs. 56, 57
  in photosynthetic rates, *see* photosynthesis
  in roots grown under low and high O_2, 137
Mooney, H. A., 148, 160
Mukherjee, B. B., 3, 24
Myers, J., 180

Nerium oleander, leaf temperature of, 99
Nicholson, Frank, iii

Nicotiana alata × *N. langsdorfi,* 84
Nobs, Malcolm A., 178
Nuttall, T., 2

Olson, Richard L., 48, 51
Oscillatoria, 181
Ostreobium reineckii
   action spectrum for photosynthesis, 181–182
   light intensity for photosynthetic saturation, 181–182
Owens, Olga van H., 181
oxygen
   effect of varying concentrations of on growth, 130–137
   inhibiting effect of on photosynthetic rates, 124–129, 179
   inhibition of photosynthetic rate in relation to temperature, 157–160
   interaction with CO_2 effect on photosynthetic rates, 124–128, 179
   method of control in growth cabinets, 131–132, figs. 34, 35
oxygen analyzers
   paramagnetic, 105
   use of, in measurement of photosynthetic rates, 105
   use of, in monitoring O_2 levels in cabinets, 131–132
   Zirconium oxide cell, 105
Oxyria digna, 148

Panicum, 178
partial genetic barriers
   within *Mimulus cardinalis,* 14–15, 60–63
   within *M. lewisii,* 12–14, 58–60
   within the *Erythranthe* section, 12–26, fig. 7
partial genetic linkages, *see* coherence
Peebles, Robert H., 24
petal reflexing, inheritance of, 32–39, table 5
petal width, inheritance of, 39–41, fig. 14
Phaseolus vulgaris, growth of, under high and low O_2 concentration, 136
phenological responses
   at transplant stations, 71–76
   differences in flowering in *Mimulus cardinalis* and *M. lewisii* in controlled conditions, 121–124, fig. 48
phenotypic adjustment in leaves of contrasting ecological races, 106–121
photorespiration, 130–137, *see also* oxygen

photosynthesis
   β-carboxylation (C-4 dicarboxylic acid) pathway, 124
   effect of light intensity on, 106–121
   effect of temperature at which plants were previously grown, 160–162
   enhancement of rate in low O_2, 124–137
   inhibiting effect of O_2 on, 124–127
   interaction between CO_2 and O_2 concentration, effect on, 126
   internal leaf factors limiting rate, 106–107
   major elements of, 102–105, fig. 36
   methods of measurement, 103–105
   modifications in rate on plants grown under high and low O_2 concentrations, 137–138, table 32
   performance of in *Mimulus* compared with other plants, 175–184
   physical factors affecting rate, 103
   quantum yields in *Mimulus* leaves, 110–112
photosynthesis, comparative
   between different clones of *Mimulus lewisii,* 170
   differences in pathway of CO_2 fixation, 178–179
   in plants with and without β-carboxylation, 178–179
   of amphiploid derivatives in comparison with parents, 170–175
   of *Atriplex patula* compared with *A. rosea,* 169–179
   of contrasting ecotypes of *Solidago,* 175–177
   of ecological races of *Mimulus* compared with other species, 175–183
   of hybrid derivatives and parents, 163–175
   on *Mimulus* leaves grown under high and low light intensities, 107–112
physical parameters in natural environments, 93–96
physiological studies on ecological races
   future investigations, 197
   present status of, 196–197
   selection of experimental materials for, 1, 91–92
   working principles, 91–93
Picken, Kathy, iii
Pinus, 194
pistil length, inheritance of, 43–45, fig. 13
pleiotropy in relation to genetic coherence, 79–80

pollen fertilities
    in intra-*cardinalis* hybrids, 14–15, table 1
    in intra-*lewisii* hybrids, 12–14, table 1
    of species and hybrids in the *Erythranthe* section, 12, table 1
Pollock, Gail H., 50, 56
Polygonium bistoroides, 160
Potentilla glandulosa, 194
Pray, Thomas, iv
Prosser, C. Ladd, 92
protein content
    in *Mimulus* leaves grown under different temperatures, 162
    in *Skeletonema costatum*, 162
Pursh, Frederick, 2

quantum yields in photosynthesis
    in ecotypes of *Solanum*, 177
    in *Mimulus*, 110–112, figs. 38, 39
Quercus wislizenii, leaf temperature of, 95

Radford, Pamela, iii
Raphiolepis ovata, leaf temperature of, 99
Reese, Jane, iv, 26
Reitsma, Jacob, 194
Rhododendron indicum, leaf temperature of, 99
ribulose diphosphate carboxylase (RuDP carboxylase)
    activity of, in leaves grown at different temperatures, 162–163, table 41
    activity of, in *Mimulus* leaves grown under low and high light intensity, 117, table 24
    relation between activity of, and photosynthetic rate, 117–120
Roberts, Karen, iv
Rydberg, P. A., 2

Satina, Sophia, 194
Schaub, H. W., 105
segregation of characters
    in F_2 and F_3 populations, see inheritance
    in spontaneous "weedling" populations of *Mimulus*, 86–89
    in survival of F_3 populations at transplant stations, 86
    morphological, in relation to transplant responses, 63
    physiological, in relation to transplant responses, 170–177
Selasphorus rufus, 19

Shields, Oakley, iv
Shropshire, F., 160
Shull, G. H., 194
Siegel, S. M., 130
Skeletonema costatum, 162
Slack, C. R., 178
Solanum dulcamara, ecotypic differentiation in, 177–178
solar energy along Sierran transect, 95–96, fig. 30
Solidago virgaurea, sun and shade ecotypes of, 175–177, 197
Sorokin, Constantine, 177
Spach, E., 2
species-complexes
    Mimulus cardinalis-lewisii, 12–23, 24–25
    Mimulus guttatus-glabratus, 3
    Mimulus verbenaceus-eastwoodiae-nelsonii, 12, 23, 24–25
    Potentilla glandulosa, 79, 81–82
    Solanum dulcamara, 177–178
    Solidago virgaurea, 175–177
Standeven, Warren, iii, 184
Stebbins, G. Ledyard, Jr., 194
Steemann-Nielsen, E., 162
Stein, Janet R., 181
Steward, F. C., 185
stomata, effects of, on CO_2 concentration inside leaves, 147–148
stomatal resistance, method of determining, 105
survival, differential at transplant stations
    of amphiploid derivatives and parents, 174–175
    of F_3 progenies, 86
    of *Mimulus cardinalis* and *M. lewisii*, 20–23, 63–67
    of parents *vs.* F_1 and F_2 hybrids, 70–71
Synechococcus, 181

temperature
    dependence of photosynthetic rates of *Mimulus cardinalis* and *M. lewisii* clones measured in low and high O_2 concentration, 161, fig. 61
    differential effects of, on growth of *Mimulus cardinalis* and *M. lewisii* races under controlled conditions, 148–157
    effect of, on Arrhenius plots of photosynthetic rate under varying O_2 concentration, 158–160, fig. 62

effect of, on growth of *Mimulus cardinalis* of alternating days and nights, 140, 153-154, fig. 59
effect of, on interaction between O_2 concentration and photosynthetic rate, 126, 155
effect of, on leaf transpiration, 96-99
effect of, on photosynthetic rates of *Mimulus cardinalis, M. lewisii,* and their F_1 hybrid under low and high O_2 concentrations, 167-170, fig. 69
effect of, on photosynthetic rates in *Mimulus lewisii, M. nelsonii,* and their amphiploid, 171-175, fig. 71
effect of, on photosynthetic rates under different light intensities, 127-128
effect of, on solubility of CO_2 inside leaves, 158
of leaves in natural environments, 93-95
of leaves in relation to ambient temperatures, 98-99
optimal, for photosynthesis in cryophilic plants, 181
optimal, for photosynthesis in thermal algae, 180-181
Thomas, William H., 181
tolerance, degrees of, in
  amphiploid derivatives as compared with parents, 174-175
  ecotypes of *Solidago virgaurea*, to differences in light intensity, 175-177
  Mimulus cardinalis and *M. lewisii,* to temperature, 148-157
  parents and hybrids, to transplanting, 63-71
  Solanum dulcamara ecotypes, to light intensity, water stress, 177-178
  Solidago ecotypes, to light intensity, 175-177
transgressive segregation
  in frost resistance, 77-78, fig. 22
  in *Mimulus,* 90
  in number of leaf dentations, 48, figs. 17, 18
  in pistil length, 43, fig. 16
  in rose, 54-55
transpiration
  cooling effect of, on leaves, 94-100

measurements of rates of, in controlled cabinets, 96-100
measurement of rates of, with microwave hygrometer, 105
measurements of, simultaneously with CO_2 concentration, 147-148
transplant studies
  differential responses of ecological races, 63-78
  flowering responses, 71-76
  methods and materials, 26-31, table 2
  of F_3 progenies at transplant stations, 86
  responses of amphiploid derivatives in comparison with parents, 174-175
  responses of parental and hybrid combinations, 63-70
Tregunna, E. B., 124, 158
Turesson, G., 162, 192

Van Niel, C. B., 171
variables, selection of, in controlled physiological experiments, 91-93
Vickery, Robert K., iii, 1, 2, 3, 24, 48, 50, 51, 56, 154

water stress, differentiation among ecotypes of *Solanum* to, 177-178
water vapor, measurement of, on attached leaves, 105
"weedling" populations from transplant stations, correlation between characters and station of origin, 86-89, fig. 28
West, Marda, 160
Wiens, Delbert, 3
Willdenow, C. L., 2
Wilson, Kenneth G., 56
Winge, O., 194
winter activity at Stanford
  inheritance of, in F_1, F_2, and F_3 progenies, 76
  yearly variation in, 76
Wood, Steven, iv

yellow lower epidermis of petals, inheritance of, 54, table 11
yellow upper epidermis of petals, inheritance of, 50-52, table 9

Zea mays, 136, 197